YEAR ONE

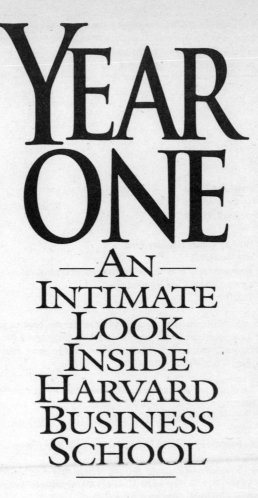

YEAR ONE

—AN— INTIMATE LOOK INSIDE HARVARD BUSINESS SCHOOL

ROBERT REID

AVON BOOKS ◆ NEW YORK

AVON BOOKS
A division of
The Hearst Corporation
1350 Avenue of the Americas
New York, New York 10019

The William Morrow edition contains the following Library of Congress Cataloging in Publication Data:

Reid, Robert, 1965-
    Year one : an intimate look inside Harvard Business School / Robert Reid.
        p. cm.
    1. Harvard University—Graduate School of Business Administration. 2. Reid, Robert, 1965-   . 3. Harvard University. Graduate School of Business Administration—Students—Biography. I. Title.
HF1134.H4R45 1994   94-5569
650'.092—dc20   CIP
[B]

First Avon Books Trade Printing: September 1995

OPM 10 9 8 7 6 5 4 3 2 1

For Chip, Doug, John, and Mike

AUTHOR'S NOTE

While this book is not a work of fiction, the principal student characters discussed within it (with the exception of the narrator) are not actual people. These characters are comprised of a cross section of attributes, opinions, and adventures representing a range of Harvard Business School experiences and viewpoints. To the extent that real persons are depicted in any detail in the book, their names have been altered. Excepted from this is a small group of individuals whose highly visible administrative posts or academic reputations have made them public persons.

ACKNOWLEDGMENTS

A number of people both within and outside of the Harvard Business School community provided me with invaluable insights and counsel when I was writing and editing this book. I would especially like to thank Patty Akopiantz, Orville Bailey, Mike Kaufman, Chip Hazard, J. R. Lowry, Eric Madoff, Sarah Jane McKinney, Daniel Muth, Chris O'Connell, Susanne Wedemeyer, and Martyna Wierzbicka for their help with this work. Thanks also to all of my first year professors, whose commitment and professional excellence created a truly exceptional learning environment for our section, and to my sectionmates, who together made the first year at Harvard a rich and unforgettable one.

Special and heartfelt thanks to my mother and father for plowing through countless drafts of this book, and for tolerating the peculiar hours I kept during my weekends at home while writing it. Thanks also to Joel Beinen, who as a professor, friend, and role model largely sparked my interest in writing, and to Clark Peterson, who in many ways sustained it. Special thanks as well to those who helped shape my understanding of the business world and heightened my interest in it, especially Tom Blaisdell, Donna Hazard, Tom Ostrander, Mani Sadeghi, David Sanderson, and Steve Skaggs.

I would also like to thank Suzanne Wetlaufer, fellow author and HBS alum, for introducing me to my agent, Alice Martell.

I would like to thank Alice, in turn, for arranging for the publication of this book while simultaneously coaxing me through my first two final exams at Harvard (and for later coaxing me through the rest of the year and the process of writing about it). Finally, I would like to thank my editor, Adrian Zackheim, and his assistant, Suzanne Oaks, for guiding the development of this book.

Robert Holliday Reid

CONTENTS

Acronyms and Abbreviations

Aldrich   Aldrich Hall; location of Harvard Business School's classrooms. Section I met in the room Aldrich 9

BGIE   Business, Government, and the International Economy (course; pronounced "Big E")

C&S   Competition and Strategy (course)

DMEV   Decision Making and Ethical Values (course; also known as Ethics)

first-year   as an adjective: anything pertaining to the first year at Harvard Business School (e.g., "the first-year courses"); as a noun: a student in the first year (e.g., "Sandra was a first-year.")

FRMA   Financial Reporting and Managerial Accounting (course; pronounced "Firm-uh")

Harbus   *The Harbus News;* a weekly publication by business school students

HBS   Harvard Business School

HRM   Human Resources Management (course)

IOC   Information, Organization, and Control (course)

Kresge   Kresge Hall; student lounge, and home to main campus cafeteria

MC   Management Communications (course)

ME   Managerial Economics (course)

MPP   Management Policy and Practice (second-year course; now defunct)

OB   Organizational Behavior (course)

second-year   adjective or noun (see "first-year")

Shad   Shad Hall; main campus athletic facility

TOM   Technology and Operations Management (course)

1

WITH SINCERE REGRET . . .

IT WAS A DARK and stormy night. Warsaw's good at cranking those out, I've discovered. And if anyone ever asks, there *are* better places to spend mid-January than Warsaw. Like Buffalo, perhaps. Or maybe Reykjavík. But for me, it was Warsaw.

I used to work for a consulting firm in a snug little office in San Francisco. Then one day, my old boss called. She was in Poland, working with a group that was helping the Polish government privatize its economy. This group was getting busy, and they needed extra hands. The idea of joining them was alluring, as I planned to start business school in a year. What better way to spend that year than watching history unfold in Eastern Europe? Besides, after six years in California, I missed The Seasons.

Four months later, the wind was howling like something out of a Hitchcock movie as the snow piled up outside. I was hunched over the office fax machine, having long since decided that I'd had it with The Seasons. "C'mon, baby, receive. Re-*ceive!*" I muttered. A tantalizing fragment of a letter had snuck through a minute ago. The university seal, the Admissions Department letterhead, a date, then nothing.

You could call it Stalin's revenge. Two years after the collapse of socialism, that Cro-Magnon communist technology was still rotting away in the telecom network. A partly received fax was perhaps more of a triumph than a letdown. But I had been waiting for that thing all night. And in January in central Poland, that meant since about three-thirty in the afternoon.

"Receive, baby, *receive!*"

Given the way the weather had been, my fixation on The Fax was pretty natural. It had grown even stronger that afternoon, when I spent an icy hour shopping for some gifts. The best place to do this was an open market by the stadium where thousands of Russians sold fuzzy hats, cheap vodka, military watches, and anything else they could push for those coveted Polish zlotys. Although the zloty was trading at about 12,000 to the dollar, they were a lot more attractive to the Russian merchants than their own little rubles. It could be worse, I thought grimly as I strolled through the frosty flea market. I could be in Moscow.

The afternoon brought a chilly winter wind. It howled in from the Russian steppe like a band of marauding Hunnish snowmen, making short work of my six bundled layers of defense. Soon I was back at the stadium gates, eager to return to the relative warmth of my office. A tram arrived. Painted red in a valiant attempt at cheer, it wheezed up to my stop and grudgingly squeaked open its doors. I joined a throng of grumpy-looking Poles inside, and gazed out the window as we crossed the icy Vistula on a crumbling, spray-concrete bridge. Warsaw, mighty ocean of gray! Demolished by the war, the entire city was redesigned, rebuilt, and redecorated by 1950s' Polish communists. The contrast with San Francisco, I noted for the umpteenth time, could not have been starker.

This unhappy comparison plunged me into an inevitable wave of homesickness. I had originally come to live in San Francisco by way of Stanford, my undergraduate alma mater. Stanford! Every icy blast of Russian wind sparked memories of Windsurfing, foothills, year-round outdoor swimming, and February sunburns. I hurried back to the office, where I hoped to learn that Stanford missed me as much as I missed Stanford. My mother had promised to fax Stanford's response to my business school application as soon as it came in, and it was due that day.

Late that night I was still waiting, although it now seemed my answer was imminent. "Receive, baby, *receive!*" I knew Mom was trying hard out there, because moments later the fax machine started its peculiar squealing tire sound for the third time in ten minutes. University seal. Admissions Department logo. Date. "Dear Mr. Reid . . ."

Mr. Reid! I thought wildly. *Personalized! They don't bother to personalize rejections, do they?* The tires squealed again. The little machine groaned. Then—

They do. They do personalize rejections.

I don't recall its precise words, but the central message of the fax was unmistakable. The Admissions Department did not write me with promises of Windsurfing, foothills, year-round outdoor swimming, or February sunburns. Indeed, they had nothing to offer me but Sincere Regret; Sincere Regret for the outcome of their Very Difficult Decision regarding my application.

A few minutes later, I wearily accepted this fate. I had gotten the green light from Harvard a few weeks earlier. While Boston lacked California's appeal at that subzero moment, Harvard was perhaps the better place for me anyway. In any event, I was now spared the trial of making a Very Difficult Decision of my own. Harvard Business School it would be; they were the only ones who let me in.

2

THE ROAD TO THE WARNING TRACK

"TEN? TEN?? *TEN???*"

My roommate burst into the living room to find me gazing catatonically at a Harvard Business School application, which had just arrived in the mail. "Ten goddamn essays!" I gasped, the application quivering unsteadily in my hands. In one week I would leave San Francisco for my nine-month hitch out in Poland. I had furniture to sell, friends to bid farewell, clothes to pack, a car to move, a tricky Slavic tongue to master, and 8,500 miles to travel in one week. And now I had ten essays to write. *Ten!*

This wasn't all Harvard was throwing at me. There were forms to fill out, postcards to stamp and address to myself, transcript requests to send to every school or program I had ever attended, and three recommendation forms (featuring seven long-answer questions) that would easily cancel out any favor my recommenders ever owed me. Then there was the small matter of the hundred dollar application fee. A hundred bucks! "They should be paying *me* to fill this thing out," I growled as I lumbered off to the kitchen for some peanut butter and crackers. It was going to be a long night.

Harvard, of course, wasn't about to pay me to fill out their torturous application. Not when thousands of other people were pulling out checkbooks, dusting off word processors, and

18

grudgingly cranking out Harvard Business School applications every year. It made sense; by requiring such big investments of time, money, and brain power, Harvard made sure that the people who ultimately applied all took their candidacy very seriously. But ten essays still seemed extreme. I flipped through the pages of my evening's entertainment, studying the big questions that would dominate my life until I hopped that rickety Russian jet to Warsaw.

> 1. *What evidence can you present to demonstrate your capacity to perform well academically in the Harvard MBA Program?*

What on earth did that mean? Couldn't they get whatever "evidence" they needed from the transcript of my undergraduate grades? I bitterly imagined a squad of Admissions Department functionaries sitting around, punching out silliness like this to reach their quota of ten questions for the application. I revved up the word processor.

> I did fine academically as an undergraduate at Stanford University, an institution located in a beautiful, sun-drenched region with far more distractions than I suspect Cambridge offers.

Moments later I hit the delete button, banishing my blasphemy from the screen. Still, I felt a bit better. A few lines down was the most famous question on the application.

> 4. *Describe an ethical dilemma you have experienced firsthand. How did you manage and resolve the situation?*

This one was a perennial favorite, not only of Harvard's, but of many of the top business schools. A similar question was certainly asked by Stanford, the only other school to which I was applying.

Many pre-business-school neophytes first became aware of their need to encounter an ethical dilemma before they even started their first job. The have-you-had-your-ethical-dilemma-yet routine was a standard joke in my office, where a large majority of post-college hires ultimately went on to business schools. Some took the joke a bit too seriously. A few weeks earlier, a nerdy new B.A. from an East Coast school confided to me his concern about his ethical-dilemma-free background. "You're applying to schools now, Rob," he said. "Where'd you find your ethical dilemma? I really kinda need one."

Harvard's dilemma was relatively easy to come up with, as it was not required that it come from one's professional life. Some schools were far tougher, demanding that applicants encounter an ethical dilemma *at work* prior to applying.

> 6. *Describe your three most substantial accomplishments and explain why you view them as such.*

We had one page for that one. Did I even have three substantial accomplishments? The first thing that came to mind was winning a model-car race in third grade. This probably wouldn't cut it.

> 10. *What are your post-MBA career plans?*

Half a page for that one. Whatever our plans were, they better be concise. I had another peanut butter-coated saltine cracker and started to write. This question was broad enough that it should be easy. Thirty minutes later I had my first sentence:

> I spent much of this year considering the disparate threads of my life and how they can best be synthesized both professionally and personally.

Disparate threads. Cute, Rob. It was clearly going to be one long night.

Fortunately, Harvard hadn't seen fit to ask something like, *Exactly why do all you people want Harvard MBAs anyway?* The honest answer to that one for me (and perhaps thousands of applicants) would have been either "I'm not quite sure," or perhaps a ten-page essay. But even unraised, this wasn't a bad issue to ponder before continuing with my evening's mission. Just what was it that drove so many of our society's young into MBA programs? And why was I joining the throng? And exactly who were my 6,000-odd rivals for admission anyway?

I had at least some insights on the last question. Although

increasingly diverse, applicant pools at the most competitive business schools were still dominated by younger professionals (two to four years out of college) who had followed one of a few traditional pre-business-school career paths.

Sandra, a woman I later got to know well, was in many ways representative of this group. She grew up in a prosperous Washington suburb, where she attended public schools. Much of her time in junior high was focused on getting good grades, which allowed her to take honors classes in high school. Much of her time in high school was focused on getting good grades in honors classes and joining innumerable clubs so that she could get into a good college. Much of her time at Yale was spent getting good grades and keeping up with innumerable clubs as well.

Things went pretty smoothly for Sandra right up until the start of her senior year of college. It was then that she first faced an uncomfortable question. Could it be that she and her peers were really just foot soldiers in a great, marching column of twenty-something lemmings? This was a sudden and jarring notion. People in her milieu, particularly those who had landed in competitive schools like Yale, always used to strike her as a decisive lot. They were the ones who aggressively cut their own paths in life, who shaped their own destinies.

But now she was struck by how little path-cutting and des-tiny-shaping she had actually done. She and almost everyone she knew had gone directly from high school to college. Whether they were to become lawyers, professors, diplomats, or social workers, this was clearly the first step to take. And while it was also a very natural step, it meant that by the time they were twenty-one, few of them had made any limiting decisions about their futures.

But their paths would necessarily diverge after college graduation. By the beginning of senior year, many people didn't know much more about where they were heading than they did as freshmen. Nonetheless, Sandra could already feel a certain peer pressure building. The idea was that while you might not know exactly what you wanted to do, for God's sake you had better do *something*. The people who were the least confused at that point were those who had followed the pre-med track or had stud-ied engineering. They typically readied to go on to the graduate schools or professional careers that they had prepared for since freshman year without too much soul-searching. After all, it would have been difficult to stick to the rigorous academic paths they had followed without some passion for the subject matter.

But for the vast group of non-technical students (or "fuzzies," as people like Sandra and me were disdainfully called at Stanford), things were far less defined. Still, as senior year wore on, a number of generally acceptable post-graduation paths emerged. One which attracted battalions of talented young fuzzies was law school. Sandra knew dozens of people who ultimately chose this route. She secretly suspected that for many of them, law school's principal allure lay in its reassuringly familiar trappings. As a senior in high school, you took a standardized test (the SAT), lofted applications to a number of schools, and attended the best one you got into. As a senior in college, you could again take a standardized test (the LSAT), go through another round of applications, and again pick the best school that admitted you.

Sandra imagined that many people went through this process precisely because it seemed so safe and formulaic. If you were confused about what you wanted from life, yet liked to view yourself as the hard-charging shaper of your own destiny, law school could be an extremely seductive option. It carried little apparent risk, and was a highly respected destination for competitive-minded fuzzies. And once the application process began, it was almost like a narcotic. Recommendations, LSATs, transcripts, essays! The long-held dread of leaving the undergraduate nest could be lost in a whirl of activity. The burning question of "what comes next?" could be neatly put to rest. You were Doing Something, dammit, and law school was it! Sandra feared that someone who got her JD out of anything other than an ardor for the law was inviting a life of professional misery. By Halloween, she had quietly removed law school from her own consideration.

Business school, meanwhile, had been completely out of the question from the start. There was once a time when a large annual harvest of young adults went directly from college to the nation's top business schools. But those days were by now long past. As the popularity of business schools heightened during the seventies and early eighties, admissions standards had tightened everywhere. And the parameter upon which they had tightened the most was that of work experience.

When Sandra was a freshman, she still heard of occasional applicants who got into the top business schools during their senior year of college, but they were unusual cases. These college admits were also strongly urged to take a couple of years off to see something of the business world before coming to school. By the time she was a senior, applying directly to business school without at least two years of post-college work experience (and preferably more) was all but futile. Harvard, for example, still admitted a handful of college seniors, but it no longer "urged" them to take time off before matriculating; instead it required them to.

So if business school and law school were not alternatives, what did this leave? One option, perhaps, was to get a fellowship or a job teaching English abroad. This would give her a couple of years' grace to figure things out under the cover of doing something. Another option, of course, was getting a job. For those who aspired to join the ranks of the gainfully employed (and for most, this was a financial imperative), a competitive hierarchy had already developed among the companies and industries that recruited on her campus. Management consulting and investment banking were viewed as being the toughest areas in which to get jobs. Overachievers uncertain of what they wanted from life were therefore often drawn, if only by their competitive urges, to those fields.

Sandra first turned her attention to investment banking, a profession she had always heard a great deal of chatter about. Only a few years before, it had rested, unchallenged, at the apogee of her campus's competitive recruiting ziggurat. Throughout much of the 1980s, droves of top students had left Princeton, Yale, and similar schools for crushing work weeks and relatively modest pay on Wall Street. Many later moved on to Harvard, Wharton, and other schools for their MBAs. The glamour of Wall Street, its boom in the eighties, and the perception that investment banking experience virtually guaranteed admission to the top MBA programs directed hordes of business-minded college grads to the Street. Many were also drawn by the thought of returning to the industry after business school, when a few more years of terrifically hard work might yield some truly titanic Wall Street wages.

But by the time Sandra was preparing to interview, the investment banks' allure had waned somewhat. Tales of Wall

Street's trying lifestyles were widespread by then, and the trauma of the stock market crash of 1987 had eroded much of the industry's luster. Business-bound seniors like Sandra had since discovered several new darlings, many of which came to pose significant challenges to the I-banks at recruiting time. Most prominent among these was the boutique industry of management consulting. Particularly coveted were jobs with a handful of consulting firms that specialized in corporate strategy.

Sandra considered the consulting option carefully. Consulting firms were said to offer better lifestyles than investment banks ("lifestyle" being a euphemism for hours worked per week). And given the expense of life in New York City (home to most investment bank neophytes), the compensation prospects of jobs in consulting came to approach those of jobs in banking. The work sounded interesting too. With client lists dominated by Fortune 500 companies, strategy consultants were often hired by top executives to investigate their companies' most pressing issues. This gave young consultants an unusual opportunity to work at high levels in a wide range of industries. Consultants also had a certain leg up if they later decided to apply to business schools. Because like their counterparts on Wall Street, all of the leading consulting firms were major feeders to the country's top MBA programs.

Sandra weighed all her options and decided it was time to get a job. And so, like countless young women and men throughout the country, she proceeded to flood her campus post office with résumés and cover letters directed at a handful of well-known investment banks and consulting firms. A continent away, many of my friends and I were meanwhile flooding our own campus post office with precisely the same letters. Winter brought a whirl of on-campus interviews. When the dust settled, Sandra had a job with Morgan Stanley, an investment bank, and I had a job with Bain and Company, a strategy-focused consulting firm.

While we were both happy with our jobs, neither of us could honestly describe them as the logical culmination of years of academic and personal preparation. Indeed, we couldn't really attribute them to interests that were more than just a few months old. Instead we had both followed the crowd to the interviewing chamber, and had emerged from it with a certain set of offers. Sandra would now become an investment banker, and I would be a management consultant. Had a certain gesture been made differently, a certain comment phrased more or less subtly, the reverse might have easily come about.

And so the Great Lemming March of the *fin de siècle* twenty-somethings began. You were able and competitive in high school, so you got into a highly regarded college. You were a fuzzie with the willpower to resist law school, so you sought employment after that. You were able and competitive in college, so you got a job in consulting or investment banking. And then you were a consultant or an investment banker, so you would naturally apply to business school two or three years into your job. The only tough decision you really had to face was which schools to apply to.

Like many of her colleagues at Morgan Stanley and many of mine at Bain, Sandra immediately focused on Harvard and Stanford. Stanford attracted her because it had a terrific academic reputation, and because she imagined it was a warm, relaxed, and generally enjoyable place to live. Harvard, meanwhile, had certain traditional measures of grandeur recommending it. Its MBA program was both older and larger than Stanford's. It also offered the highest average graduating salary of any MBA program in the world, had the largest endowment, enjoyed the greatest alumni representation at the top ranks of America's largest corporations, and its students had more job offers to choose from on average than their counterparts at any other school.

And while Harvard and Stanford were similarly regarded in MBA-rich consulting firms and investment banks, Sandra felt that no school approached Harvard's name recognition in the broader world. In short, Harvard was the Mother of All Business Schools; what Coke was to soft drinks, what McDonald's was to fast food, what Mickey Mouse was to animated rodents, Harvard was to the MBA.

Harvard Business School (or HBS, as the school was widely known) had also made a number of signature contributions to the business world, which added to its aura. Central pieces of the jargon-happy consultant's conceptual tool kit, such as the "marketing mix" and the "discounted cash flow," were pioneered at Harvard. But perhaps the school was best known for its popularization of teaching business by the "case method." A case is a ten- to thirty-page description of an actual managerial situation, which is used to illustrate business principles and lessons. It was generally accepted that the use of the case method was first pioneered at Harvard (although a Canadian friend of mine swears it was developed at McGill).

Regardless of its origins, the business case had long since become synonymous in most minds with Harvard Business School. While most leading business schools had adopted the case method to some degree, few embraced it as unreservedly as HBS. Other schools maintained that certain things, such as cost accounting and basic finance, could not be covered thoroughly by examining a few dozen business situations. Not Harvard. At Harvard, *every* class was taught by the case method.

I ultimately applied to only Harvard and Stanford as well. The reason for my own narrow focus was perhaps environmental. Close to 75 percent of the professional staff in my office had MBAs. And something approaching 90 percent of this group had received their MBAs from either Harvard or Stanford. With such a skewed sample, you could almost trick yourself into thinking that only people from those schools got jobs.

This was not, of course, the case, and Harvard and Stanford were by no means the only business schools in America. Indeed, theirs were only two of more than eight hundred MBA programs in the country, and, in the minds of many people, they were by no means the best. *BusinessWeek* made this clear whenever it published its biannual survey ranking America's MBA programs. This survey never viewed Harvard and Stanford as kindly as Sandra or I; Harvard had ranked as low as third, and Stanford as low as ninth in recent years.

But while *BusinessWeek* and certain other observers didn't view them as being the country's top programs, Harvard and Stanford were statistically the most difficult ones to gain admission to. Every year, Harvard attracted more applications than any other business school. But because its entering classes were so much smaller than Harvard's (350 compared to 800), Stanford was, numerically, the most selective school in the land. Still, getting into Harvard was no cake walk, and most applicants passed their share of unhappy hours fretting about their odds of making the cut.

I was certainly no exception to this. My concerns about my own candidacy centered on the key area of professional experience. Before I started working, Bain had granted me a year's sabbatical to pursue an independent research project in Cairo. This meant that I had less than two years of corporate work behind me when I began my application. A few years before, this would have been fine. But by now, the once-standard two-year stretch of work between college and business school was going the way of the dinosaur. Most people in my office applied to business schools during their third or fourth year at Bain, which did not make me feel like an entirely ideal candidate.

Not everybody had such worries when they sat down to apply to HBS. The whole process was significantly more relaxed for William Simmons, a man who would later spend hundreds of hours just a few seats away from me in class. He was, after all, the perfect HBS candidate. He spent his undergraduate years at Harvard College. He was business manager of the *Harvard Crimson*, an outstanding student, and a leader in the African-American student community. He followed this with three (*not* two) years at one of Wall Street's premier firms. To cap it off, he had an actor's sense of poise and presence, and a sonorous voice that was enough to make any BBC announcer yearn to speak with an American accent.

After his time on Wall Street, William decided to head off to Paris, where countless challenging work opportunities would surely await him. But Paris, like everywhere, was mired in recession when he arrived in August of '91. He had a few interviews, but nobody was hiring. So he started French lessons at the Sorbonne, Espresso sessions at a certain café, and pursued his general edification at the city's many museums. Summer turned to autumn and then to winter. On those rare occasions when somebody asked, William confirmed that he was, ah . . . looking for work.

Whereas I raced to file my HBS application before the first deadline, William was almost blasé about the process. He ended up physically handing it over at the Admissions office moments before closing time on the last deadline date in late March. He was somewhat alarmed when someone called asking that he come in to interview with Laura Fisher, the dean of Admissions herself. An interview? thought William. This was most concerning. It was rumored that interviews were typically required of borderline candidates, or of candidates who had something unusual enough in their application that it required clarification. "Borderline" was not a word commonly tagged to William Simmons. Clearly, it was the latter case.

After William settled down in her office, Ms. Fisher told him she found it most unusual that so motivated a young man would take a whole year off just to *do stuff* in Paris. William's rich voice boomed in response; despite his best efforts, work was simply not to be found out there. Fisher just nodded. Then she asked rhetorically if he thought his status as a former *Crimson* business manager automatically qualified him for a slot at the business school. William shifted uncomfortably in his chair. It *was* true that no former *Crimson* business manager had been denied admission in living memory, but perhaps this wasn't the time to point that out . . .

Fisher pressed harder. "Why is it," she asked, "that so qualified a person couldn't find work in one of Europe's leading cities?"

William knew everything depended on his reaction to Laura's parry and thrust. With images of *Risky Business* dancing in his head, he slowly removed his steel-rimmed spectacles and stared contemplatively at the wall. "Quite frankly Laura," he said, "everyone in Paris assumed that I would be enrolling at Harvard Business School this fall. I suppose they were just reluctant to hire somebody who would be transient by nature." It wasn't a pleasant day for William, but it wasn't a disastrous one either. In the end he cleared this final hurdle, and took his rightful place in Harvard Business School's class of '94.

While William and I may have found Harvard's application process to be draining (and perhaps even scarring), as American citizens we were spared its fullest fury. International students applying to HBS faced administrative hurdles that would make a wily Washington bureaucrat shudder. Hans was an Austrian who attended university in Germany, and later became my classmate at HBS. When he first considered applying to American business programs, he never suspected that some of graduate school's greatest challenges would come months before he even got his acceptance letter.

"It all started with those standardized tests," he later lamented. "The TOEFL and the GMAT." The first of these, the Test of English as a Foreign Language, was naturally not required of the likes of William and myself. The second was a standardized SAT-style aptitude test. Of all the top business schools, HBS was alone in not soliciting GMAT scores (indeed, Harvard refused to even look at them). But like most of us, Hans applied to other MBA programs that did, and so was obliged to take it.

Hans was working in Germany when he took the GMAT, and the nearest test site was an American military base about an hour's drive from his home. On the test day he awoke at sunrise and made his way to the base, clutching a quiver of those distinctly American instruments known as number-two pencils. The base, he found, was a little slice of Americana deep in the German heartland. Jimmy Buffett crooned from a GI's car stereo. American flags fluttered in the breeze. The commissary sold Budweiser. But the most striking American trapping of all was the baseball game which raged just outside his exam room's windows.

At first Hans regarded the game as a enchanting prequel to the American odyssey he hoped to embark upon. But its charm quickly diminished as the occasional *crack* of batting practice gave way to the roar of a growing throng of spectators. By the time Hans started the GMAT's second quantitative section, a dramatic contest between two expatriate American high schools was under way. Hans had never realized how distracting the seemingly peaceful game of baseball could be to a person trying to concentrate. He also never imagined how much noise a tiny complement of American cheerleaders could generate.

The cheer-led ball game was not the last of Hans's pre-Harvard trials. The assembly of his application was a consuming chore that became a minor industry for local translators and notaries. As a foreign student, Hans had to provide certified English versions of all his transcripts and diplomas. This was no easy task. He had pursued his higher education at a German university, where he received individual certifications for completing many of his *courses*. Once he had finally located all eleven of these documents, each had to be translated into English, notarized, and then sealed in an envelope by a university official. It took three months and two numbing cross-country drives to see this little adventure through to its conclusion. But in the end, all of Hans's hard work paid off with an acceptance letter from Harvard. And unlike William, he got to this point without being subjected to an interview.

Unfortunately, the road to HBS did not end with the re-

ceipt of Dean Fisher's happy missive. For many of us, this was
when the hard part really began. Because suddenly, there was
a big decision to be made. His harrowing encounter with Laura
Fisher notwithstanding, my friend William was lucky in this
area. For him, the decision to attend was not an agonizing
one. A member of Harvard College's class of '88, William first
realized that he wanted to attend HBS sometime in the early
1970s. But many other Harvard admittees found themselves
facing a much tougher decision.

Sandra was one person who went through a particularly
acute bout of pre-Harvard ambivalence. She didn't want to end
up defaulting her way through life, automatically basing her
professional choices on competitive urges. It seemed all too easy
to heed the siren song of the Lemming March right after college
and then get pulled along for decades. And the more she
thought of it, the more it struck her that she had been marching
to its numbing beat for some time already.

Why, after all, did she make the decision to work for Morgan Stanley? Did it stem from a fascination with finance, or a
detailed examination of her long-term professional goals?
Much as she wanted to believe in such high-minded motivations,
Sandra feared the real reason was far simpler. As had been the
case with Yale, as might now be the case with Harvard, she went
to Morgan because it was "the best place that she got into" when
it came time to apply to the next stage in life.

Now she often quietly wondered why she had been in such
a hurry for so long. After college her two best friends set off to
work their way around the world, beginning with waitressing
jobs in Honolulu. Sandra passed on the voyage, opting for the
working week. Now, with her HBS acceptance letter in hand,
she again found herself on the verge of doing the conservative
and responsible thing. And this begged an obvious, but unsettling question. Just why did she want a Harvard MBA anyway?

Several plausible reasons did, of course, suggest themselves. First, there was the simple issue of earning power. The
average salary upon graduation from HBS exceeded $80,000 a
year at that time (including bonuses), an impressive figure in a
recession. Sandra also knew that business school would greatly
increase her professional flexibility. While she could get pro-
moted to an MBA-style position after another year or two on

Wall Street, it would be far more difficult to find a comparable job in another industry without the degree.

HBS students, on the other hand, seemed to face an array of possibilities that was almost dizzying. Hundreds of firms from scores of industries were known to recruit at the school for middle- to upper-level jobs. Without an MBA, a person might have to work in one of these industries for years to establish credentials; with the MBA, it almost seemed that credibility would be conferred automatically. Sandra ultimately found this fact to be decisive, as by now she realized that investment banking was not right for her in the long run. It was time to do some soul searching, to discover what else the business world offered, and to develop her credentials. A two-year hiatus from working life coupled with the training, contacts, and resources that HBS provided seemed like the ideal way to achieve this.

Like Sandra, I also did a good deal of pondering after getting my acceptance letter. And like her, I had my reservations about business school. I fervently liked to think that I had avoided the Lemming March up until then. After all, Cairo and Warsaw were fairly unusual ports of call. But even if I had partly avoided the March to date (and this was a fact not entirely in evidence), going to business school seemed frighteningly close to putting on my walking shoes and joining in.

Even worse, getting an MBA would be tantamount to finally acknowledging adulthood. It would mean letting go of that extended adolescence that can come with being young, educated, and unattached. Because after business school, jobs no longer have the soothing temporary quality they have when you know you'll eventually be headed back to school, or moving on to something more permanent. It becomes more problematic to tell yourself that you're really going to be an artist, or a teacher, or a television reporter. With a new set of education loans, you can forget about spending that year teaching English in Madrid, or falling in love in Sweden, or running a surf shop in San Diego.

But like Sandra, William, and Hans, I ultimately came down on the side of going back to school. While I enjoyed living in Poland, I was ready to go home, and was interested in learning about some of the many professions in which an MBA could be an asset. I was also twenty-six, going on twenty-seven faster than I cared to admit. Dozens of my classmates from Stanford had started business school a year before, some had even dashed off to it two years earlier. Of course, I liked to imagine that I was above devoting my life to "keeping up with the Joneses." But in the end, it was hard to ignore the call of my peers' thundering feet.

3

SUMMER CAMP

IT WAS LATE August and high time I laid eyes on the place. Orientation week would start in eight days, and I was finally driving down the Massachusetts Turnpike for a glimpse of the campus that would be home for two years. I was heading up to visit Tyler and Mandy, two old friends from California, and to run a couple of HBS-related errands. I had returned to the States about a month before, looking forward to some low-stress time with my family. The month had been nice, but there was plenty of mail from HBS to keep things from getting boring. There were pictures to send in, forms to fill out, housing lotteries to enter, and reams of booklets and pamphlets to plow through.

A particularly disturbing manila envelope had come about a week before. The cover letter inside it explained that recruiting for summer jobs would begin early in the year, and ominously warned that "once you are on campus, your extracurricular time and attention will be very limited." It went on to "sincerely urge" us to come to school with our résumés either completed or close to completion. Summer jobs. Here it was August, and the summer job search was already on! I'd hoped for at least a bit of respite.

It was dusk before I got to Tyler and Mandy's place. They had gotten married a year ago, just before Tyler started at

33

Harvard. Combining the first year of marriage with the first year of HBS seemed like a daunting proposition, but they had fared beautifully. Our evening centered around dinner with Torrance and Sally, another young HBS couple. Torrance was from Tyler's section. The section was a very important part of HBS life, as students took each of their twelve first-year classes with the ninety-two people in their section. Each section met in the same room for the entire year. The professors, not the students, changed rooms between classes.

"It sounds like my elementary school!" I said as we sat down for dinner. We were at the closest thing to a Mexican restaurant in Cambridge. Adorned with murals evoking Latin vistas, the place was generously fitted with East-Coast-goes-borderland paraphernalia.

"That's nothing," said Torrance. "When was the last time you sat in an assigned seat?"

I strained to think. Junior year English in high school? No—Sophomore. Sophomore English. "You're joking, right?" I said hopefully. Mandy and Sally exchanged knowing glances.

"Well," Tyler said, trying to soften the blow, "they're not assigned, per se . . ."

"Yeah," added Torrance helpfully, "you do pick your seat . . ."

"Once," Tyler finished.

"Once?"

"Hope you don't plan to sleep much the night before classes," Sally told me.

And so I learned of Darwinian seat selection, a great and aged tradition at HBS. The night before classes began each year, the building housing the school's classrooms was left un-locked. At some ghastly hour of the morning, the zombies' march of first-year students would begin. The seats in each section's classroom were available on a first-come, first-serve basis. If the first person to stumble into the room happened to do so at three-thirty in the morning, then that was the will of the market. The only restriction was that once you sat down, you sat down for good; under no circumstances would anyone be allowed to switch seats for the rest of the year. Three-thirty was the winning time in Tyler and Torrance's section the year before. At that hour a particularly ambitious sectionmate of theirs entered the room and had his pick of locations. What seat did he decide would best personify and position him for the next nine months?

· "The joker took Power Deck, Left Field!" said Torrance with disdain. Tyler, Mandy, and Sally all shook their heads disparagingly.

After a moment's hesitation, I gave my own head a knowing shake. "Power Deck, Left Field," I muttered. "Such foolishness."

"You better get there before five," Sally counseled.

"Yeah," said Tyler. "You can count on the Sky Deck filling up by five-thirty."

I decided that feigned agreement wouldn't do after all. "Sky Deck?"

And so I learned of another great HBS tradition. Sky Deck was the name of the last and most elevated row in each classroom. It was there that the self-appointed slackers, jesters, and ringleaders would sit. Early in the year, the Sky Deck would traditionally launch a series of weekly "section awards." These were meant more to keep people in line than to laud exemplary behavior. Popular honors included the Shark Award for the week's most ruthless remark, and the Invisible Hand Award for someone who spoke without being called upon by the professor.

Sky Deckers had fun compiling their weekly lists of awardees. Seated far from the professor's watchful gaze, they also enjoyed the diversion of a vibrant note-passing culture. Top Ten lists, sardonic reviews of other students' comments, and critiques of professorial appearances and deportment flew through the Sky Deck daily. Politically correct irritability was generally not welcome in that most elevated of decks. "Those notes kept me sane during four months of Marketing class!" Tyler recalled. Sky Deckers often viewed themselves as the section's elite; they got away with having the most fun, and their grades rarely suffered as a result. Sky Deck, in the opinion of everybody at our table, was the only place to sit.

"I made a huge mistake last year," Torrance confessed. "There were still a few Sky Deck seats left when I came in on the first day. But I was worried about getting a bad image with the professors or something, so I sat in the Warning Track."

"The Warning Track?"

And so I learned the names of the other decks of the Harvard Business School. The Warning Track, named after the brown patch of packed earth which brackets the fringe of a baseball outfield, was one notch below the Sky Deck in both altitude and prestige. Next was the Power Deck, so named because its residents sat at eye level to professors, and could therefore most easily fix them with a penetrating, knowledgeable gaze. Below that was the Garden Deck, so named because gardens are found above worms, as the sniveling inhabitants of the front row, or Worm Deck, were known. The decks were horseshoe shaped, and together they bracketed the Pit, where the professors stood during class. The room was divided into three sections by two staircase aisles (known by some people as the Atlantic and the Pacific, because they were particularly difficult to pass notes across). These sections were called, predictably enough, Right Field, Center Field, and Left Field, based on the perspective of a professor facing the class.

In the opinion of the experts at the dinner table, Left Field, Power Deck was a laughable site for someone to pick at three-thirty in the morning. "Where you really want to be is Right Field, Sky Deck," Torrance noted sagely.

By now the Sky Deck's desirability was self-evident. But Right Field?

"You don't want to be in Center Field. A professor's more likely to call on you out of the blue if you're in his line of sight," Tyler explained.

"But you want to get called on when you raise your hand, so you don't want to be too far out of sight," Torrance cautioned.

"And since most professors are right-handed, they tend to look over their *left* shoulder into *Right* Field when they're writing on the board, and that's when they'll be looking for hands," Tyler finished. Thus Right Field. "But you don't want to be too far off to the right, or you'll really be buried. You'll never get called if you're all the way over on the Foul Line."

"I see. So the best place is Sky Deck, Right Field, but on the extreme *left* side of Right Field so that I'm sitting on the aisle and am more likely to be seen." I felt like I was getting the hang of this. Aisle seat! Just like on an airplane. In the unlikely event of a sudden change in cabin pressure . . .

"No, no!" Torrance said. "You don't want to sit next to the Pacific!" (Pacific, I thought. Aisle between Right Field and Center Field. Gotcha). "That'd make you the interocean mailman. The professors would see you passing other people's notes all day long. They'd end up thinking you're a total hack even if you're not!" He rolled his eyes, looking at Tyler. Was this kid really gonna cut it?

"Okay, now I get it," I said, eager to salvage something of my reputation. "I want Sky Deck, Right Field, one seat *away* from the Pacific."

Tyler smiled broadly and nodded. "Best seat in the house. Worth losing some sleep over." At that point the fajitas came and the conversation shifted. I didn't learn much about classes, study groups, how to crack business school cases, or a variety of other subjects, but somehow I felt that Tyler and Torrance had imparted the most important advice one could hope for.

The next morning I navigated my way through Harvard Square and across a little bridge to the Boston side of the river where the business school was located. Orientation week was only a few days away, but the campus looked like a strip mine. It was a maze of trenches, pits, and piles of debris. Mature trees with burlap sacks of dirt tied about their roots dotted the walkways like so many potted plants. I had heard of this phenomena before. HBS was said to put itself through a traumatic bout of capital improvements every summer. A hurricane zone two days before students arrived, it always returned to pristine normalcy in the nick of time.

Despite the construction work, it was clear that the campus was a lovely place. Most of its buildings were red-brick, ivy-clad Georgian structures. The main library, Baker, was eerily reminiscent of my red-brick, Georgian-style junior high school (with the exception of its Greek columns, which my junior high lacked). After a while I found my way to the office that administered the dormitories. I had applied to live in a dorm, but had heard their rooms were notoriously tiny. I was therefore anxious to see the room I'd been assigned before agreeing to live in it.

The woman in charge of assigning dorm rooms introduced me to the fellow who would show me the room I was allocated in the housing draw. "If you don't like that one, just check out a couple others," she said. "There are still a few rooms open, and I'm sure you'll find one you'll like."

In the summer sunlight, the exterior of my would-be dormitory was handsome enough. But inside it was a grim-looking place. Its long, tiled hallways seemed out of a 1950s psychiatric ward, where sociopathic doctors would give bellicose patients electric shocks. Worse, my room was so small I could hardly stand in the middle of it with both arms outstretched. My guide chuckled as I tried this. He'd seen it before. Eventually he showed me a much larger room on the top floor of a dormitory called McCulloch. It got plenty of sunlight, and was on the upper floor of a spacious two-level suite made up of several other rooms. So this was it; the McCulloch attic. Not a bad place if you could handle a fourth floor walk-up.

A week later I was back again. I met Tyler at his house, then headed over to a parking lot where we met Torrance. The guys had generously volunteered to be my move-in committee. This was lucky, as I had filled my father's pickup truck with as much stuff as I thought could be crammed into my tiny new penthouse pad. When we got to McCulloch, Tyler and Torrance made the requisite jokes about how my stuff would never fit into the room, but it eventually did. When we finished unpacking, they sent me along to one of the hourly campus tours the second-year students were giving. The group waiting for the tour was comprised of young, professional-looking men and women. Most were fairly relaxed, although one or two looked as nervous as college freshmen preparing to bid their parents farewell.

A strapping, bearded second-year walked up to our group and greeted us. "Mornin' folks, and welcome to Harvard Business School. My name is Mike Profit." Mike *Profit*? I already knew the dean of the MBA program was named James *Cash*. This couldn't be real.

Mr. Profit guided us around the campus. The high point for me was Shad Hall, even though it was closed at the time. The building was named for John Shad, the former chair of the Securities and Exchange Commission. Mr. Profit told us that Shad made a $20-million contribution to help foster the teaching of ethics at the business school. And now we had Shad Hall. It was one of New England's finest athletic facilities, and I had often heard of it from atrophying alumni who recalled it with misty-eyed fondness. Just seeing the building's exterior was like a pilgrimage for me. Warsaw was barren of health clubs, and I had hardly hefted a barbell since leaving San Francisco. HBS would be different. Shad Hall was simply massive. Here's to ethics, I thought.

After our tour, Mr. Profit took us to a typical classroom. It was a windowless room, with five horseshoelike rows bracketing the professor's territory in front. Just like Tyler and Torrance had described it. Sky Deck. Worm Deck. Atlantic. Pit. I felt like a veteran already.

That night brought a series of welcoming parties. The biggest was held in a massive tent in one of the fields. Most of the first-year class was there by eight o'clock. The tent was cramped, humid, and packed with beer-swilling bodies. So this was the class of '94. Soon I was in the midst of an endless series of three-minute conversations. Where are you from? Where did you work? Where did you go as an undergraduate? Next!

One of my longer conversations of the evening was with a guy named Rick, who grew up less than ten minutes away from me in Connecticut. He came from Stamford's black community, a world more distant from my own than the four highway exits separating our childhood neighborhoods would suggest. Eight years before he had become the first person from his immediate family to attend college. Now that his two younger brothers had followed suit, he was leading the charge again by becoming the first to enter a graduate program. He was one of roughly forty black students in HBS's class of '94. Rick and I made vague plans to have brunch the next morning, then continued on our random paths through the crowd.

Not long after that I met Hans, the Austrian whose GMAT test was so enlivened by the chants of Rhineland cheerleaders. He was a 6'3" ectomorph with owlish horn-rimmed glasses and a distinctly uncomfortable air about him. We chatted briefly about his background. Although Austrian, Hans had chosen, for a variety of reasons, to study in Germany. He completed a course in economics, and then went to work for a large commercial bank in Bonn. Throughout our conversation, he seemed out of sorts and none too certain about where he would fit into things.

Months later he would tell me that he had indeed found much of orientation to be awkward. He'd had some American acquaintances in Austria and Germany, had seen his share of American films, and had traveled briefly to the United States as a teenager. But none of this had readied him for an orientation week which was as American as the baseball game that raged throughout his GMAT exam, much less two years of Boston. Hans found the week to be short on events to mitigate these feelings. Orientation did feature a modest reception for international students, but it came too late in the week to help Hans and his peers form the kindred cliques of like-minded orientationeers that developed quickly among the Americans. "It was as if they tossed you into an American sea without first checking to see if your gills worked," he later observed.

That sea frothed thicker as the evening wore on. Faces and backgrounds blended together. It seemed that more of my classmates graduated from college in 1989 than any other year, meaning that they had been out for three years. A handful had been out for two, while a big group of people were pushing or beyond their thirtieth birthdays. The younger folks tended to have gone the consulting or investment banking route, although many had worked in manufacturing, marketing, or other fields. A lot had been in the military, and there was a huge group of foreign students. I met people from at least a dozen countries, including such remote points as post-Soviet Georgia and Vietnam.

I found myself gravitating toward the younger consulting/I-banking types, partly because almost everyone I met from this group seemed to know somebody I knew. Either it was a classmate from Stanford who worked at their company, somebody from their high school who went to Stanford, somebody from their college who worked at Bain, or some other odd connection. There were also quite a few people I knew personally; at least a dozen alumni of Bain San Francisco were in my class, as well as about forty Stanford graduates. It was nice making all these connections. Such a small world, we marveled; we're practically all related!

Not surprisingly, some people had a very different take on the night. Jerry, a person I later got to know quite well, hated the tent party. He grew up in Montana, went to a public university in New Mexico, and had spent his professional life in the army. Unlike me, he wasn't tied to half of our class through college, work, or other friend-of-friend connections. "That night, I thought this was the most unfriendly place on earth," he later told me. "People had barely heard of my university, they seemed to have little professional respect for the army, and nobody had ever been to my home state. It was three strikes and you're out. I don't think I held anyone's attention for more than a minute."

Thinking back on the night, I don't think many people were being deliberately exclusionary. It's natural to bond with people of similar backgrounds in a new environment, particularly when they are people you already know or are friends of people you know. Still, if I wasn't calculatedly cruel to people like Jerry, I probably was guilty of being overly focused on people like myself. For better or worse, I ended up heading across the river for dinner with about twenty people who generally fit the typical mold of the younger students. The bridge to Harvard Square was packed with other roving bands of fifteen to twenty-five HBS students. Each was a loose alliance of people who vaguely knew one another, united in a collective alcoholic fog and a general desire to get fed. For the third or fourth time that day, I had the uneasy feeling that this was an extended flashback of my freshman year of college.

The next morning I was nursing a college-sized hangover when a pounding came from the door. It was Rick, the guy who grew up ten minutes west of me, and he was hungry. We set off to Kresge. This was the main student lounge-cafeteria, and was conveniently located about a hundred yards from McCulloch's front door. The breakfast pickings were unspectacular but adequate. Rick was rebounding from a similar night to my own, but we still managed a decent conversation.

Rick went to Rensselaer Polytechnic Institute (RPI) in Troy, New York. There he studied industrial and electrical engineering, eventually graduating to a job with United Technologies Corporation in Connecticut. He worked at UTC for just under four years. One day, the thought of applying to business school came to him almost out of the blue. "I was talking on the phone to a buddy of mine from college. His roommate was working for some software house, and had just gotten into Stanford Business School. And the guy was a year younger than me. That started me thinking about doing it myself."

Rick knew that UTC had hired its share of MBAs over the years, so he started paying close attention to their trajectories within the firm. Eventually he determined that getting an MBA, particularly one from Harvard, would be invaluable to his own career. This wasn't an immediately obvious conclusion to draw, as he had been doing remarkably well in his job since college. "I knew I'd been targeted by the senior folks to do well in the business unit I was working for. And while that felt good, it kind of blinded me to the big picture. But when I looked at things closely, it seemed like I was ultimately headed for a professional plateau. A respectable, comfortable plateau, but a plateau nonetheless. This wasn't the case with the MBAs, especially the ones from Harvard." Rick applied.

Pragmatism generally dominated Rick's thinking about the degree. "I guess you could cynically look at it as a certification, like a stamp in your passport or something. But like it or not, the MBA used to be something that made you stand out. Now it's just something that brings you to the table with everyone else." For this reason, he found Harvard particularly attractive. "Where I come from, the Harvard brand name can still differentiate you. Where you were working, places like Stanford might have had the same effect. But I'm heading back to United Technologies after graduation for sure, and it's a pretty East Coast place."

After lunch, Rick and I walked over to Burden, the main auditorium. There, a big lineup of speakers was on hand to give us our official welcome to the business school. The program featured most of the heavies from the administration, as well as some student leaders from the second-year class. For me, the most interesting speaker was Laura Fisher, our dean of Admissions. She got the hearty welcome one would expect from an audience of eight hundred people who feel they owe their station in life to the speaker. She congratulated us all, then gave the anatomy of our class. The average age of our group was 26.2, almost precisely my age when I cranked out my essays in San Francisco. Nobody was younger than 23. A few people were well beyond 30. We had an average of 4.1 years of work experience, or roughly 3,200 years among us.

Our classmates hailed from almost every state in the country as well as over fifty foreign lands. Among us were a medalist from the Barcelona Olympics, HBS's first blind student, and a man who had been exiled from South Africa for his political activities. Fisher was particularly proud of our international credentials. Not only were 25 percent of us from foreign countries, but a huge percentage of the Americans had spent time studying or working overseas. Competition for admission had been tough our year. Over 5,000 people had applied for the 800 places in our class, and of those accepted, over 80 percent had matriculated. Her talk was heavy in statistics, but I didn't find it dry as it gave me a good sense of who we all were.

That night featured another big party in the tent, where the day's speeches were a big item of discussion. "What did you think of Laura Gordon Fisher?" people asked. By now, Ms. Fisher's middle name was often invoked; an honor usually reserved for certain American presidents (and occasionally their assassins).

The next day's main event was the HBS Olympics, or the Intersection Sports Day. This was a seminal moment, as it was then that we finally discovered who else was in our sections. The nine sections were creatively named after the first nine letters in the alphabet. I was assigned to Section I along with ninety-one other people. The formation of the sections from the 800 incoming students was by no means a haphazard process. Each was said to be a hand-selected, meticulously balanced cross section of our class. Section I, then, was a scientific mix of consultants, marketers, foreigners, investment bankers, social workers, singles, married people, African Americans, Asians, people over thirty, Californians, and (I am certain) lefties.

Over the previous two days there had been a certain amount of excitement and perhaps some anxiety over the prospect of the sections' first meetings. After all, we were unlikely to see much of anyone else for an entire year. Section I would take each of the twelve classes in the first-year curriculum as a group. Between us we would spend almost 50,000 person-hours together in the same room. Romance, camaraderie, rivalry, treachery; we were sure to have it all within a week or two. I headed over to the HBS Big Top with Rick, who also turned out to be in Section I. Soon we identified our section T-shirts, which would color code us for the rest of the day. Section I's color was a revolting shade of near-neon green. There would certainly be no mistaking us on the playing field that day.

Section I was shunted off to the far left edge of the field, as its position at the bottom of the alphabetic barrel dictated. Soon I was in a sea of shocking green shirts. "Leapfrog!" somebody hollered. "Get ready for leapfrog!" The Olympics were on, and we now had three minutes to field a team of twelve leap froggers for our first group effort as a Harvard Business School section. Somehow I got volunteered to leap. Moments later I found myself wearing a red jersey. I would be no ordinary leap frogger; this jersey now designated me as an Anchor Leap Frogger! My subgroup of three would be the last trio to leap for Section I in the day's opening relay. I felt my anchor status merited a demonstration of Leadership Skills as the section gathered to shout encouragement to the first group of leapers. "GIVE ME AN I!" I yelled.

Several dozen throaty voices responded. "I!!!"

"WHAT'S THAT SPELL?"

"I!!!"

There were chuckles all around, and our first section cheer was born.

By the time our trio was ready to leap into the relay, Section I was losing badly. Our group made up all the lost ground and even edged ahead by sprinting seventy or eighty feet between "leaps." This may not have been traditional leapfrogging, but it hadn't been specifically forbidden. We were thrilled with our come-from-behind triumph, but the Olympic committee refused to dignify our victory with official acknowledgment. The name of a rival section boomed across the loudspeakers as the sanctioned victor.

"Hey, we won that," someone groused.

"Section I got screwed," somebody else muttered.

Soon another cheer was born. "I GOT SCREWED! I GOT SCREWED!" we chanted.

The next event was a potato sack relay, and Section I approached it in a similarly subversive manner. We designated a squad of petite women to be our sack-hoppers. When the starting gun sounded, each of our racers was lifted by her shoulders and physically carried the length of the field, potato sack dangling about her feet, by a pair of brawny men. Not surprisingly, our entire team was done before most of the other sections finished the first leg of the race. Less surprisingly, we were again robbed of victory by an Olympic committee with a limited sense of humor. The "I GOT SCREWED!" cheer was launched again, and Section I delighted in becoming the bad boys and girls of the HBS Olympics. We proceeded to concoct our own approaches to almost every event, and were disqualified from most of them.

I was pleased with my first glimpse of Section I. The group

certainly came as advertised in terms of being a microcosm of HBS. Among us were fighter pilots and venture capitalists, avowed Libertarians and former civil servants, as well as HBS's first blind student. We had fun playing our Olympic outlaw role, although when the day was over I realized that none of the other sections had paid much notice to it. Each section was an island unto itself that day, and most people were oblivious to outsiders.

The evening's activity was a gathering at a Boston pool hall large enough to accommodate our whole class. It was a fairly low-key affair, as most were regaining their wits after the previous night's debauchery, or husbanding their energy for the next evening, which would feature the first of many "section pub nights." I met a number of people from my section that night including Jerry, the guy from Montana who had had such a miserable time at the tent party.

A towering man with a shaggy mane of dark hair, a pulverizing handshake, and the glimmer of a musky backwoods twang, Jerry was a person whose background could hardly have differed more from my own. He had spent eight years in the army after getting an engineering degree at the University of New Mexico. One of the oldest people in the section, he was also married. While military backgrounds were less common than business backgrounds at HBS, they were by no means unheard of. The class of '94 included dozens of alums of the U.S. military, at least one officer still on active duty, and countless foreign nationals who had served in their own countries' armed forces.

While it hadn't taught him how to develop financial models or marketing plans, Jerry's job had given him something most of us lacked; real managerial experience. During his last tour of duty, he had commanded an armored company in Germany. This made him responsible for fourteen tanks, an assortment of other vehicles, and over a hundred soldiers. The level of authority and responsibility he held over his troops far exceeded that exercised by any management consultant or investment banker. I ended up enjoying Jerry's company quite a bit, although he was a bit soft-spoken at first (perhaps a hangover from his unpleasant evening at the tent party). Once he warmed to someone, he had a quick, sardonic wit and seemed very perceptive. I also met his wife, Melissa. A tall, pretty woman with jet black hair and dark blue eyes, she was quite vivacious and had Jerry's sharp sense of humor.

The next day was mainly a time for moving in. Rick and I wandered over to Harvard Square to buy push pins, desk supplies, and other essentials for the approaching academic year. I had been up to Harvard a couple of times in high school and was glad to find the Square was as interesting a place as I remembered it. The area was dense with bookstores, CD outlets, little boutiques, ice cream parlors, and bars. A ratty folk singer was parked in the midst of it all, belting out outraged, politically correct anthems as a small crowd nodded in sympathy and occasionally tossed a coin in his guitar case. Rick and I watched the singer, wandered through a bookstore or two, and had a leisurely lunch of pizza slices. "It's a pretty fun area," Rick observed. "It's good we're enjoying it before the storm hits."

That night was the long-heralded Orientation Show, featuring a contingent of second-year students performing silly skits and songs about the coming year. The most memorable part of the performance was the finale. A few months before, we had each been asked to send in a photograph accompanied by a brief summary of our experiences and interests. The pictures and information, we were told, were for a class directory. Somehow the organizers of the Orientation Show had gotten an advance copy of this directory, and found in it a gold mine of material.

"You know," the emcee said, "a few of you have some pretty bizarre hobbies. Like this guy." A picture of a rather reserved-looking fellow flashed up on the cavernous auditorium's screen. Beneath it was a yearbook-style listing of the information he had sent in about himself. "His hobbies include travel, running, and THRILL SEEKING!" Sure enough, Thrill Seeking was up there in his list of interests. The Thrill Seeker's 800 new classmates erupted in laughter. I broke into a cold sweat. *What did I put down as my hobbies?* Another picture flashed on the screen. Not mine.

"This man's favorite hobby is karaoke! For those of you who don't know, karaoke machines play popular songs without the words, so a ham like this guy can get up, grab a microphone, and sing along for his friends. Now we saw this and thought, what a terrific pastime! Why don't we give him a chance to show it off to all of his new friends!" The room filled with anticipatory laughter. The emcee asked the unlucky student to come down to the front of the auditorium, which he nervously did. They handed him a lyric sheet and the band struck up "I Write the Songs," a sappy mid-seventies hit. The guy luckily rose to the occasion; he swaggered about like a Las Vegas lounge artist and even had a pretty good voice. He was awarded with a standing ovation.

About a dozen other people were roasted for their hobbies, their old employers, or their pictures. A woman who had listed an interest in "Silly Hungarian Folk Dances" had to come down and demonstrate her art. A British student who wrote that he enjoyed "traditional English ales" was invited to chug a can of American beer as the band played the Budweiser theme. The segment was clever and not mean spirited, although I couldn't help but wonder if it hadn't dashed a fragile ego or two.

After the show, everyone headed to their respective section pub nights. Section I was at the Hong Kong, an establishment whose specialty was Scorpion Bowls. These globe-sized glasses of grog were known to be perennial favorites with the HBS populace. I found Jerry at the end of one of the tables. He was talking to a guy who introduced himself as a member of "Old I," our section's second-year counterpart. He had learned that "New I" (my section) was meeting at the Hong Kong, and thought it would be fun to pass by and check out the freshmen.

"So," he scowled, after we had been introduced, "have you heard about the seating assignments?" I nodded. A rumor that circulated all week had just been confirmed: The days of the late-night rush for Sky Deck seats were over. This year, our seats would be assigned. "Totally ludicrous," the second-year muttered darkly. "When I was a first-year, you had to be up by five in the morning just to avoid Worm Deck!" Here it comes, I thought. For decades I listened to my father tell me how he walked five miles to school in the snow as a child. Now I could look forward to a year of war stories from second-year students about how rough they had it claiming seats on the first day of school.

Jerry was happy with the change. "At least we'll be able to sleep tomorrow night!" he pointed out. This was a common view among my classmates. In fact, I knew of almost nobody other than myself who was displeased with the new regime.

Most people felt the old system constituted an unnecessary burden on what was already a stressful first day of classes. While this
was probably true, I personally saw little advantage in gaining a
few hypothetical hours of sleep on a night that was likely to be
steeped in insomnia for most of us anyway. I also thought that
to focus on the issue of sleep before the first day of classes was
to miss the real question.

The real question was why did we need a "one year-one
seat" rule anyway? It wasn't to help professors remember our
names; all of us would sit behind name plates, which would be
enough to prompt even the most forgetful teachers. The best
explanation I heard was that Harvard was trying to foster a
"boot camp" mentality among the first-years, which would
somehow build our characters and help us "bond" with one
another. This seemed like an awfully lame reason to confine
somebody to one seat for twelve courses. But given that it was
reality, I would have preferred to control my own seating destiny. The place for me was Right Field, Sky Deck, one seat
from the Pacific. I could probably have nabbed that spot just by
braving an early morning wake-up call. Now my chances of
getting it were one in ninety-two.

The man from Old I eventually gave up on trying to sell
Jerry on the virtues of Darwinian seat selection. "You'll be singing a different tune when you walk in there and see your name
tag in the Worm Deck," he grumbled.

By now our first Scorpion Bowl had arrived. A suspicious
mixture of pinkish liquid and crushed ice, it was garnished
by several two-foot straws that sprouted from it like so many
tentacles. We each grabbed one of these and inhaled. Looking
like a clutch of junkies around a hookah pipe in an opium den,
we soon finished with a massive slurp. For now, at least, the
perils of Worm Deck Roulette seemed remote.

4

THE WARNING TRACK

THE NEXT DAY was gray and drizzly. The morning was taken up by registration, an approximately fifteen-step process which featured the settlement of over $9,000 in tuition charges. This was by no means the only thing to be paid for. There were charges for food, for housing, for health insurance, for access to the student medical center, and for the right to use the on-campus athletic facility. There was a $1,050 bill for roughly 200 cases, a mysterious $40 fee payable to the "Student Association," and a $550 billing for the privilege of leaving my car in a dimly lit outdoor lot which was said to be plagued by thievery. The people living in Soldiers Field Park, a pricey complex of on-campus apartments, were particularly incensed about parking. They were required to use an indoor facility that rented its spots at $90 a month; this came on top of the extravagant cost of their leases.

And registration wouldn't be the only time we'd face bills from HBS. Harvard had its own telephone system, and those of us in the dorms would pay substantial "hook-up" charges even though our rooms were permanently wired to the same phone numbers every year. Later on everyone would dole out approximately $150 for "section dues." Also on the horizon was a $20 fee to have our résumés included in the HBS résumé

49

book, which would later be sold to interested corporations for $295 per set. "These guys are like a credit card company, collecting money from both sides of the transaction," Jerry groused upon hearing of that little racket. Harvard Business School may have been a not-for-profit organization, but it certainly wasn't running at a loss.

One of the last steps in the registration process was collecting a copy of the class Prospectus. This was the directory our Orientation Show emcees had mined so effectively for material. Attractively designed and intelligently formatted, it was a photographic guide to the class of 1994. Along with our yearbook-style photographs and thumbnail résumés, the Prospectus included several appendices that cross-listed us by school, previous employer, industry expertise, home state and country, and several other affiliations.

A casual inspection of the Prospectus's pages revealed a number of interesting trends. Our class's professional profile was particularly striking. As expected, people had come from consulting and investment banking firms in droves. In total, there were well over 200 consultants in our class of 800, and slightly less than 200 investment bankers.

No other industry approached these levels of representation. Together, just four investment banks (First Boston, Goldman Sachs, Salomon Brothers, and Morgan Stanley) and four consulting firms (McKinsey, Bain, the Boston Consulting Group, and Booz Allen & Hamilton) had sent more people to HBS than all of the companies in the Fortune 500 combined. Representation from within the ranks of America's industrial giants was similarly skewed. Just four companies (IBM, Procter and Gamble, General Electric, and General Motors) accounted for roughly half of our Fortune 500 alums. More HBS first-years came from Bain, McKinsey, and Goldman Sachs alone than the other 496 companies on Fortune's venerable roster.

Not surprisingly, HBS's biggest feeder school appeared to be Harvard College itself. Sixty-four of my classmates were Harvard graduates. Stanford placed a very distant second, sending thirty-five of its own, followed close by Brown, the University of Pennsylvania, Princeton, and Yale. The eight Ivy League colleges together with Stanford and MIT accounted for roughly 35 percent of my classmates.

After registering, we spent the afternoon at the Student Clubs Fair, a recruiting rally for on-campus organizations. Most of these were industry or regional focus groups, existing principally to sponsor lectures and informational seminars and to help students get jobs. Some, like the Finance Club, regularly signed up high percentages of the student body. Many of these larger clubs touted the fact that they assembled their own résumé books, compilations of member credentials that were solicited by industry leaders at recruiting time. Some also sponsored industry career fairs that attracted more big-name employers than some whole schools could lure during an entire year.

The more popular clubs focused on areas such as marketing, management consulting, manufacturing, venture capital, entrepreneurial management, arts and media, and finance. The Finance Club was a bit notorious due to a scandal the previous year, in which a student reportedly rigged his own election to the club's presidency. The incident, which was covered on the front page of The Wall Street Journal's Marketplace section, was well known to members of my class. This didn't stop us from signing up in droves, however. For a mere $35 we could get a two-year membership, which included a spot in their famous résumé book. They also threw in a ninety seven-page survey of the industry and its leaders and a club T-shirt.

A few clubs were actually unrelated to students' professional objectives. Many of these were connected to athletic endeavors. Others, like the Harvard Political Forum, touched on more cerebral pursuits. One organization that caught my eye was The Harbus News, the HBS newspaper. I occasionally enjoyed writing for Stanford's campus paper as an undergraduate, so I signed my name to their list of interested students and got a plastic Harbus mug for my troubles.

Near the Marketing Club's booth I ran into Sandra, the Yale graduate who had worked at Morgan Stanley. I recognized her from the potato sack relay. She was perhaps 5'4" tall and had thick strawberry blond hair.

"Joining any clubs?" I greeted her.

"I dunno," she answered guardedly. "I heard a lot of these people are really just selling twenty-five dollar T-shirts." I nodded. Some of my second-year friends had warned me that the main activity offered by many of these clubs was writing the membership check. "I joined the Marketing Club, but I think that's where I'll stop," she finished.

"What about the WSA?" I asked. The Women's Student Association was one of the more highly regarded clubs, and seemed to be enjoying a successful membership drive.

Sandra looked somewhat perplexed. "I don't know. . . . I don't think so. It seems like a bit of a crutch, doesn't it?"

I gave her a baffled look.

"I mean, I didn't need a women's association to get through Wall Street," she said, a bit more forcefully. "So I don't see why I should need one to get me through HBS." This response surprised me, and I decided not to press the issue.

I ran into Jerry on my way out of the fair, and he accompanied me as I hiked toward McCulloch to face the inevitable. The orientation schedule, so full of happy events for the past week, had a single gloomy entry for the next day: "CLASSES BEGIN. You'll start your academic career at HBS with a double session of Ethics. Classrooms open at 8:15 A.M. Class is from 8:30 to 12:30." The double session of Ethics referred to two consecutive classes of Decision Making and Ethical Values (DMEV), the only class that would meet on that first day. DMEV was an odd offering. Just three weeks long, it was the only ungraded course at HBS.

The irony that Ethics was a brief, ungraded subject was not lost on Jerry. "Who's this school's PR guy?" he said as we strolled toward McCulloch. "I mean, how many business people get convicted every year? And they make Ethics the smallest part of the curriculum! Some reporter's gonna get hold of this and run with it."

We discussed this as we waded through the humid summer air. I thought it would be problematic to grade people in so subjective an area as ethics. Jerry agreed, but thought the course should at least meet as long as something like Organizational Behavior, which would be in session for months. "What the hell is Organizational Behavior anyway?" he asked, shaking his head.

I said good-bye to Jerry, climbed the four flights of steps to my floor, and walked into my cramped, humid room. The next day's ethics case, the first of the roughly 800 cases we would read, analyze, and discuss over the next two years, was waiting expectantly on my desk. I looked at the title, *AT&T and Mexico*. It was about fifteen pages long, by no means an imposing amount of text. Still, its length was a minor issue, as the challenges of HBS cases would come not in reading them, but in preparing to speak about them. In the classroom, each case would be taught in the forum of a dialogue between a professor and the section. Students would read and analyze the case, and present their conclusions when invited by the professor. The professor would shape the discussion, and ideally drive the class to some sort of consensus, or at least a few conclusions about what the case illustrated.

I picked up the case and began reading. It was intriguing, and I was done before I knew it. A manager had to decide whether to build a new answering machine factory in Mexico. Among the ethical issues it touched upon were the export of American jobs, the exploitation of Third World workers, and the definition of proper conduct in an environment rife with bribery and corruption. The central question of the case seemed like a no-brainer to me. Having once lived in a developing country with a stagnant economy, I found nothing wrong with bringing higher-than-average wages and better-than-average working conditions to poor, hungry areas. The question precisely of how to deal with corrupt local practices was a murkier issue.

I read the case twice more, taking detailed notes in the margins and on separate sheets of paper. I spent perhaps a half hour pondering the three study questions, each of which demanded a good deal of thought (for example: *What decisions should* [the protagonist] *make about wage levels, benefits, waste management, teenage workers, gender-based hiring, and bribery in the event that he chooses a Mexican site?*). Then it hit me—what if I got cold called? The odds were slim—one out of ninety-two, to be exact—but I wasn't in a risk-taking mood. Cold calling was a legendary fact of business-school life, which I had known about for years. If the promise of high-paying jobs was the carrot that dragged thousands of HBS students through two grueling years, the ubiquitous threat of a cold call was surely the stick. Most classes, I had been told, would begin when the professor selected an unsuspecting student to "open the case." This student would then be expected to speak for five to ten minutes, summarizing the pertinent points of the case, presenting an analytical framework for understanding it, and developing a plan of action for addressing the situation it described.

The cold-called student might then have to defend this analysis against potentially damaging assaults from the rest of the section. All the while the cold callee would be keenly aware that much of his grade was hanging in the balance. I could see two ways of dealing with the ever-present possibility of a cold call. One was to assiduously prepare every case every night. The other was to strive for a more balanced life by sometimes giving cases a more cursory treatment, thereby playing occasional rounds of cold-call Russian roulette. The former approach seemed more appropriate to the first day of classes, so I set out to make a detailed outline of what I would say if asked to open the case. I finished after about a half hour, and was about to type it into my computer when I realized I was getting hopelessly carried away. This was an ungraded class! Besides, it was time to meet with my first study group.

Study groups were almost as much of a tradition at HBS as the section system itself. They met late at night or early in the morning before classes. People went to them to discuss the day's cases, to make sure they didn't miss anything important, and to float their more bizarre ideas in a safe environment. Most first-year students joined one for at least the first few months. At first I wondered if it made sense to join a study group at all. I had survived without one in college. Still, study groups were said by many to be central to the Harvard socialization process; not going to one for at least a few weeks would mean missing out on part of the "HBS Experience."

Because all sections took the same classes at the same time, any random group of first-years could team up to form a study group. The past few days had been like choosing partners at an eighth-grade dance, as people shyly sidled up and invited one another to join their groups. I had met a lot of people during orientation and was asked to join four. My plan was to sample all of them over the next few days, and then decide which was the best fit.

Whichever group I joined, I planned to join with Alistair. I first met him at Stanford, and later worked with him in both San Francisco and Warsaw. A good study group was said to be the key to a successful year, and I knew Alistair was someone I could count on. That night we planned to sit in with a group convened by Natasha, a Russian woman I met during orientation.

I met Alistair in front of Kresge Hall, the dining and meeting center, and soon we found Natasha and her cohorts. The group was huge because many invitees had brought along friends, just as I had brought along Alistair. I recognized at least one other person from Section I. This concerned me, as I had been warned that forming a study group with people from my own section would be the kiss of death.

The second-year student Jerry and I met at that first section pubnight at the Hong Kong restaurant told us that he had a disastrous experience with this. Early in the year, he used to discuss all his best ideas with his study group, which was composed solely of people from his section. It wasn't long before they started parroting his ideas back in class, usually before he could give voice to them himself. "Damn plagiarists!" he scowled, still bitter about it a year later. "At HBS, a good in-class comment is a zero-sum game. If someone else says it, you can't. If you've got a brilliant idea and someone beats you to saying it, it's aggravating enough. But it's outrageous if they got it from you in the first place!"

He eventually decided to withhold all his good insights from his study group. The other members responded by guarding their ideas just as jealously, which soon defeated the purpose of even meeting. They disbanded in early October, and he felt his relationships with the rest of the group were poisoned ever since. This is not a good situation to be in with people who will take every single class with you during your first year of business school. "The one thing that could be worse would be sleeping with someone in your section," he growled.

Alistair and I sat down at the big table, and Natasha started the session. She asked everybody to say what they would recommend to the AT&T manager and why. There were relatively few differences, but we still managed to spend about an hour agreeing with one another. Carter, the other person from my section, was sitting across from me. He was quiet, and seemed somewhat unsure of himself. By the end of our meeting it was clear we had all generously overprepared for the next day's class, and everybody left in a relaxed frame of mind.

I slept fitfully that night, and woke up at seven the following morning. Around eight, I dragged myself across the lawn to Aldrich Hall, which housed all of our classrooms. Section I would be in Room 9 until June. This was in the basement, but it didn't matter as all the classrooms were identical and windowless. When I arrived, there was a small knot of people gathered around a seating chart posted next to the door. This was it! I raced up to find my name, scanning the Worm Deck first. Great! Not one of the unlucky ones. I continued my search. Not in the Garden Deck. Not in the Power Deck. Could it be? I eagerly skipped up to the Sky Deck. No such luck. Finally I found my name. It would be Warning Track, Left Field, right on the Atlantic's dangerous coast.

Standing by the door was a wild-looking man with longish hair and a flowing beard. He was wearing a suit in the frumpled style of William Buckley. I started to pass him on my way into Room 9 when he caught my eye and thrust out his hand. "Mornin', Rob!" he said. I smiled, greeted him, shook his hand, and started across the room to my seat. *Mornin' Rob?* Then it hit me—this crazy-looking dude was my professor! Over the summer I filled out a little questionnaire about myself which I sent back to Harvard with a picture (this was separate from the photograph and information used to tease people at the Orientation Show). An accompanying letter said the questionnaire would be used to acquaint professors with my background. This, then, was a professor, one who had memorized everybody's name and face before we got to class that morning.

I climbed up to my seat and looked around. We all had little white nameplates in front of our seats to identify ourselves to the rest of the section, making the place look like an assembly room at the UN. I recognized some people from orientation, but most of my classmates were still strangers. To my right was a German guy I hadn't yet met, to my left was an aisle. I wasn't happy about the aisle, having been warned about the note-passing problem by Tyler and Torrance. Still, the Warning Track was nothing to complain about. I was glad to notice that Jerry was my neighbor, only one row behind me and a couple seats over. Sky Deck, the lucky dog.

People were chattering idly, but most seemed pretty tense. There were a lot of bleary-eyed faces. The people assigned to the Worm Deck looked particularly shell-shocked. What a drag! Aisle seat or not, I was grateful not to be in their shoes. Across the room I spotted Hans, the Austrian. A tall, thin man, he was particularly tall and thin from the waist up, and towered over his diminutive American neighbors. He kept nervously adjusting and readjusting his glasses, and had brought enough note paper to see the lot of us through several months of lectures.

At precisely eight-thirty, our professor strode into the room. Not a seat was vacant; everyone had made it on time. He stood in the middle of the floor (or the Pit, I reminded myself) and started staring at us. All conversation hushed. He glowered theatrically for a few moments more, then leapt into the air and landed in a fighter's stance. "LET THE ADVENTURE BEGIN!!!" he bellowed. A few people giggled nervously, but most held their tongues. "We have a *lot* of ground to cover today, but before we get started I want you *all* to give yourselves a *big* round of applause, because you've all done some re*mark*-able things to get here today, and you de*serve* it!" That one broke the ice. The room rattled with clapping hands; few disagreed with the man.

The professor, Sam Lubbock, went on to tell us a bit about his background, about the course, and about Harvard Business School. He had a terrific presence and worked the section like a performer. I was impressed; this was going to be fun after all. Then he started talking about us. He rattled off some things about our backgrounds that he gleaned from our little questionnaires. He didn't name any names, but demonstrated with his quotes and citations that taken together, we were quite a group. At this point I started to feel uncomfortable. How seriously were those questionnaires taken, anyway? I recalled writing mine out a few months before. We were sternly instructed to type them, but our office in Warsaw had no typewriter. The only one I could find was in another office downstairs, and it was designed for typing in Polish. So while the keyboard included every letter in the Latin alphabet, their positions were hopelessly scrambled. My questionnaire ended up as a barely legible mess. Would that awful wreck really be my professors' first and lasting impression of me?

Professor Lubbock was still talking about us. "One of you," he said, "wrote a remarkable thing on his questionnaire this summer, and I'd like to share it with all of you." He began to quote from somebody's card: "I enjoy challenge, growth, and stimulation." As he said this, he drifted up the steps toward the Warning Track on the right side of the room. "Push me—" he paused dramatically, "to develop my fullest potential." He stopped in front of a guy in Center Warning Track whom I recognized from one of the orientation parties. "Mr. Clarke," Lubbock continued. "Would opening the first class of your MBA career constitute an adequate . . . challenge?" The poor guy almost fainted, while the rest of the class erupted with laughter. Lubbock's delivery was flawless; we had David Letterman for Ethics, and it was going to be a good year.

Lubbock's cold callee struggled a bit, but ended up presenting a good analysis of the case. He concluded that opening the factory in Mexico would be the right thing, provided that Mexican employees would work in conditions comparable to those in AT&T's American plants. Lubbock thanked him for an exemplary job, then asked the rest of us if we had anything to add. At least seventy hands shot into the air. The race for *airtime* was on.

I had been amply warned of the airtime obsession by Tyler and Torrance. Once a class's cold-call lamb was left quivering in a corner, they told me, the battle for air would begin. One would accumulate airtime whenever speaking in class, whether the comment made was a shining insight or a pedantic truism. Although my professors were sure to insist that class participation grades were not based upon the quantity of a student's comments, I could bet that many people would risk alienating their peers by zealously trying to "get in" as often as possible.

These students would be Section I's devotees of the "chip shot," the golfing term for an easy whack to the ball. A chip shot, they told me, was an innocuous comment that gives class discussion a paltry push forward. Wiser students would shun the chip shot, trying to make a genuine contribution every time they spoke. Others would derive elaborate strategies governing when to speak, how to speak, and how often to speak. What's the best tactic? To supportively "build upon" another student's remark? Or to ruthlessly "shark" somebody who made a foolish oral blunder? Ultimately, people's reputations and friendships would be driven to a large degree by their conduct in class discussions. And the stakes were by no means trivial; up to 50 percent of the final mark in any given class would be determined exclusively by class participation.

And now the first discussion was on! I remembered Tyler urging me to launch at least one comment during this maiden run of Ethics. "It's good to get used to talking when you know you're not getting graded. Besides, most people are too intimidated to speak up on the first day, so you'll have an easy time getting in." He was right about the desirability of learning to speak up in a low-risk environment, but Section I was anything but intimidated. No sooner would one person finish making a point than dozens of hands would shoot into the air. A lot of people even kept their hands up throughout other people's comments. This seemed a bit rude, but was said to be a common practice.

Lubbock did a great job of working through the key issues. There was relatively little ground for conflict in the case; American jobs would not actually be threatened if the factory was built in Mexico, and it was clear the new plant would be a windfall to its host community. The main point of contention was the issue of bribery. A Latin American student said that corruption in his part of the world was so endemic that AT&T would have to play along if it wanted to build the factory. Another student cited the Foreign Corrupt Practices Act, saying any indiscretion could get the company in trouble in the United States. Two camps formed on the issue, the pragmatists, who felt a small amount of bribery was acceptable if it advanced the higher end of opening the factory, and the idealists, who felt none should be tolerated. There were also a few people who supported the idealist position for pragmatic reasons, believing that once a factory paid off any official, it would be forever subject to further extortion.

The discussion went on for almost four hours which, it turned out, was closer to the duration of three normal classes laid end to end, rather than just two. This was more time than we needed to cover one case, but it was the first day. By the time the session was over, almost every person in the section had spoken at least once. I made some minor point supporting the hybrid "pragmatist-idealist" stance, and didn't get in again. But Tyler was certainly right. It was good to experience speaking in class before the first graded discussion on the next day.

Lubbock wrapped up the case by telling us what actually happened. AT&T did build the plant in Mexico. It gave a tremendous boost to the local economy, and quickly achieved productivity levels that surpassed the company's expectations. Before starting construction, AT&T made it clear to all relevant officials that the factory would absolutely not pay out any bribes. By establishing this position up front and adhering to it, corruption never became a problem. Lubbock thanked us for our attention and told us we did a great job. Everyone applauded and started congratulating the section's first cold callee on his opening.

By then we were all famished and aching to stretch our legs, but had to remain seated for another hour. It was time to meet Karen Trumble, our "section chair." She was the nominal head of Section I's faculty, although our professors actually reported to their respective academic departments. As the year unfolded, we would learn that the section chair's main role was to act as an interface point between the administration and the students. Trumble would also teach us a course in Human Resource Management starting in January.

After giving us a few minutes to unwind, Professor Trumble launched more or less immediately into the Harvard hard line. "You will *not miss classes*, folks," she told us. "It just *won't* happen. There are only three acceptable reasons for missing class; a serious *ill*ness, a serious illness in your *fam*ily, or a *death* in your family. That's *it*."

Hoo boy, I thought. My high school was more lenient than this.

"You should view your classes as *business* meetings," she continued. "Which is why you will not be late to class. You would never be late to a business meeting, would you? So you will never be late to class. That's also why you will not eat in this room. You wouldn't eat in a business meeting, would you?" I looked back at Jerry, who rolled his eyes in horror at this outburst.

Trumble wasn't finished. "You're going to want to establish some norms as a section. Is it acceptable for people to speak without raising their hands? Is it acceptable for people to raise their hands when somebody else is talking? These are issues you should resolve as a group."

Now she's onto something, I thought. Hand-raising while people were talking was sure to bother everyone, and I hoped Trumble would help us shake that habit quickly. Invisible Hand comments (in which somebody speaks without getting called on by the professor) would probably be even more annoying, but fortunately those hadn't cropped up yet.

Trumble continued. "You might also want to establish a way of greeting guests. You're going to have all kinds of guests coming through here this year. Last year there was a section that greeted people by doing The Wave [a small-scale version of the stadium antic in which people in one row stand up, followed by people in the next row, then the next, etc.]. You'll just have to ask yourselves if greeting people like this is appropriate professional conduct."

A number of people raised their hands to talk during the meeting, but the discussion didn't really go anywhere. Those who spoke mainly repeated one another on the subject of "section norms," affirming that they, too, thought hand-raising should be restrained when other people were talking.

Before hitting the books (or "the pamphlets," which our cases resembled more closely), I made my inaugural visit to the inside of Shad Hall, our exalted athletic center. The first stop on the way in was a guard desk, where nonmembers of the HBS community were screened out. Shad was as legendary to nonbusiness students at Harvard as it was to us. To our unhappy counterparts on the undergraduate campus and at the other graduate schools, it was a forbidden garden of physical delights. Their banishment from the facility led to a widespread case of Shad envy, which served to increase the general resentment the rest of Harvard seemed to bear toward the business school. "Let them eat cake," I muttered as the guard waved me through to the rarefied air of the interior.

Inside I found a beautiful, towering atrium which stretched up to skylights far overhead. I collected a towel from a staff member, and entered the men's locker room. It alone was almost as big as the diminutive athletic facility I once frequented as an undergraduate. There were rows of spacious lockers, as well as a well-kept bathing area which included over a dozen private showers, all fully stocked with shampoo and body soap. There was also a huge hot tub and a sauna. Outside the bathing area was a row of shining white sinks, each complemented by an electric hairdryer. And the locker room was easily Shad's least impressive area.

Just outside its doors on the first level were five squash and four racquetball courts. One level up were two aerobics studios, three full basketball and volleyball courts, and a fitness room. The fitness room was packed with the latest weight machines, as well as treadmills, rowing machines, ski machines, Life Cycles, and StairMasters. Also on that floor was HBS's franchise of Au Bon Pain, an upscale French deli. Its dining area was vast, and was furnished and decorated stylishly enough to keep pace with Shad's ritzy tone. On the top floor of Shad was the indoor track.

Eventually I made my way back to the less glamorous world of preparing cases. The next day would be another big one, as it would feature a session of Marketing, our first graded class. Marketing would be followed by a single helping of Ethics. Tyler had tipped me off that class participation would count for about a third of our grades in Marketing. The more I thought of it, the more ludicrous this seemed. How could you tell a room of ninety-two overachievers that their evaluations would be based largely upon how often and how articulately they spoke? If the double header of Ethics was anything to go on, the competition for air would be murderous once talking started to count toward grades.

My other big concern at that point was the grading policy. Professor Trumble reviewed it for us, but I had already read about it in a mailing we received over the summer. There were basically three grades a person could get in a class, a 1, a 2, or a 3. Ones were good; 3s were bad. It was theorctically possible to get a 4, but these were only doled out in extreme circumstances. Grading would be on a strictly forced curve; in each course, at least nine people in every section would get a 3. Even if a section contained the ninety-two greatest marketing wizards in human history, nine of them would still have to get 3s in Marketing. Conversely, no more than eighteen people would ever get 1s. This would leave a vast band of people in the middle with 2s.

I supposed the forced curve was a natural companion of the section system. Without it, sections blessed with 1-happy professors would tend to graduate people with better marks than other sections. Still, the policy seemed fraught with risk. The people in our section would spend a sometimes-claustrophobic year together. The competitiveness fostered by this would surely be worsened by a zero-sum grading system in which a person could only avoid a bad mark at the expense of someone else getting it.

With this in mind, I gloomily opened a Marketing case entitled *Hurricane Island Outward Bound*. As the title suggested, it concerned a branch of Outward Bound, the organization devoted to teaching wilderness survival skills in the context of grueling outdoor treks. Managers of the Hurricane Island location needed to bolster attendance in the slack winter months, and were worried that certain trips were losing money. What was the best way to promote the school, and what was the optimal mix of trips to offer? As I flipped through the pages, I saw it contained many numerical exhibits; clearly this was no Ethics case. I revved up my computer and crunched through a spread sheet for the first of many times at HBS.

That night I attended a study group organized by a guy I used to work with, while Alistair checked out a group set up by an old friend of his from Stanford. My group began by looking at the Marketing case. We analyzed it into the ground, much as Natasha's group had done with the AT&T case. Together we concocted a strategy for opening it, covering ourselves for the one-in-ninety-two chance of an early-morning crisis the next day. We spent very little time on Ethics; on day two, the course's ungraded status was already making itself felt. I was pleased with the group, but was concerned that it was already a bit large. I had been warned to study with no more than five people, which would leave no room for both me and Alistair in this group.

Marketing went well the next morning. Our teacher was Frank Cotton, a very tenured professor who had started his career at MIT. Like Lubbock he was bearded and bespectacled, but was much more kempt and conservative in appearance. His style was also more reserved, which was admittedly not saying much. Before class started, I noticed him drift over to Center Warning Track and chat briefly with a woman I knew from orientation. A few minutes later, after he had introduced himself and said a few words about the curriculum, he invited her to open the case. I had heard of this practice from Tyler; it was a warm call. Certain professors, like Cotton, believed in giving students a few minutes to collect their thoughts (or say their prayers) before launching an opening. This made sense to me; for most, even a few moments of frantic preparation would result in a better opening. This would get the class off to a better start, to say nothing of what it would do for the opener's

self-image. At least on this day the tactic worked, as both the
opening and the rest of the class discussion went well.

That night, I marveled that it had only been six days since
I lugged my suitcases up the McCulloch steps. It seemed more
like a month. The next day, Friday, would be a big one too,
as it would feature three graded classes. We would start with
Marketing, move on to Technology and Operations Management (TOM) in the late morning, and conclude with Management Communications (MC) after lunch.

The Marketing case was another interesting one. It concerned a company called Dominion Motors, a manufacturer
of oil-well pump motors. Dominion had just learned of new
regulations from the Canadian power authorities, which would
impact their customers. The company had to decide whether
to respond to these regulations by introducing a new product.
Obscure as the subject was, the case was rich in issues and
subtleties. And like the Hurricane Island case, it was also rich
in numbers. I crunched through some more spread sheets, and
eventually hit upon what seemed like the heart of the case. The
new regulations would make a certain type of motor incredibly
cheap to operate relative to other motors on the market. It
seemed that if Dominion could develop a pump motor with a
certain starting torque and horsepower, they would develop a
huge edge in the Canadian oil-pump motor market.

For MC we didn't have a case to prepare at all. Instead we
had a longish article to read about Digital Equipment Corporation. It discussed how DEC's founder and longtime president,
Kenneth Olsen, was finally stepping down. His successor, Robert B. Palmer, would sadly have to begin his tenure with a
massive layoff. I read the article carefully, making a slew of
notes. I also outlined responses to the study questions that accompanied it, but felt rather mystified about the object of the
exercise.

The TOM case was tough. It concerned a manufacturer of
printed circuit boards that was having a hard time pushing
production through its factory. Several steps in the manufacturing process were bottlenecks, and certain others were underuti-
lized. The case required both numerical and qualitative analysis,
and I didn't fully conquer it before it was time for study group.

That night, Alistair and I attended a group organized by
Carter, the guy we met through Natasha. I went despite my

reluctance to join a study group with a sectionmate. While somewhat quiet in the classroom, Carter was an otherwise outgoing
and relaxed person. I felt certain he'd pull together an interesting bunch. I also felt his background would mesh well with
mine and Alistair's. A graduate of Emory College, Carter had
spent three years working as a commercial banker in Atlanta
before coming to HBS. His understanding of finance, I reasoned, should nicely complement the backgrounds Alistair and
I had in corporate strategy.

Carter was in his dormitory's lounge when we arrived,
along with a few other people from different sections. We began
our meeting by discussing TOM. Alistair and Carter were on
top of this case, I had mastered about half of it, and at least one
of the other attendees was quite lost. It was then that I really
began to appreciate the value of the study group. Carter and
Alistair talked us through all of the case's tricky points, and
after about twenty minutes I had a much better grip on it.

Then we started on Marketing. Alistair and I were both on
top of that one, whereas Carter hadn't picked up on how the
regulations would transform the motor market. Alistair and I
explained the situation, and Carter and the rest of the group
seemed appreciative.

Carter became even more appreciative early the next morning. Right before Marketing started, I noticed Cotton approach
a student sitting two seats away from him. Clearly another warm
call. Soon enough, Cotton "publicly" asked Carter's neighbor to
open the case. The guy got the discussion off to a good start,
but didn't hit on all of the points our study group had explored.
As soon as the opening was over, Carter's hand shot in the air.
He was just a few feet away from the warm callee, and Cotton's
eyes went straight to him. "Okay, Carter," he said affably, "do
you have anything to add?"

Carter went on to rattle off much of the analysis that Alistair and I had laid out the night before. By the time he was
done, I felt like I had nothing left to say about the day's case.
Nothing! I understood Carter's zeal to jump into the fray of
class discussion, as I also felt it keenly. But wasn't he stealing
thunder that could have been mine? The second-year's grim
warning from our night in the Hong Kong came back to me,
and I resolved to heed it. It suddenly seemed that it would be
wise to avoid study groups with people from my own section.

Our next class, TOM, was taught by Joseph Stanley, a towering man whose credentials were even more impressive than his physical stature. Stanley had gotten his MBA at Harvard before going on to several years at a top strategic consulting firm. He later left consulting to help start a technology-intensive manufacturing company. Some time after his company went public, Stanley chose to heed a longtime desire to teach. He returned to Harvard for a Ph.D. and now, having just completed his degree requirements, was teaching his first class as a Harvard Business School professor.

If I hadn't known Stanley was new to his job, I wouldn't have guessed it from his teaching. He clearly illuminated the key points of a case that had initially overwhelmed many of us. TOM, it seemed, would be a survey of industrial engineering, a field I knew little about. Stanley had an affable, patient demeanor, which made this new territory significantly less threatening. When people spoke, he tended to engage them in a brief dialogue, probing to see how well they had thought out their positions. He managed to do this in a nonconfrontational manner, which made people push themselves further rather than squirm under pressure. The only sign of Stanley's inexperience was that he ran low on time at the end of the class, and had to rush us through his last few points.

At lunch I dined at a long table which was packed with Section I people. I sat down between Rick and Hans, both of whom were as impressed with Stanley as I was. "The guy must have made a bundle when his company went public," Rick observed. "He could be doing anything in the world right now."

"Which means he's doing what he wants to do most," I said.

"Yeah, and it shows," said Rick. "It's sure nice to find a professor with that kind of commitment."

I nodded in hearty agreement, as I had been considering this very issue all morning. At least so far, our school seemed particularly apt at hiring professors who genuinely enjoyed teaching. This was a welcome change from what I had encountered on my undergraduate campus, where many classes were taught by superb researchers who were unenthused or mediocre as instructors. By all accounts, Harvard's undergraduate program was even worse in this regard than Stanford's, so I expected a similar situation at HBS. I was very pleased to find the opposite.

I mentioned this to Rick and Hans. "Ah, you once attended Stanford," Hans responded. "So pretty a place. I have seen pictures."

"Yeah, it's great," I answered. "Did you think of going there for business school?"

"Yes, and I was even admitted. But sadly, it was never a realistic choice." Rick and I looked at him quizzically. "You see," Hans explained, "for the Austrian, simply getting an MBA is a very . . . rather strange thing to do. For us it is typical to attend university for several years, and graduate with the equivalent of one of your Master's degrees. Going back to school after some years of work is unusual enough. And most people, they have never even heard of this MBA.

"So one who gets this degree will always find himself explaining to people just what it is he has gotten himself. But if he went to Harvard, well, it's easier to get away with that. The normal man on the street, as you say, he has surely heard of this Harvard. He may not be an expert on the school, but he knows it, and he respects it. But Stanford? The University of Penn? Far fewer people know them, aside from the most educated and internationally-oriented people. If you spent two years studying business administration in America, you might have to talk yourself green in the face explaining to people that this was rather a valuable thing to do. And even then they might be skeptical, and suspect you were just trumpeting your own horn. But should you say you studied business at Harvard, well that's probably easier to explain, even to one not familiar with the MBA."

Rick nodded. "You know, it's funny, but it was a lot like that for me too. Because even though I'm from here, going off to business school was about as radical for me as it was for Hans." He looked over at me. "A lot of you pretty much got here by following the path of least resistance," he said, only half jokingly. "If you grew up in a rich suburb, went to an Ivy League school, and then ended up somewhere like McKinsey or Wall Street, HBS was an easy next step because it's what everybody expected of you.

"But me, I was really kind of breaking the mold when I decided to come here. I didn't have many precedents to look at within the engineering ranks at United Technologies. And then there was my family. I'm sure almost everybody here made their parents' day when they told them they were coming to Harvard Business School. Not me. My parents flipped out. They figured I was making good money at UTC, and had pretty decent job security. It just wasn't logical to them that I'd jettison that to take on a ton of debt for another degree. Maybe they felt that way because they've both worked hard to support themselves since high school. They're pragmatically minded, and they don't like the idea of betting heavily on intangibles like the career benefits of an MBA. You know, it's kind of ironic," he added reflectively. "It seems like a lot of people like you come here because they're risk averse." I nodded, as this was certainly true of me. "But me," he concluded, "I think I'm here more because I'm a risk taker."

Eventually it was time to leave Kresge and head off to Management Communications, the last class of the day. The course was intended to make us more effective business writers and speakers. I came to class with my note-laden articles on DEC, still not sure of what to expect. I certainly didn't anticipate what happened next. Moments after I sat down, our professor walked up to me. "Hi, Rob, my name's Al Golden. I'm your MC professor." I smiled and nodded. Why the special treatment? "In a little while I'm going to ask you and two other people to head out of the room for about ten minutes. When you come back, one of you is going to give a speech as Robert Palmer announcing the layoff of 25,000 people at DEC. Don't panic— it won't necessarily be you." Whoa! I thought. What did I type on that Polish typewriter that earned me this?

Golden started the class. Like Lubbock he was a bit of a comedian, and moved energetically about the room as he spoke. He told us about the course; we would have two speeches to make, a group presentation, and a few papers. Then he launched a class discussion about the future of DEC. I paid little attention to any of this, as I was desperately trying to collect my thoughts. *What do you say when you're laying off 25,000 people?* I had once fired a housekeeper in Egypt, but that was my net experience in terminations. After a short while, Golden asked two other students and me to exit the room as promised. We would have ten minutes to prepare our speech, and would then have to choose one of our number to give it.

The other students were a woman from worm deck and a woman who sat a few seats away from me. "So, who wants to do the honors?" my neighbor asked after we sat down. I said

I'd do it if nobody else wanted to. One of my projects at Bain involved a fair amount of speaking before large groups, and I felt up to it.

Out came the articles. We decided it was important to cast the layoff in as positive a light as possible, saying it marked a "new beginning" for DEC rather than an ending. This was perhaps a bit trite, but would have to do given our time constraints. We thought the speech had three principal audiences; the employees, the investment community, and the computer industry. We tried to balance the requirements for speaking to each group without offending the sensibilities of the others. We agreed to emphasize the material steps DEC would take to soften the blow for the people being laid off.

The moment we finished preparing we were asked to come back into the room. I didn't know what the section had been talking about for the last ten minutes, but was fairly certain they'd agreed on what I should say and how I should act. As we stepped into the Pit I was more nervous than I expected to be. So this was what we looked like to our professors! Seen from the front of the room, Section I was a sea of upper torsos, heads, and white name tags. I launched into the layoff speech. Get into your role, I reminded myself. Remember—you're their boss! If you don't like the way certain people look at you, fire 'em!

The outline we had crafted was logical and easy to remember, and I felt comfortable within moments of starting my speech. I went through the Sincere Regret, the New Beginning, and the DEC Will Never Forget Its Own routines. At the end I was treated to a relieving round of applause.

By then there were only a few minutes left in the class. Golden kicked off the postspeech analysis. "Okay folks, what *didn't* you like about Rob's speech?" Dozens of hands went up.

"I didn't think he said enough about what DEC's new strategy would be."

"I didn't think he sounded sincere enough."

"I think he should have said which departments the cuts would come from, and how many people each department would lose."

"I think he should have said more about how DEC will help people find new jobs."

This lively Rob-bashing went on until the class ended. It didn't bother me that people threw out all those negative comments; after all, Golden solicited them by specifically asking what people didn't like. What did bother me was that Golden didn't also take a minute or two to ask what people liked about my speech. After all, it was only the first week of class and hardly the time to be tossing people to the sharks.

After class I was surrounded by people telling me I had done a fine job. This was becoming standard treatment for anyone after a cold call (although the ten-minute team prep session had made mine about as warm as a cold call could get). Still, people seemed sincere. As I was walking out of class, Sandra came up to me. "Super talk, Rob," she told me as we headed toward Baker 20. Baker 20 was a small office near our classroom, and visiting it was a daily ritual for every HBS student. It was there that course materials, class schedules, official pronouncements, and other important items were handed out.

"Thanks. It was pretty easy, given the lead time we had . . ."

"No, I mean it. You were very poised. I think it's lousy the way everyone took it apart afterward."

"Hey," I said, "Golden wanted them to, didn't he?" We passed by the desk in Baker 20, collecting a computer disk filled with supplementary spread sheets for Marketing cases.

"Yeah, I guess so," Sandra said, unconvinced. "It just seems that people around here are a bit too eager to swipe at somebody when they get the chance." I considered this for a moment. Even though I was the object of the swiping, I couldn't quite agree. I wondered if Sandra was overly sensitive about things, or if I was just naïve.

After saying good-bye to Sandra I found Jerry over at Kresge, where we had agreed to meet for a snack. The most suitable offering available in the upstairs grill seemed to be frozen yogurt.

"*Frozen Yo*gurt," he whined. "I know I'm a civilian now."

"At Stanford we called it Fro-Yo," I pointed out. Jerry rolled his eyes pityingly. "And it looks like you definitely are a civilian," I continued. "And while we're on the subject, I've been curious to know why a guy would leave Uncle Sam for Harvard Business School."

"I wanted to grow dreadlocks. And guess what, the jerks kept making me cut them off." I chuckled obediently at this quip. "Actually," he continued, "it's a pretty long story." As neither of us was in a particular hurry, he began.

Jerry spent much of his childhood assuming he would eventually join the military. His father had been in the army for the requisite two decades before leaving it for an unglamorous white collar job in Billings, Montana, where Jerry spent most of his childhood. An ROTC scholarship made college affordable, and when Jerry graduated he went straight to Fort Knox. After six months in the basic course for Armor branch officers, he was sent to Fort Hood in Texas, where he immediately became a platoon leader.

Now with four tanks and roughly thirty soldiers under his command, Jerry already had more subordinates than anybody but the most senior person in my old San Francisco office. "That was the best thing I'd ever done up to that time," he recalled. "I liked leading people, I liked responsibility. And guess what, they overloaded me with both of those things right off the bat." After about a year and a half with the platoon, Jerry was assigned to a more administrative position supporting a company commander. Although this job made him second-in-command over more than 100 soldiers, he didn't find it as engaging as leading a platoon. "The new job involved too much logistical nonsense," he remembered. "It was the company commander and the platoon leaders who had the really direct leadership responsibilities." But disappointing as his new assignment could be, it did give him a real flavor for what the company commander role would be like.

When his four-year ROTC obligation ended, Jerry was within eighteen months of becoming a company commander himself. This fact proved decisive as he pondered the issue of staying in the military. "Ever since ROTC, I'd thought that being a company commander would be the greatest job in the world. And four years of the army hadn't changed my mind about that." By then Jerry was married. He and his wife spent many long nights weighing their options, and ultimately decided in favor of the army. "Melissa had just completed her teaching credentials," Jerry recalled. "This meant she could stay mobile and still have the job she wanted. That made the decision easier." Jerry chose to serve another tour.

After several months in an advanced officer course back at Fort Knox, he was sent to Stuttgart. About a year later, he took command of his own company. His new dominion was larger than that of many factory managers. The physical assets he answered for were impressive enough; sixteen tanks, other assorted military vehicles, stoves, tents, desks, tables, radios, and countless other items were essentially signed out to him.

But it was Jerry's personnel responsibilities that were truly awesome. Over 100 soldiers were now under his direct jurisdiction, and his authority was almost total. He could tell them when to stand, when to sit, or when to leave the room. He could put them in jail, remove them from jail, give them their pay, or withhold their pay. He made promotion decisions for many of his lower-ranking soldiers, and provided counseling and evaluations for lieutenants and sergeants. He also had to deal with problems that would make even the most seasoned management consultant blanch. Troubles with alcoholism, spouse abuse, illiteracy, fighting, thievery, bad food, leaky roofs, inadequate heating, and ugly haircuts all fell under his purview. But draining as all this could be, Jerry found the life of a company commander to be a heady one.

When his command ended after almost two years, it was again time to decide whether or not to stay in the military. "This was much tougher the second time around," he recalled. At that point, the army was prepared to send him on to graduate school. He would likely spend two years in an academic program (perhaps even getting an MBA), and acquire another four-year service obligation in the process. "It was pretty much a career decision at that point," Jerry said. "I'd been in for almost eight years. Two years of grad school and another four of the army would make fourteen. And when you've been in for fourteen years, you know you're going the full twenty for your pension."

Jerry found this reckoning unpleasant to contemplate, as he had never intended to become a career soldier. Further, it would be many years before he would be up for another command (this time at the battalion level), and it was by no means guaranteed that he would get one even then. Jerry also felt that spending cuts and personnel reductions were making the army a place of diminishing opportunities. And meanwhile, his long-standing frustration with the army's lack of a merit-based promotion scheme was really getting to him. "Your first shot at an early promotion comes after you've been in for *eleven* years," he said. "At that point you might go from captain to major *one* year early, if you're lucky. Of course, that's how the army works, and I knew it when I went in. But after eight years, I was ready for more of a meritocracy.

"And that's why I'm sitting here eating *Fro-Yo* with a Stanford guy who's probably never even fired a howitzer," Jerry concluded. He got up, flicking his empty cup into a garbage can. "And I know it's just Friday, but I've already got three new cases on my mind, doctor, so it's time to work!"

That evening brought yet another party under the big tent in the field. Most of the section was there. Everyone was talking about what a busy week, what a *great* week it had been, and how great it was that the busy week was finally over. Sandra incited several people to bring me beers in celebration of my successful layoff speech. Eventually I cornered her and begged her to stop. It was only nine, and I hoped to still be standing at midnight.

Sandra and I chatted for a while, and I got to know her a bit better. Like me and many of the younger people at HBS, she was still a bit perplexed about what she wanted to do when she "grew up."

"I liked some aspects of investment banking," she admitted, "but not enough to go back to it for the rest of my professional life." One field she had started to consider more seriously was marketing. This first interested her when she was at Morgan Stanley, where she worked with several large consumer products companies. These companies all benefited from innovative technology, top manufacturing expertise, and superior financial management. But their real competitive and strategic strengths, she felt, were rooted in their marketing departments. "I found those companies and the way they competed to be fascinating," she said. "I don't think I'd mind working inside one for a while."

But she did have one concern about this. Marketing powerhouses like Procter and Gamble, Colgate Palmolive, and Kraft/General Foods were vast corporate monoliths. Having grown accustomed to Morgan Stanley's flat meritocracy, she feared that she'd find such companies to be stultifyingly bureaucratic.

"I interviewed with Procter and Gamble when I was a senior at Yale," she recalled. "It was for a job in sales rather than marketing, but I think what I saw was indicative of the company as a whole. They flew me out to Cincinnati for a day of interviews. At one point in the process, I met this guy who was maybe four promotions into his career. I think his position was called Field Manager, or something. Anyway, the junior people I talked to were all in awe of him. He was a real mover and shaker, they told me, because he'd made it to Field Manager in nine years instead of eleven." Sandra tossed her empty beer cup into a garbage can. "Eleven goddamn years!" she marveled, slowly shaking her head. "And I'd say he was still three or four levels away from having any real influence.

"I was twenty-one at the time. I remember thinking Christ, eleven years ago I was in fifth grade. Grade school! I tried to remember my fifth grade teacher, my friends from that year, and what we used to do. And I realized that if I went to work for this guy, Yale would be just as remote as Miss Kelly's class at Sanderson Elementary before I held his position." Sandra still planned to interview with P&G and similar firms, but she was far more attracted by the idea of getting a job with a smaller, more entrepreneurial marketing firm.

"Look at us," Sandra said suddenly, surveying our surroundings with mock dismay. "We've got 800 young energetic people without a care in the world until Monday morning and nobody's dancing. We're not on the suburban cocktail party circuit yet!" We discussed this state of affairs and agreed that the ambiance was to blame; even with a lively DJ, a crowded, brightly lit circus tent with airplane-hangar acoustics could never encourage much more than sipping and chatting.

With this in mind, Sandra corraled about fifteen of us and herded us off to the Hong Kong restaurant, which featured a small dance floor along with its famed Scorpion Bowls. Later, much later, I ended up in my suite's living room with an Eastern European who had escaped to the West a few years before communism collapsed, and some guy from Indiana. We stayed up until the wee hours heatedly debating the future of Central Europe, the advantages of Japanese production methods, and the merits of Tekkno, a strain of hyper-synthesized dance music coming out of Berlin.

My guests finally weaved off around three in the morning. It had been a good night, one reminiscent of those easy days of orientation. But by now, orientation was long over. Indeed, those heady moments of Olympic leapfrogging already seemed like they had happened weeks ago. A lot had gone on since

Wednesday. And drained as all of us felt, this had only been a half week of classes, one which kicked off with a unique twin session of our sole ungraded class. As I drifted off to sleep, my last uneasy thought was that the first *real* week of HBS still lay ahead of us.

5

THE BATTLE
FOR AIR

On Sunday afternoon, Alistair and I decided that enough was enough; it was time to settle on a study group. Natasha's group was out of the question, as it had self-destructed after one day. Everybody in it, Natasha included, was so concerned about its burgeoning size that they affiliated elsewhere. We ruled out teaming up with Carter, since the episode in Marketing class had left me uncomfortable with the notion of joining a study group with someone else from my section. This left the group I had attended without Alistair, which was perhaps too large, and the one he had attended without me. This last group was started by Spencer, a friend of his from Stanford, and he urged me to give it a look.

While I hadn't known Spencer at Stanford, I had heard his name more than once. After graduation, he had taken a job in the strategic planning unit at Disney. Managed largely by ex-Bain people, this was known to be one of the company's hardest-working departments. Within moments after we arrived at his apartment, it was clear that Spencer's study group was going to be one tightly focused crew. "We've got two objectives," he announced after we settled down. "Avoid 3s, and wrap it up in less than an hour every night."

"We should get it down to a half hour by Thanksgiving"

added Gary from the kitchen. He was Spencer's roommate; they had grown up together in Indiana. "By the way, we've got Molson, Sam Adams, Saint Pauli Girl, Bud, Heineken, and Lite. What'll it be?" He opened the refrigerator door revealing that they had little else.

"Anything. Let's get this over with," Spencer said as Gary tossed us some refreshments. With Spencer as our taskmaster, we charged through the three cases in less than forty-five minutes. I immediately appreciated Spencer's focused leadership, and saw that Gary would also be an asset to any study group. He had spent several years in banking after graduating from college, and had a better grasp on financial issues than the rest of us combined.

New on the academic horizon that night was the mysterious Organizational Behavior class. In the course guide, OB was said to focus "on managers and managerial behavior. It seeks to help students better appreciate what is the true nature of managerial work, what will be required of them in a managerial career, and how they can best equip themselves to meet these intellectual and interpersonal challenges." Other issues to be explored in the course included "creating healthy corporate cultures" and "managing a managerial career."

"Sounds like a bunch of puff to me," Spencer observed suspiciously. He may have been right, but that evening's case was no pushover. It concerned the challenges a manager encountered in restructuring the cumbersome and overwhelmed back office operations at Citibank. The case was written several years before, and its main protagonist, John Reed, later became the bank's CEO. Then head of the bank's Operating Group, Reed faced office culture problems and a tangled physical work flow which would have challenged a TOM professor. The case was long and detailed, and I had already spent almost three hours analyzing it and preparing an opening.

"Big mistake," Spencer the veteran observed after I mentioned my extensive preparations. "You just *can't* put together an opening for every class. Your odds of getting cold called are one in ninety-two. So on the average you'll have to wreck ninety-two nights just to look a little bit better once every three months. And most classes only meet thirty or forty times anyway, so you may never get cold called at all! Think of how stupid *that* would

make you feel." By now the other guys were nodding like pa-
rishioners at a Baptist revival meeting. "One out of ninety-two!"
Spencer repeated.

"Ninety-one," I corrected him. Section I already had its
first casualty, a contemplative fellow who had spent several years
at a top consulting firm. There was all kinds of grim speculation
about why he was leaving us; we eventually learned that a business he had started was suddenly going great guns and needed
his attention. A few other sections had also lost people by now.
The circumstances surrounding these departures were universally murky, although most were rumored to have been motivated by academic terror.

But despite the recent erosion in our section's cold-call
roulette odds, Spencer's argument against readying openings
for every class was still persuasive. Preparing an opening could
take a while, and I wasn't sure how much I learned from the
process. Besides, I'd found that once I had a detailed opening
worked up, it was almost disappointing *not* to get cold called.
I'd feel like I'd gone through a ton of stress and preparation
for nothing.

Spencer went on to pitch his study group. "Basically, we're
perfect for someone who wants to have a good time and isn't
worried about being a Baker Scholar." He was referring to a
distinction granted to roughly five percent of the students from
each graduating class. It was conferred mainly on the basis of
academic performance, although other nebulous criteria were
rumored to be considered as well. I shared Spencer's indifference to the honor. Almost every HBS alum I had talked to
maintained that actively seeking Baker Scholarhood was a
bad idea. The costs of doing this, after all, were quite steep, as
HBS was competitive enough that good grades were hard to
come by.

And if two years of toil brought you just short of the Baker
threshold, your mighty efforts would have little professional
relevance. This was because prospective employers were pro-
hibited from seeing the grades of first-year students at Harvard,
and many didn't bother to solicit grades from second-years.
This "no grades to recruiters" policy took a lot of performance
pressure off of those who surrendered the Baker field early,
which was a good argument for doing just that. Unlike undergraduates, whose academic abilities were pinpointed by grade

point averages, HBS grads were widely viewed as coming in two flavors; Baker Scholars and non-Baker Scholars. And there was certainly no shame attached to the latter category, as the overwhelming majority of HBS alums came from it. So if Spencer's study group was premised on a disinterest in Baker Scholarships, this was fine with me. By the time I left his apartment, I had made up my mind to sign up.

Unfortunately, I soon learned that the general irrelevance of grades at Harvard had a catch. The bearer of this grim news was Sandra. "Aren't you interested in making First-Year Honors?" she asked me over breakfast the next day.

"First-year . . . Honors?" I prayed that this was just another distinction for a triflingly small group of prodigies.

"Sure, haven't you read the *Academic Standards* guide?" I vaguely remembered a booklet with that title cluttering my desk over the summer. "Fifteen or twenty percent of the class gets First-Year Honors. It's based on grades. You have to get something like five 1s to make it." She leaned closer, whispering in a mock conspiratorial manner. "I heard McKinsey won't hire *anybody* who doesn't make First-Year Honors." McKinsey. This was strong stuff. McKinsey was to consulting firms what Harvard was to business schools. And since consulting was clearly among the industries of preference on campus, McKinsey's opinion of First-Year Honors carried considerable weight.

The fact that I was at all concerned about McKinsey's views was absurd to a certain degree. I had already worked at a good consulting firm, and if I wanted to return to the field, I could probably go back to Bain regardless of McKinsey's opinion of me. Still, to consulting, McKinsey was the pasha, the *generalissimo*; the granddaddy of 'em all. If McKinsey attached this importance to First-Year Honors, what did Goldman Sachs think? Morgan Stanley? Bill Clinton? The Sultan of Brunei? I suddenly felt the beat of the Lemming March, thrumming deep in the bowels of the dining hall. You were a bright kid. They put you in Unified Math in seventh grade, Honors Physics in eleventh. Then you made it to a good school, got a good job, and got into HBS. So what do you do for an encore? Get an offer from McKinsey? Goldman Sachs? *Better make First-Year Honors, kid!* Fairly panicked about grades for the first time in years, I walked into OB class.

Our professor was a nice, mustachioed man named Bob

Rosenthal. He had a tempered but focused demeanor, and seemed particularly attuned to how he worked the room, to whom he called on and when. At the end of the class I still wasn't entirely sure of what OB was, but had a feeling I would enjoy it. Rosenthal gave us the lowdown on the course, which would run a few weeks shorter than the others and end in November. Unlike Marketing and TOM, OB would have no midterm. Grades would be derived entirely from our finals and class participation. This was a bit worrying. How do you grade comments in a fuzzy class like OB, I wondered.

My general concern about class participation increased throughout the week. The airtime war in Section I escalated considerably, and I quickly lost my stomach for it. At every pause in the conversation it was hands, hands, hands. It became increasingly difficult to "get in" in any particular class. Each day I came fully prepared, which made me especially eager to talk, as I felt I had worthwhile things to say. My urgency was heightened by the fact that grades (and First-Year Honors! And McKinsey! And the Sultan of Brunei!) depended so heavily on in-class commentary. And of course there was the natural desire to establish myself with my new peer group. All of this had me bursting to talk in class. But of course, nine times out of ten (or was it ninety times out of ninety-one?), I wasn't asked to speak when I raised my hand.

So those first days at HBS were soon dominated not by excitement, apprehension, shock, elation, or perplexity, but rather frustration. Never before had I been in a conversational setting with ninety other people. Never had I been required not to speak unless spoken to for such long and frequent stretches. Not even as a child had I been seen but not heard for such a high proportion of my waking hours. To be sure, this came with the territory, and I knew what I was getting into when I decided to go to Harvard. But still, it was grimmer than I'd expected.

I certainly wasn't the only one going through this frustration. Everybody felt it to some degree, some far worse than me. In those first strange days, the subject of class participation caused serious agitation. The opportunity to speak was such a precious commodity that most people were terrified about blowing it by saying something shallow, repetitive, or (God forbid) stupid when they were finally called on. Those who were lucky enough to get frequent airtime risked alienating their more frustrated counterparts.

It was easy to let this cause you to lose your perspective. Since every day's conversation counted toward final grades, every class could seem like a midterm. Every comment, then, could seem to have profound implications for your class standing and professional prospects. Soon enough, this attitude gave rise to overly aggressive or opportunistic behavior, as all of us were sometimes willing to bend the implicit rules for some airtime. Some did this by parking their hands in the air for minutes at a stretch, regardless of who had the floor. This was a violation of our section norm to not raise hands when others were speaking, but the practice started and snowballed quickly.

A rarer and more dramatic way of defecting was the Invisible Hand comment. This was a costly way of getting in, as it was universally regarded with disapproval. The first such comment came during TOM. Stanley posed some question to the class, and before he could call on someone to answer it, a young engineer piped in with an extended soliloquy about the case.

As he spoke, I got my very first note in class, a drawing from Jerry's able pen. It featured a reasonable sketch of our aggressive sectionmate. Eight hands sprouted from his torso and waved in the air like tentacles, evoking an Indian deity. Jerry appended a caption to this inspired illustration: THE HIDDEN HANDS OF POWER DECK: AN ARTIST'S IMPRESSION. I thought it was clever, so I passed the note to my right and it quickly traveled the length of the Warning Track. A minute later it came back, covered with other scribbled commentary. KEEP YOUR HAND ON YOUR WALLET WITH THIS DUDE AROUND, advised one wit. I'LL BET HE CAN TYPE LIKE A BANSHEE noted another.

Annoying as it was, the Invisible Hand routine occurred rarely enough that it remained a minor issue. A form of defection that was often more annoying was the Deliberate Tangent. Deliberate Tangents plagued every class we sat through, and at times afflicted several comments in a row. These were comments that had nothing to do with the preceding discussion or which (more flagrantly) completely ignored a direct question

from the professor. A typical exchange would go something
like this:

PROF. COTTON: Okay, who has some insights on the
                  way Toshiba manages relations with
                  its distributors. . . . Maxwell?
MAXWELL: Their distributor relations are intrigu-
                  ing. But I think their media strategy
                  is more significant. In their media
                  strategy, Toshiba has . . .

There was no anointed king of the Deliberate Tangent, as almost all of us indulged in it to some degree. The implications
of this for the quality of class discussion were devastating. Conversation jumped from topic to topic so whimsically that it was
often difficult to forge any consensus or synthesis at all.

Deliberate Tangents emerged because people often came
to class determined to air their one or two biggest insights about
a case. You'd first raise your hands when the conversation
touched on an issue you had thought about. But with dozens
of other hands in the air, you'd probably not get a chance to
speak at that particular moment. You might then keep your
hand up indefinitely. When finally called, you would say what
you meant to say twenty minutes before, dragging the conversation backward or into a radical new direction in the process. At
any moment there could be dozens of us waiting in the airtime
queue to make some prepackaged observation.

A related, less common, but more egregious category of
conversational misconduct was the Reopening. This happened
when a student, called on to speak in the middle of class, would
prattle on for several minutes running. In most cases, these
filibusters were used to present openings outlined the night
before in anticipation of a cold call. While this practice was
understandable (it was frustrating to craft detailed openings for
weeks without ever getting the gratification of presenting one),
it was wildly annoying to almost everyone in the class. Many
suspected that it irked our professors as well, and yielded few
if any class participation points. Still, a few people reopened
cases with depressing regularity.

Frustrating as all of this was for most of us, the challenges
of this period were all the greater for the non-native speakers

of English in our ranks. Hans later told me that he found the first weeks of school to be long on stress and short on sleep. Because while a particularly diligent American might spend three hours on a case, including one hour of reading and two of pondering, Hans often spent three full hours just reading a case.

While Hans's English struck most of us as being fluent and almost flawless, every case featured words and phrases that sent him running for the dictionary. TOM was particularly onerous in this regard. What, after all, were *Ladles? Nozzles? Epoxy?* A *blind loop?* Did one wear a *solder mask?* Did one shop in a *milling department?* And if Benihana restaurants were, in fact, a *fad,* did this make eating in one of them a dangerous act?

Another bogeyman for Hans was abbreviations. From the very first day of class, he found that his sectionmates were conversing in a sort of secret code. ROE. NPV. IPO. IRR. American business was swimming with peculiar three-letter words that no English-German dictionary seemed to contain. Worse, many HBS cases were rich in acronyms peculiar to the companies or industries they examined. (To decipher one TOM case, for example, Hans had to master such designations as SCT, TAT, DC, UW, RAP, RAIN, RUN, and RERUN.) Defined once at the beginning of a case, these acronyms would crop up throughout the following pages, and would never fail to perplex an already baffled Austrian. In class, Hans found his sectionmates livened up their comments by using these case-specific wordlets with alarming regularity.

Hans soldiered on bravely. He struggled through each of his cases until he had them cracked, even if this meant getting four hours of sleep and dining on Domino's Pizza for the third night in a row. He didn't join a study group for fear that his own difficulties would act as a drag on everybody else, but he did get occasional sympathetic help from the other people on his dormitory floor. Each morning he was one of the most meticulously well-prepared students in the room. His cases were thick with underlinings in four colors of ink, and he was always armed with pages of detailed, typewritten notes.

But despite his exemplary preparation, Hans had one key downfall. He couldn't bring himself to speak in class. And at a school as obsessed with class participation as ours, this was a problem. Before coming to HBS, Hans had acknowledged that the academic honors he once garnered easily in Austria and Germany would be out of reach in a foreign setting. But he never anticipated this unwelcome bout of muteness, nor its potentially disastrous consequences. For the first time in his academic career, Hans was starting to panic.

The guys in my study group, meanwhile, weren't scared, but they were frustrated. The lurching, disjointed class discussions that plagued my section, it seemed, were common to all the sections during the early months of the year. Each member of our group soon had a large store of anecdotes pertaining to this problem. "You should see the way some of those people go on!" Gary complained. "My favorite phrase is 'building on.' When someone says they want to build on someone else's comment, you can bet they're gonna completely change the subject."

We all nodded in disgruntled agreement. Our study group had become a model of temporal efficiency, and we expected nothing less from our classes. Every night we would rocket through all the study questions attached to our case assignments, then zip through the other main issues the questions didn't cover. Class discussion didn't always focus on the study questions (which was fine with us). But when it did, it was a rare day that each question was actually covered in the allotted eighty minutes.

Needless to say, each of us was probably just as guilty of deliberate tangents and other forms of in-class misconduct as any other first-year. But these antics were easier to contain in small-group settings, allowing many study groups to rocket through material that brought full sections to a grinding halt.

"W'hell. Whatta ya'll say we go into Cambridge to drown our sorrows?" This suggestion came from George, our study group's latest addition. George was from Alistair's section, and came to us under his sponsorship. He was a remarkably relaxed individual, and spoke with an appropriately sluggish Georgian drawl. He had spent several years working in finance, both domestically and internationally.

George's motion for adjournment met with unanimous approval, and soon we arrived at HBS's on-campus student pub. This was actually Au Bon Pain, the Francophile eatery in Shad Hall. The irony that Shad, a shrine of physical improvement by day, was the center of corporeal unravelment at night was not lost on us. We swaggered into "ABP" around ten-thirty, which turned out to be quittin' time for a few hundred other first-years. With the music playing and the bodies packing in, the place quickly acquired a suitably festive ambiance.

This was a relief to me. I had heard countless stories about the *old* student pub, a squalid little place tucked beneath one of the dorms. Decrepit as it was, it had endeared itself to generations of HBS students as a place where you could unwind without needing to worry about chipping the crystal or spilling beer on the mahogany. It was shut down, though, when Shad opened. All the fond tales I had heard about the old pub led me to regard its upscale successor with suspicion. Au Bon Pain looked more like a yuppie wine bar in Greenwich than a casual campus hangout, and somehow I've always found it difficult to trust a student pub where you can't carve your initials into the furniture. And Au Bon Pain's *faux* marble tables would make short work of even the toughest blade.

We ordered a few pitchers and started socializing. Shad's last call was around midnight, far too early for anybody's taste. We figured this shut-down time was chosen to discourage people from heading into town at closing, as Cambridge bars only stayed open an hour after this. Had this actually been the logic, it didn't work with us that night. By 12:05 we were racing across the bridge toward Harvard Square.

Soon we were at The Boathouse, a bar with low ceilings, sticky floors, dim lighting, and the rank smell of a brewery. It was packed, the crowd liberally sprinkled with other refugees from Au Bon Pain. Eventually even The Boathouse had to shut its doors. Exiled again, and with nowhere to go but home, we joined a convoy of HBS students headed across the river.

The next morning was a bleak one. It kicked off with a special two-hour session of TOM, which meant class started at eight instead of the usual eight-forty. As TOM wore on, my thoughts turned back to the talk we had prior to our Shad run. The quality of class discussion was really getting me down. People were much more concerned about making the points they wanted to make than they were about following the direction of class discussion, and I was certainly no saint in this respect myself. During somebody's laborious reopening in the last moments of TOM, I resolved to clean up my own act as much as possible.

About a half hour into OB, I had a chance to put this

resolution to the test. OB had been frustrating to me, as I had only been called on once in the first few classes. That day, I found the case discussion to be particularly engaging and was eager to get in. But the class started with a depressingly familiar pattern. Rosenthal frequently glanced my way, but never called on me. Finally, when one student was finishing a point, he gazed right at me for a few seconds. I had a strong opinion about the other student's argument, and eagerly raised my hand the moment he fell silent.

Rosenthal's usual style was to let four or five people talk on an issue before nudging the conversation in a new direction with a question or comment. But he must have just tired of the current line of questioning, because at that moment he posed a question to the class about a completely unrelated subject. As he started asking this question I lowered my hand, but he had already seen it raised, and called on me anyway. "Well, uh, actually," I stammered, "I'd raised my hand to talk about something else."

"No problem," Rosenthal said affably. "I'll get back to you in a bit. Anybody else care to address this issue?" The usual kelp garden of tentacles leapt into the air. Man, that felt lousy. I had been bursting to speak in OB for days, and now I'd surrendered a chance to do just that. The usual tactic would have been to make a truncated response to Rosenthal's question, then segue back to a lengthy discourse on the previous issue. So had I just exhibited a laudable degree of self-restraint, or a laughable degree of naiveté?

Rosenthal didn't end up getting back to me as he promised, and this made me furious. So much for hiking my airtime standards! Anybody paying attention to my burst of self-control would have come away with one clear lesson; speak when you get the chance or forever hold your peace. At least, that was the lesson that I came away with. After class I headed over to lunch with a couple of people who had drawn this very conclusion. "You kinda showed some inexperience there," Carter said, a bit condescendingly. "So he didn't see you drop your hand as he was asking the question. So what? He called on you, that's the important thing. I mean, who cares *what* question he asked! If you get airtime, you take it, right?"

If you get airtime, you take it. Who cares what question he asked. These certainly seemed to be the day's little lessons. I was tempted to set up a meeting with Rosenthal to lodge a complaint. The next day I found a note in my pigeonhole that spurred me to make an appointment straightaway. It was from Rosenthal. GOOD POINT IN CLASS, BUT TRY TO STAY A BIT CLOSER TO THE TOPIC OF DISCUSSION it said.

Now what was this, I fumed to myself. I had pushed my self-restraint to the limit, and now here I was getting hate mail from my professor! When I called, his assistant told me to come by the next afternoon, which gave me twenty-four hours to stew about the situation. Soon enough, I was far more worried than angry. Maybe some bizarre rule said that when asked a different question from the one you raised your hand for, you still had to answer. Maybe Rosenthal had given me some weird kind of midclass cold call. Rosenthal's note constituted the first bit of "performance feedback" I had gotten from a professor, and it was hardly flattering. So was I messing up in OB? If I was, did this mean I was messing up in all my classes?

And what if my professors talked to one another? Hell, they probably did; they were all members of the Section I faculty. Surely they had meetings. And surely they talked about problem students. So if Rosenthal had some kind of hangup with me, he'd probably bring it up at the next Section I faculty meeting! "That Reid kid's a problem," he'd say. "You should've heard what he said in class today!" The other professors would nod in grim agreement. Those who hadn't had a bad run-in with me would start viewing me as a troublemaker.

Fortunately, my little bout of paranoia proved to be unfounded. In our meeting, Rosenthal told me that his note referred to my one true moment of OB airtime, which had come a few days before my encounter with *comment interruptus*. We discussed the comment I made that day, which Rosenthal thought was inadequately linked to the discussion. After we had chatted for a moment, he said that all was forgiven and I should forget about the note. I told him that I originally thought the note referred to my declining to answer his question.

"No, not at all," he laughed. "Sections always have a tough time sticking to the point at the beginning of the year. I actually wish more people would do what you did." We chatted awhile longer. He told me that professors rarely met by section, but rather met by department to discuss each day's cases. When faculty members from the same section did meet, they strictly

avoided discussing particular students. This policy was followed
to prevent one professor's opinions from tainting a student's
reputation with other professors (the very situation I had
feared).

When I left Rosenthal's office I was relieved to the point
of jubilation. It was then that I realized how much I really *did*
care about grades. After all, I really got worked up about that
little note. Thank God the ordeal was over. I'm okay in OB! I
thought triumphantly. The Section I faculty doesn't hate me
after all! As I glided toward the elevator, I took a few moments
to marvel at the edifice that housed Rosenthal's office.

This was Morgan Hall, home to most of the faculty offices at
HBS. One look at the building made it clear that HBS professors
were not forced into the mold of the self-sacrificing academic
so familiar to undergraduates. Whereas a Stanford history professor was likely to have a cramped private office and one secretary to share with fourteen colleagues, even junior faculty in
Morgan had stately offices that would turn most upper-middle
managers green. Untenured, Rosenthal had an office more
than twice as spacious as that occupied by the program *chairman*
of my undergraduate major. Come to think of it, it was also
larger than most partners' offices at Bain.

Morgan Hall's opulence didn't stop in the professors' quarters. From tip to toe, the building whispered of Harvard's cod-
dling of its business faculty. It had been recently renovated at
a cost exceeding $20 million, a sum which could have provided
almost a year and a half of full-tuition scholarships to every
member of my graduating class. The building's exterior harmo-
nized well with the rest of the campus's Georgian tone. But
inside, it was a shining modern office complex, complete with
massive skylights, card-key doors, designer furniture, and a
beautiful atrium which soared majestically toward a distant ceiling. At the base of this atrium was Morgan's centerpiece. This
was the Tethys, an inestimably valuable 500-square-foot, 14-ton
tile mosaic. The Tethys hailed from the ancient city of Antioch
and dated back to the fourth century A.D.

Even the building's nondescript exterior doors were luxurious in their own peculiar way. They weren't exactly automatic
doors, as it certainly wouldn't do for Morgan to pop open like a
grocery store every time someone walked by. They were rather,
well, semi-automatic. Tug gently on a handle and slowly, si-

lently, dramatically, they would swing open by themselves. It was all eerily reminiscent of *The Addams Family*.

"And it's not just fancy doors they're getting," Jerry observed over lunch the next day. "A lot of the professors here pull in over $100,000 a year."

"What?" Rick almost gagged on his soup.

"Hey, you can't expect them to graduate kids who're gonna immediately make twice as much as they do!" Jerry observed sardonically. "And remember, a lot of them have consulting practices on the side which really let them rake it in."

I nodded. This particular form of moonlighting was widely known. Professors did well by their consulting franchises, and not all of them were small. Monitor, one of the better-known strategic consulting firms, was cofounded by Michael Porter, a renowned HBS professor. The author of many top-selling books about business strategy, Porter was quite a celebrity in consulting circles, and enjoyed considerable notoriety in the broader business world.

"So," Rick said, steering the discussion away from the disturbing specter of plutocratic professors. "You guys thinking of running for anything?" He was referring to the election of section officers, which was to take place in a couple of weeks. The officers of "Old Section I" had recently briefed us on the duties and rewards of their respective positions. The equivalent of our section's president would be its General Affairs Council (GAC) representative. This person would sit on a board with counterparts from the other sections to discuss issues affecting the school and the student body. The GAC rep would also have the unenviable chore of administering our daily diet of in-class announcements.

The other big position was that of education representative. Our ed rep would help mediate between disgruntled students and the professors. This person would also publicize academic policies, help set up study sessions, and perform other related chores. Oddly enough, it would also be the ed rep who would distribute our grade reports. The other positions were less glamorous. We would have a treasurer, a student clubs representative, a technology rep, and some other officers.

Our discussion of elections gradually flowed into one about how our section was developing. Jerry and Rick were both concerned about the directionless nature that class discussion often exhibited. Certain people's mannerisms were also getting on everyone's nerves. Each of us had his favorite scapegoat, but it was generally Invisible Hands, tangential comments, and arrogant attitudes that raised our ire. Also unpopular were those who indulged in unwarranted apple polishing. Immediately after every class, a subset of the section would surround the professor and pelt him with questions. While most of this did arise from genuine confusion or curiosity, we all suspected that a good deal of fawning was going on in those groups as well. And certain people seemed to join the fray after almost every class.

"And what about *Callie*," Jerry asked in a baffled tone. Rick and I shrugged our shoulders helplessly. A few days before in OB, we read a case set in a high school with a so-called "house" organization. Callie, a contemplative woman who had worked in education, came to class the next day with an unusual exhibit. She had attended a house-style high school herself, and wrote up a detailed summary of her experiences for the section's edification. Rosenthal made copies of this available to the section after class.

"I don't know if she was trying to score points with the professor, or if she's just a compulsive memo writer," commented Rick. Callie had left me baffled too. I liked her quite a bit, and couldn't quite figure out what had moved her to do this. And by no means had hers been the only unexpected stunt in Section I. One student came to class with overhead slides prepared about the case. He even managed to get the professor's blessing to put them on the projector for everyone's enlightenment.

Other people had genuinely put the section off. One student had recently made an awful gaffe during an OB session that focused on a dispute between two female coworkers. After we viewed a videotape of the protagonists, he had unwisely stated that it left him favorably impressed with the "good taste" of one woman's boss. The other woman was overweight and not especially attractive. A shudder rippled through the class, and he became a rather unpopular figure with most of the women and many of the men in Section I. A few days later he dug himself in deeper during TOM, by contending that backward practices at a certain French factory were due to the "stubbornness and general resistance to change" of the French people.

"After all," he argued in support of his point, "it took them two hundred years to remodel the Louvre."

"You've really gotta try hard to pull off a culturally insensitive remark in TOM," Jerry concluded. He was right, but somehow this guy had done it. And this wasn't the only unlikely feat that we would see.

6

SAVING THE SADHU

Jerry, Rick, and I weren't alone in pondering instances of extreme in-class behavior. One night, I was accosted on my way to dinner by a squad of chuckling Section I men. Among them was Carter. "Ever seen the Academy Awards, Rob?" he asked me.

"We need you to help us brainstorm," said another guy.

Carter's crew, it turned out, had heard of the long-standing tradition of weekly section awards at HBS. They were eager to get the ball rolling in Section I on Friday.

They told me about the awards they had already thought of. One woman was slated for the Obvious Really Does Begin with OB award for making a particularly self-evident remark in Rosenthal's class. A guy was designated the Statue of Liberty award for keeping his hand in the air for what seemed like days at a stretch. Yet another guy was to get the Corporate Relations award for making cutting remarks about Reebok's advertising when a high-ranking official from that company's marketing arm was visiting our section.

The Shark award, an HBS classic, was given to someone who made a notoriously aggressive Invisible Hand comment in Marketing. The Computer Literacy award, meanwhile, was designated for several people who habitually peppered their remarks with numerical references.

When he doled out the awards in class, Carter took extra precautions not to offend anyone's sensibilities. He toned down some of the more cutting citations, and added a couple of mocking awards for himself. His delivery was good, and the presentation had a friendly, chiding tone to it. By all accounts it was a big success. At the end of the session Carter was careful to remind everybody that it had all been in fun, and if anyone was offended they could talk to him privately and we would quit giving out awards immediately.

Unfortunately, somebody took him up on this. Almost two dozen people got awards that week. One person who received a relatively benign citation came away hurt and offended by the whole process. True to his word, Carter recommended to the rest of us that we nip the tradition in the bud. When Jerry heard about this he was incensed. "What the hell kind of place is this, anyway?" he blasted. "Just because one person got pissed off about something, nobody else can do it? Whatever happened to the first amendment? Section One's starting to look like a pretty uptight place."

Jerry might have been right, and the awards fiasco was not the only sign of this. The second meeting we had with our section chair, Karen Trumble, was another. In it, a couple of people argued that class comments should be more closely monitored to prevent "insensitivity to diversity." While based on noble sentiments, these lectures had a disturbingly Orwellian ring to them.

To be fair, class discussion in Section I was by no means paralyzed by politically correct orthodoxy. Still, certain people had at times sought to delineate the range of opinions that could be expressed in class. Booing and occasionally hissing erupted in response to in-class comments that these people found unpalatable. Most of these incidents occurred around issues that were peripheral to business matters. Still, the badgering sometimes touched on core issues to the cases.

Several of us felt this behavior was contrary to the section's interests. It took guts to express an unpopular opinion when your grade was on the line and a bevy of eager sharks was ready to take you down. So it didn't take too many self-righteous hissing fits to make some people shy away from saying anything controversial. Still, things could have been substantially worse. In another section, the self-appointed vanguard of morality was said to be truly out of control. Dismayed by the occasional scowls his sectionmates displayed when hearing comments they didn't agree with, somebody had reportedly proposed that all *facial expressions* be banned during class. Luckily, nobody in Section I got so carried away as to suggest this.

The other big issue at our meeting with Trumble concerned computers and exams. Our first midterm was still over a month away, but people were already worried about how computer users would print their essays (we would have the option of handwriting our answers or using a word processor). Neurotic as such a priori fretting may seem, we had good reasons to be concerned.

The problem's roots stretched back to early summer, when we all got letters from Harvard inviting us to buy computer packages. It was well known that computer ownership was a prerequisite for attending HBS. Many homework assignments were given electronically, and Harvard had required business students to invest in pricey hardware packages for years. The summer mailing trumpeted Harvard's "educational discount." I was excited about this, as I had enjoyed terrific prices on Macintosh equipment as an undergraduate at Stanford. Unfortunately, it appeared that most of the discount that Apple granted Harvard didn't benefit us, but rather flowed to the school's swelling bottom line. I visited friends at Stanford over the summer, and had found that their computer prices were substantially lower than Harvard's. More disturbingly, I had also found discounters in New York who offered comparable or better prices than Harvard on a lot of equipment. Our school surely enjoyed significant discounts from computer manufacturers. But unless Stanford and J & R Music World were accorded substantially better treatment, Harvard was making a fat profit before passing some thin savings on to us.

But at issue in Trumble's session that day was not computer prices, but computer printers. The summer mailing had also indicated that we would need portable printers "for exam use" at school. At this urging, many had purchased a certain type of portable printer from the school. Fortunately, Tyler had warned me that these little devices were worthless for the purposes of HBS students. The printers were known for taking an eternity to print embarrassingly messy pages. This made them useless for producing résumés, printing term papers, and most of the other computer-related tasks typically faced by HBS students. Unwilling to pay hundreds of dollars for printers that were all but useless to them, a majority of first-year students had boycotted the shoddy products. This was the first time this problem had existed so extensively at the school; in previous years, word about the printers had not spread so wide or so quickly among the new students.

Trumble told us that using laser jets (which many of us had purchased instead) would not be permitted, as these might blow a fuse in the exam room. Yet we all felt that buying a portable printer was by now out of the question, as the printer's uselessness outside of the exam room had by then been verified by those who had gotten it. Writing exams by hand was likewise unacceptable. Most of us had stopped writing lengthy documents in this manner while still in our teens, and weren't about to start again just because the administration wasn't up to the task of setting up a printing station. Grousing about the printer situation took up the rest of a contentious and unpleasant meeting with Trumble. She tried valiantly to calm our worries, and wrapped up with a promise to get some kind of closure on the issue before our next meeting.

The one class in which we would never have to worry about printing exams was, of course, Ethics. Our third week of classes saw the end of this ungraded stub of a course, which we had all enjoyed so much. Monday featured one of the most interesting cases in the Ethics curriculum. It concerned the notorious Salomon Brothers bond trading scandal of 1991. At that time, Salomon was the unrivaled king of the U.S. Treasury bond market. The auctions in which these bonds were issued were governed by a number of regulations. Prominent among them were government-set limits on the proportion of bonds that a single entity could acquire in any one auction. These limitations were meant to keep dominant firms (like Salomon) from acquiring monopolistic positions on certain issues.

The mechanisms governing the auctions and enforcing their rules were quite informal in some respects. This made the issuance of federal debt a less bureaucratic and expensive process than it might otherwise have been, which was good news for the American taxpayer. Unfortunately, it also made the process vulnerable to subversion. In February of 1991, a high-ranking Salomon trader allegedly exploited this weakness by secretly bidding for Salomon's account under another institution's name, thereby boosting Salomon's position in a certain auction beyond the legal limits. The ensuing flap ended the careers of a number of prominent Salomon executives, including its chairman, John Gutfreund.

Like most people in the section, I had read about the Salomon conundrum back when it unfolded. But I hadn't followed the events very closely, and had only a rudimentary understanding of the mechanics of treasury auctions. This made the case fascinating to me. Just learning about the quirks of the auction process merited the time I spent on it.

The next day as I walked past the rack of first-year pigeonholes, I noticed they were all stuffed with little white envelopes emblazoned with the Salomon Brothers logo. I found the one addressed to me. What could this be? I wondered as I pulled it out. A refutation of the facts as presented in the case? An outraged plea of innocence? We had been on campus for only a few weeks, and already there was a full-blown scandal in the works! I ripped open my envelope. Inside I found not a rebuttal, but an invitation. Salomon was offering to treat the entire first-year class to dinner at one of Cambridge's most expensive restaurants.

I knew employers had big budgets for recruiting at the MBA level, but this was more extravagance than I expected in the first month of school. After all, interviewing season was still five months off. I had a feeling that Salomon would enjoy a good turnout. This would be our first chance to sample the circus of summer recruiting. It would also be many students' first opportunity to encounter an investment bank in person. All this aside, the inflated costs of on-campus eating meant that free food would never be dismissed lightly.

The Salomon letter drove home the fact that while summer was still remote, the issue of job hunting was quite immediate. In a few weeks, recruiting fairs and on-campus company presentations would begin in earnest. Dinners like Salomon's would proliferate. And already, the deadline for handing in final versions of our résumés for the résumé book was only a couple of weeks off. Relaxed as orientation had been, they sure didn't waste any time around here once things got rolling.

The conclusion of our Ethics training with Sam Lubbock

was another milestone indicating that the year was really under way. Our final case with him was a hallmark of the course. It concerned a successful investment banker who took a sabbatical from work to make a lengthy trek through Nepal with an old friend. He had hiked the Himalayas before, and had long dreamed of following this particular route. Its high point was an 18,000-foot pass, which they reached a month into the journey. There was no guarantee of clearing this hurdle, as the banker had previously succumbed to altitude sickness at a much lower elevation. Fortunately, the morning of the climb saw promising weather conditions.

Partway up the pass, when the altitude was starting to take its toll, a man from another climbing party came down the hill. He was carrying a nearly naked pilgrim, or *sadhu*, whom he dropped at the banker's feet. "Look," he said, "I've done what I can. You have porters and Sherpa guides. You care for him." The banker and his companions clothed the sadhu from head to toe, then spotted a Japanese party coming up behind them with a horse. At this point the banker, concerned about the altitude, moved on. The others from his group followed after carrying the sadhu a bit farther down the hill. The Japanese refused to give up their horse, but fed the sadhu and gave him something to drink before starting up the pass themselves. While everyone helped him a little, no one had taken full responsibility for the sadhu or his safety. And nobody knew if he survived to complete his descent.

The case raised a host of ethical issues about every protagonist's behavior, and resulted in a spirited discussion which Lubbock moderated masterfully. At the end of the session, he wrapped up the course with a brief speech. "Why are you all here, folks?" he asked rhetorically. "C'mon, admit it!" he reached into his pocket and whipped out a thick roll of bills. "Y'wanna get rich!" he bellowed. Everyone laughed self-consciously. When the laughter died down, Lubbock said that of course there were many things that brought each of us to HBS, of which the promise of wealth was only one. And there would be a variety of factors governing our careers and decisions after graduation, of which money would again only be one.

He urged us not to get so caught up by the monetary side of our decisions as to lose sight of their moral ramifications.

Then he gave us his vote of confidence. "I read the little cards you sent in. Now I've seen you grapple with issues for three weeks. And I have faith in you. I believe in Section I. I'm . . . investing . . . in Section I." With that he slapped the roll of money onto a desk and slipped out of the room. There was a thunderous applause followed by a moment of chaos. *What in the world did he mean, and what were we supposed to do with the cash?* For days, hardly a meal went by without the subject of the money (which turned out to be one hundred one-dollar bills) coming up.

A number of theories soon emerged about Lubbock's intentions. Some guessed that he wanted us to pick a worthy charity to fund. Others thought he wanted us each to take one dollar and contribute it to the cause of our choice. Still others thought it was some kind of test of our moral fortitude, and that we were supposed to return the money. The fact was that Lubbock didn't intend for us to do anything in particular, but sought to stir up exactly the type of discussion and debate we were now engaged in. Between us we spent countless hours discussing the money and how it could best be deployed at school or in society.

Gradually, the concept of a "Sadhu Fund" took form. The idea was to use the $100 as seed money for a fund we would all contribute to over the years. Somebody figured out that if we each donated $10 to the fund in the first year, $20 in the second year, $30 in the third and so on, it would compound to around eight million dollars by our twenty-fifth reunion, assuming a fairly conservative rate of return on the investment. What we would then use it for was open to question, but the basic idea was appealing. The concept quickly gained support, and the fund was tacitly accepted as the vehicle for investing Lubbock's riches and saving future sadhus.

The evening after the sadhu case was the first of what would be many black-tie occasions during our two years at HBS. This was the Harvard Ball, sponsored by the European Club, and most of the first-year class turned out for it. It was held across the river at Harvard's Memorial Hall, a cavernous venue that looked like a Gothic gymnasium. There was a DJ and a band, but the acoustics evoked a discotheque in a bus station.

One of the first people I came across was Sandra. She was magnificently bedecked in a burgundy dress she had made back in college ("a little project from the days when I had a real life," she recalled wistfully).

"Welcome to the prom," she greeted me.

"Hey, are they gonna play "Free Bird"?"

"That would be about par for the course," she replied, suggesting a frustration that went beyond the evening's unglamorous venue.

"How's that?"

"Oh, I don't know. It's just that ever since orientation I've felt like I've stepped back four years socially." I nodded, having felt this way more than once myself. "I guess despite everything, I kind of liked being an investment banker. There were lots of people to go out with from work, and somebody always seemed to know where the fun places were. Every time we closed a deal we'd celebrate with a big night out, and those were always really elegant. And while it wasn't easy with the hours I put in, I still made it to a lot of shows. And now it's suddenly back to paper cups and keg parties! Tonight's splendor notwithstanding, of course," she added facetiously.

"Yeah, this isn't exactly the Limelight," I said dismissively, hoping that the one New York club I'd actually heard of hadn't gone out with Reagan.

"The *Limelight*," she said with a forgiving smile. "You're so bridge and tunnel it's adorable." *Bridge and tunnel.* I assumed this was Manhattanese for *suburban.* At that point some starstruck guy from another section came up and sheepishly asked Sandra to dance, and with a burgundy flash she was gone.

All told, the European Club's soirée was a success, although a number of people griped about what their sixty-dollar admission fee got them. We had expected a "dinner buffet," but the food offerings turned out to be a table covered with enough cold cuts and sliced vegetables to satisfy perhaps a few dozen people. Not much could have been paid for the facilities, and from the sounds of them, the band and DJ probably came cheap too. In short, the European Club made a killing off of us. The event was said to be in support of some charity, but many attendees still felt financially misused. A number of them retaliated by trying to "amortize" their ticket prices at the open bar. Have just one drink, and you paid sixty dollars for it. Have ten, and they were only six bucks apiece, a far more reasonable price. I ran into a barely coherent guy in the men's room who claimed to have hit the $3.52 mark. "If I can put away three more beers before last call, then sixty bucks isn't such a bad price," he said triumphantly.

The following week was a tough one. With Ethics over, we were now taking only graded classes. By then, my life had settled into something of a routine. It was classes in the morning, Shad and errands in the afternoon, cases at night until study group at ten o'clock, and then either to bed or back to Shad to meet some people. Whether for exercise or socializing, Shad was usually the high point of the day.

One morning, perhaps two weeks after the section's first mock awards session, I asked Carter if he wanted to grab lunch. I had seen little of him since my truncated tenure in his study group, and wanted to see what he was like outside of class. We chatted throughout a quick lunch at Kresge, and continued our conversation over in Cambridge where we both had errands to run.

Carter turned out to be what my father would call a "limousine liberal." From a wealthy background, he subscribed to a strain of left-leaning political idealism, that he had already voiced once or twice outside of class. This by no means placed him in the politically correct camp. He was rather an old-style privileged democrat of the Kennedy or Roosevelt school. After a while, our conversation turned to the inevitable subject of classes and class participation. In the first days of school, Carter had been among the section's more vocal members. But by now he had mellowed considerably in class, to the point of being almost silent. I asked him what brought on this transformation.

"Oh, I dunno," he answered. "I always come out swinging hard in a new situation. Maybe now you're just getting a better look at my true state."

At that point, Carter's true state with respect to HBS could best be described as one of increasing concern. Now that his early zeal had diminished, some deeper anxieties which it had masked were closer to the surface. "To be honest with you, almost everything we're doing except for a couple concepts in TOM mystify me. Every time I read through one of those damn Marketing cases, I don't even know how to *begin* thinking about it! Then the class discussions are so meandering, I walk out feeling like I haven't learned a thing about how to approach them. If Cotton ever cold called me I'd keel over in shock."

Carter was less worried about OB discussions, which he felt were generally "vague enough to be safe." Still, his peers' performance in this class often intimidated him as well. "Sometimes, Rosenthal calls on somebody who says the exact same thing that I have in mind. But they say it so articulately and forcefully that I just thank God he didn't call on me! That's happened four or five times, and it's getting to the point that I'm afraid to even stick my hand in the air." Carter found his sectionmates' oratorical fire to be no less intimidating in TOM, a class he had felt on top of early in the year. All of this had led him to be dangerously silent in every one of our classes since the first week of school.

It seemed that when he wasn't obsessing over airtime, Carter was a person with a wide range of general and career interests. At Emory he had developed a real passion for Latin American history and the Spanish language. He stifled an urge to move to Buenos Aires after graduation, and spent his three years as a banker feeling that he'd somehow shortchanged himself. Another of his fancies was what he called the Save the World sector. In college he had been an energetic organizer for countless charities and causes, but the demands of working life had since compelled him to neglect this side of himself as well.

Carter said his main "traditional HBS career interest" was investment banking. "I think almost every young commercial banker harbors a secret awe of Wall Street," he confided. "I interviewed with a couple of the big firms when I was a senior at Emory, but never quite made the cut. My grades were good enough, but I always got tongue-tied in the interviews. Kinda how I get in Marketing class, you know?" This time through, he hoped to do better. He planned to send his résumé to all of the leading investment banks well before summer job interviews started.

After we had finished our errands in Cambridge, I asked Carter if he wanted to head over to Shad for a workout. He begged off, saying that he needed to get home to test a new cure for his daily terrified silences in class. "It's called ultra-excessive overpreparation," he said, with a hint of irony. "I figure that if I spend *hours* thinking about every little angle of every single case, I'll be sure to have something to talk about in class." His unenthusiastic tone hinted that he wasn't convinced this would actually work.

"But it's only three o'clock," I protested. "You don't really plan to do cases straight through to bedtime, do you?"

"I do," he answered grimly. "And thank God one of tonight's cases is OB, or else I'd really be screwed."

Thank God one of tonight's cases is OB. I thought about Carter's observation as I trudged through my daily jaunt on the Stairmaster. It was an accurate one; so far, OB was clearly the least menacing of Harvard's graded offerings. OB cases were, after all, notoriously fuzzy and qualitative. Reading one was like flipping through a good magazine article, and the aid of a computerized spread sheet was never required.

A number of people had come to view the course as a bit of a joke because it was so undemanding. I tended to view it as more of a Godsend. It was nice to have discussions that weren't so numbers-driven, and we were all less inclined to come to OB with the canned comments that drove discussions from tangent to tangent in other classes. The first weeks of the course had focused on the nature of managerial work and the role of the general manager. Our cases examined not only corporate titans like Citibank and Apple Computer, but also a small food-service company, an inner-city high school, a declining British chemical manufacturer, and other diverse organizations.

I enjoyed the cases in OB, but was less impressed with the outside reading. For a few sessions we read from a book by one of the department's professors that many people found silly. Based on time spent with a handful of business people, the book offered an array of bubble charts, terminology, and rules about the habits and practices of general managers. One twenty-four-page passage climaxed with the startling twin conclusions that 1) general managers' jobs are extremely demanding and 2) they are getting *even more demanding* with the passage of time (this second revelation was based upon "a casual look at business trends").

Another riveting section discussed "The Twelve Visible Patterns in How [General Managers] Used Their Time." Here we learned the astonishing facts that the managers observed by the writer *spent most of their time with others*, that in conversations they *typically asked a lot of questions*, and that their discussions *typically contained a considerable amount of joking, kidding, and non-work-related issues.* Shockingly, this kidding was often *about others in the organization or industry.*

Passages like this had by now led some people to dismiss the course entirely. Jerry, for one, maintained that OB was nothing but fluff. "It reminds me of college sociology too much," he said. "Talk about making a science out of the obvious!" Jerry did have a point; the OB curriculum certainly featured some exhaustive ruminations on commonsensical points. Still, I found the course to be worthwhile overall. Many of the cases were fascinating, and classes were often a pleasure. Rosenthal's note was a bit of a wake-up call that led me to compose my comments more carefully. The quality of my own participation benefited from this, and I felt more engaged in the discussions as a result.

Marketing classes had a more formal tone to them. Cotton's style was relatively polished and subdued, and the early cases tended to be technical in nature. The course's first module focused on marketing communications policy, which encompassed advertising, promotional campaigns, and other ways of reaching the public. Again, the subjects our cases explored were refreshingly diverse. We studied such things as lemons, the French construction industry, and the Massachusetts lottery, as well as companies with large marketing arms like MCI and Reebok.

My favorite course at first was TOM, because almost everything it covered was new to me. Its first weeks focused on process analysis at the factory level. The concepts were more familiar to those with industrial engineering backgrounds, but nobody found the cases easy. We studied the merits of different manufacturing configurations, approaches to inventory management, and effective quality assurance strategies. Perhaps the best aspect of the course was Professor Stanley himself. He was a sincere, supportive, and patient teacher; invaluable traits given that half of our section was terrified by the rigorous curriculum of his course.

Stanley was also quite funny, but in a far subtler manner than our showmanlike Ethics and MC professors. Most importantly to me, he had one of the keenest intellects I had ever encountered. His manufacturing career had been nothing short of brilliant, and he was able to relate many of the topics we covered to his own experiences. This enlivened the course and made some difficult concepts easier to grasp. Stanley quickly became the section's most popular professor; quite a feat given the competition and the fact he taught a class that many were inclined to dread.

Difficult as TOM was, MC may have caused even more consternation in our section, as the course initially focused on the unpopular chore of public speaking. Early in the year, the section was broken into small groups that met once a week to give speeches under the supervision of Professor Golden. In the first week, I was in a listening group, and sat through nineteen or twenty speechlets. (Sandra's joking label for this exercise was "clapping for credit.") Many speakers were quite polished. Many others needed some MC training. A couple of people were downright terrified, despite the informality of the setting and the friendliness of the audience. Luckily for them, this was an ungraded practice speech. It was also videotaped, so that people could watch themselves afterward and get feedback from Golden.

One of the speakers I saw was Jerry. He was always a pleasure to listen to because he spoke in a tone that positively brimmed with force and confidence. This was a trait he shared with many of the section's military people. And of course this made sense; a few years of making dozens of adults jump with one's utterances would tend to bring a person to speak with conviction.

Jerry's speech was about why he left the military, a subject the two of us had discussed once before. After the speeches were over, I caught up with him and we headed over to Shad together. "Great talk, Captain Jerry," I told him. This had become his nickname after the section learned of his most recent military rank.

"Thanks, but it was easy. I've given it a few times in the past month."

"Yeah, and it showed. But there's one thing you never got to." Jerry looked at me blankly. "Why business school? You talked about why you left the military, but you never really got to why you came to business school."

"Well that's a good question, doctor," he replied as we cleared the security guard at Shad. "Officers who left the army at my age had two principal options. One was to go to grad school, and a lot of people did that. The other was to get a job with a big company. I'll bet you didn't know this, but there are lots of little recruiting firms out there that specialize in placing military folks into the private sector. I talked to a few of them, and even had interviews with a couple of companies. Most of the jobs I saw were in sales or factory management.

"Now guys like me are a pretty good deal from the companies' perspective. They get organized, experienced people who know how to manage a work force. Meanwhile, they don't have to pay much more than a postcollege wage. I didn't end up finding this corporate route attractive for two reasons. One, I was already eight years out of school and didn't feel like starting off at the bottom somewhere. And two, most of the jobs they showed me had very long time horizons. The companies were looking for people who would become lifers with them, you know? And I hadn't left a twenty-year track with the army just to start a thirty-five-year track at General Motors.

"Luckily I sent out some B-school applications before I started interviewing for jobs, just to keep my options open. Then Harvard gave me the nod, and here I am."

The next week it was my turn in MC. I chose to speak about virtual reality (VR), an emerging technology that interested me. It was an exciting time for VR, as it was finally on the threshold of commercial viability. I focused my speech on defining the technology as I understood it and discussing some of its potential uses. The speech went fine. I used ample hand gestures and a few pictures, tactics I knew Golden liked. It was also helpful that I was relaxed while I was speaking. After running the gauntlet with that DEC layoff speech, I was pretty tough to rattle in MC.

The next night was a time to celebrate, not only because my second public MC trial was behind me, but also because it was my twenty-seventh birthday. It was early enough in the year that everybody still had dozens of "best friends," so about sixty people turned out for the event at a nearby restaurant/micro brewery. Our reservation was only for forty, which created a logistical problem that overwhelmed the staff. A few people in our group were put off by the bumbling and at times rude treatment we subsequently received. One surly man repeatedly growled the mantra of our Marketing class. "Hey, the Customer is King!" he reminded us. "I said King!"

"Yeah, didn't anyone teach these clowns about the importance of quality management and an efficient process flow?" grumbled another person, echoing TOM's dominant themes. There was an unspoken smug certitude that our Harvard business training would forever protect us from the pitfalls that plagued this establishment. Our faith was shaken a bit when we learned that it was owned and operated by HBS graduates.

The evening was ultimately a success. I was glad to get a big turnout from the section, and was particularly pleased to have another night out with the guys from my study group. These studious alliances, it seemed, could be as central to one's social life as they were to one's academic life. By now, it appeared that most of my sectionmates had affiliated with a study group without too much difficulty. Still, a few stories had emerged about groups that were laughably serious about engineering their own composition.

Sandra, for one, had tried to join a group that was forming around a former coworker of hers in another section. When she asked if she could sit in on one of their sessions, she was told, without a trace of irony, that her background as an investment banker disqualified her from membership. "We already have a banker in the group, which is me," her friend explained earnestly. "We also have a consultant, an engineer, and a marketer. What we *really* need is someone with a human resources background."

"What a dork," she laughed when she told me about the incident. "He came up and asked me to dance at a party last weekend. I told him, forget it, I've already danced with an investment banker and a consultant. But if you can find me an engineer, hey, I'll go wild."

Jerry had an experience similar to Sandra's, although it was perhaps more painful and less comical than hers. He was rebuffed by no fewer than three study groups before he found one that would accept him. "It's like there was a price on your head," he later recalled. "If you weren't a consultant, a banker, or from one of the big marketing firms, nobody wanted to see you." This quickly resurrected the alienation he felt that first night under the tent, when we "fast-track Ivy Leaguers" seemed far too busy fawning over one another to notice that we weren't the only ones at the party.

But by now the dust had settled, and virtually everyone

who wanted to be in a study group was safely tucked away in one. The conventional wisdom was that most groups would meet with diminishing regularity as people became more accustomed to HBS and acquired confidence in their ability to crack cases alone. This tendency would become apparent in some groups as early as Halloween. After the Christmas holidays, many groups would meet only infrequently, and by spring break, most would suspend operations altogether. Study groups, then, were viewed as temporary sources of academic succor rather than as permanent centerpieces of HBS life.

Despite the problems potentially inherent within them, many section-based groups existed and thrived. Section I had several groups that were partly or entirely composed of Section I members. Luckily, anxieties of the sort that I had experienced with Carter in Marketing class turned out to be rare. Volatile situations were usually identifiable early on, and risky membership configurations were quietly abandoned during those first few days of jockeying.

The following week saw the start of Financial Reporting and Managerial Accounting (FRMA; pronounced "firm-uh"), which would be the last course to begin during the first semester. This was good news for Carter who was relieved that "something commercial banking had actually taught him" was now in the curriculum. Over the summer we had all received a self-taught course in accounting fundamentals and a letter requesting that we master it by September. For the bankers in the section, the review was rudimentary enough to be safely ignored. But for those from less financial backgrounds, accounting was a strange new art. Jerry was in this group. "Yeah, I got that *Essentials of Accounting* book," he said. "But they weren't really *serious* about us having to read it, were they?"

Evidently, they weren't. The first cases in FRMA examined the most basic tenets of accounting, and were understandable even to those who had assiduously ignored *Essentials of Accounting*. Throughout the first week we investigated such fundamentals as T-accounts and the structure of a balance sheet. These classes were quite interesting from a pedagogical point of view. I had frequently wondered how HBS would teach a detailed, formulaic subject like accounting by the case method. As it turned out, the early cases were more like accounting-book problem sets than studies of actual business events. Each was

supplemented by a "note" on a related accounting subject. The
notes were like chapters from a textbook. In this manner, HBS
crafted a case-based course that could provide a background in
accounting to the uninitiated.

This was a relief to people like Jerry. But to those who
weren't at the beginners' level, it was a serious annoyance. Sandra was particularly irate about the subject at lunch one day. "I
spent three years running cash flows and analyzing financial
statements, and I do *not* need to be told what a balance sheet is!
We're paying something like $50 a class to be here. And FRMA
is a *total* waste of my money.

"And how do they ever expect the whole section to ever end
up at the same level?" Sandra continued. Here was a problem I
saw no near-term solution to. Some people in our class were
eager to debate the finer points of LBOs, while others were just
trying to master the difference between a liability and an asset.
The likely result of this was a course that would bore some
people while racing along at a dizzying pace for others. In the
end, nobody's interests would be served.

"At least the instructor's interesting," I suggested to Sandra. She laughed, and agreed that if she met Cindy Toddson
at a party and had to guess her place of employment, the accounting faculty at HBS wouldn't be the first thing to come to
mind. Poised, witty, and spirited, Toddson was younger than
many of her students. UNDER 30, said a note from an informed
source at the start of FRMA's first session. SHE'S UNDER 30, AND
IT'S HER SECOND YEAR AS A PROFESSOR HERE! Toddson was clearly
not somebody to be trifled with.

This became even more evident a few minutes into the
class. Toddson turned out to have a canny wit that kept us all
in line. "Ooops!" she said after somebody fumbled an answer.
"Could we maybe hear from somebody who read the case?"
Later she shut down one of our tangent kings by saying "Gosh,
Frank, that's fascinating, but could you do me the honor of
answering my question?" She had great delivery, and a no-
nonsense temperament that kept everybody on their toes.

While most of his sectionmates saw Toddson as a lively
breath of fresh air, Hans was more inclined to view her as yet
another disturbing sign that he was a stranger in a very strange
land. So young a person teaching so comfortably and command-
ingly at the Harvard Business School? This was not what he had

expected! But by now, Hans had grown accustomed to periodic bouts of culture shock.

Many of these sprang from encounters with his sectionmates. Certain aspects of his fellow students' conduct often puzzled Hans, and at times struck him as downright rude. Some people, he noted, were wont to put their feet on their desks during class. Others liked to sit through classes with their shoes off (although they were usually decent enough to keep their feet on the floor when they did this). Such behavior was simply unacceptable where he came from. The aggressive, almost hostile posture some students took when responding to other people's comments in class also struck him as undignified. And this custom of calling professors by their first names was nothing short of bizarre.

Disturbing as he sometimes found all of this, Hans could take some solace in the notion that his state of alienation was, after all, quite natural. Americans who experienced similar feelings did not have this consolation. Rick was in this group, although the "culture shock" he sometimes experienced came on a professional rather than an international level. "Think about it," he said. "After four years at Rensselaer Polytechnic, and another four at United Technologies, this is the first place I've been that hasn't been dominated by engineers."

This was jarring for a person who first started viewing himself as a budding engineer early in high school. "The idea of a nonengineering academic environment was always alien to me. At least, that was my perspective in college. I didn't go there to broaden my horizons through a liberal arts program; I went to get trained, to become something tangible with a defined skill base." The environment he encountered at school and at work deepened Rick's feelings about engineering. "For eight years, I was surrounded by people who derived their status and economic well-being from the fact that they were good engineers. In college, I hardly even laid *eyes* on a history major. And at work, my peers, my bosses, and their bosses were all engineers. I was never really encouraged to respect nonengineers, by and large."

Rick was shaken to find this familiar hierarchy of prestige virtually turned on its head at HBS. "I'm used to places where an electrical engineering degree from MIT would make you a god. Around here, people are much more impressed if you studied History at Princeton, or Economics at Harvard. Some folks almost seem to equate engineering with *vocational* training." Worse, Rick found himself questioning his own suitability for an academic program for the first time in his life. "I felt incredibly behind at first," he recalled. "Accounting, Finance, Marketing. In class it was obvious who had been doing these things for three or four years, and I'd never cracked a book on any of them."

Disconcerting as he found all of this, Rick eventually acclimated to his new peers even as they acclimated to him. The Princeton Historians and the Harvard Economists gradually came to respect the particular strengths of the Rensselaer Polytechnicians. Meanwhile, Rick not only kept pace, but became a vocal leader in the section's academic life. While he didn't lead the charge in our more technical FRMA discussions, his eight years of engineering gave him insights in TOM that benefited us all immensely. Likewise, Jerry's experiences as a company commander made him a terrific resource in OB discussions, our section's sole CPA often bailed Toddson herself out of technical quagmires in FRMA, and ad agency veterans raised the level of discussion in Marketing. This synergy was the central strength of the section system. Everybody brought something unique to our classes, and everybody had something they uniquely needed to take away.

Eventually, Hans overcame his alienation just as surely as Rick. After he got settled, he found at least one aspect of Harvard's academic environment that he could embrace for every one that he found jarring or distasteful. He never expected his sectionmates to be quite as friendly and supportive as they were. And the interactive nature of class was terrific after years of sitting mutely in cavernous lecture halls. Even this first-name routine with the professors wasn't so bad once you got used to it.

In fact, he found the whole tenor of student-teacher relationships to be quite pleasant. "I'll never forget that first day of Ethics," he told me once. "When I walked in, Professor Lubbock greeted me by my first name. Can you imagine that? That was fantastic! Such a thing would never happen at home." Even more impressive to Hans was the personal interest that so many professors seemed to take in him. When he hadn't conquered his reluctance to speak after almost a month of class, it was

becoming obvious to most observers that he was in trouble. One
day he found a note in his pigeonhole from Professor Cotton
asking him to come by his office. Hans was horrified. At his old
university, this could mean nothing but trouble.

When he arrived for his appointment, Cotton greeted him
warmly, sat him down, and asked if he was having trouble
speaking in class. Hans responded cautiously in the affirmative.
Cotton urged him to speak up more frequently. By way of
encouragement, he promised to call on him promptly when he
next saw his hand in the air. He then gave him some tips on
how to steel his nerves to speak up, and on what constituted a
good in-class comment. Hans left the appointment astonished
by what had transpired, and with a redoubled respect for his
new academic home. In his earlier student days, most of his
professors had acted as remote and unapproachable demigods.
Such a meeting, particularly at a professor's behest, would have
been inconceivable.

This experience emboldened him to make an appointment
with Professor Stanley. TOM was shaping up to be Hans's academic Waterloo, and he felt in desperate need of help. His
meeting with Stanley went just as well as the one with Professor
Cotton. Stanley encouraged him to come in as much as he
needed for tutoring. Hans turned up on each of three or four
consecutive weeks, and was soon feeling in far better command
of the material. It wasn't long before he was chiming in with
increasing regularity during class.

"It's amazing what one can accomplish with the help of
these people," he observed one day, referring to our professors.
"Now I can see that even a foreign student can excel here."

At about that time, word came out that quite a number of
Hans's cohorts had done just that. On that Monday, *The Harbus*
published the names of all the second-year students who had
received First-Year Honors. Over a third of the people listed
were foreign students. Accompanying the list was a statistical
analysis of the honorees. Several interesting trends were evident.

Some groups were underrepresented in the honors ranks.
Women, 29 percent of the class, accounted for only 17 percent
of the anointed ones. Certain other groups were proportion-
ately overrepresented. Of all professional fields, consulting
seemed to offer the best preparation for the HBS curriculum.

Alumni of the top seven consulting firms accounted for 24 percent of those who made honors, but only 12 percent of the class as a whole. International students were also overly represented (24 percent of the class vs. 38 percent of honorees). But this group's success was largely driven by students from the United Kingdom, an astonishing 58 percent of whom had made honors.

There was a good deal of joking about the tendency of Brits to make honors at HBS, a trend which had been evident for many years. The smug British explanation was they tended to be brighter and more motivated than their American counterparts. The standard American rebuttal was that professors, overly weaned on episodes of *Masterpiece Theater*, were disposed to find anything uttered in a clipped British accent to be utterly *brilliant*. Given the emphasis grading placed upon class participation, such a bias would certainly influence the honors list.

That week also brought a milestone to the first-year class, in the form of our section elections. On the first day of polling, Section I only managed to elect its General Affairs Committee representative. The nomination process had been informal; interested parties needed only to submit their names and post a "position paper" in the classroom a few days before. There were quite a few candidates, including Bob Kimball, a guy who sat a couple of seats away from me. Bob was from America's mighty northern plains, was older than the norm in our section, and was married. This put him in several HBS minority groups. Most of Bob's prior work experience was with a small company specializing in conflict management, which put him in at least one more.

Bob was not someone I immediately expected to enter the GAC electoral fray, and the field was not an easy one. Five people, including the formidable William Simmons, ran against him. But Bob was the dark horse victor, due largely to an emotional speech which he ended with the slogan "Together, 'I' can do it!" A touch sappy, perhaps, but Bob sold us on his sincerity.

His conflict-management background may have been an asset to us all, because not long after his election, Section I started to relax a bit. Significantly, the awards deadlock was resolved peaceably, with the one malcontent withdrawing all objections to the process. Carter thereupon took charge of administering the flamboyant weekly sessions, which let us laugh at ourselves and relax a bit ("this is about the only airtime I ever get," he often joked). The rule was that anybody could submit nominations based on the week's gaffes and other memorable moments. Awardees would be warned in advance that they were slated for recognition, and could veto this if they found it embarrassing.

The awards sessions were so popular that Jerry felt moved to bring the section his own Friday diversion. This was Section Bingo. He programmed his computer to randomly generate dozens of cards every week. These were like traditional Bingo cards, only instead of numbers they were covered with the names of people from the section. He told me how the game would work the night before its debut. "To play, you buy a bingo card for a buck on Friday morning. Then, whenever someone on your card speaks in class, you cross out their name. As soon as you cross out five names in a row, you've got Bingo. But in order to win, you have to raise your hand, get called on by the professor, and make a comment that somehow includes The Phrase That Pays." The Phrase That Pays would be printed on the bottom of each card, and would, of course, be exceedingly difficult to utter with a straight face. The first person to get Bingo and use The Phrase That Pays would win all the money, minus a 10 percent "tax" that would go into the Sadhu Fund.

The first game was a huge hit. Over fifty people played; the phrase ("*This reminds me of something I saw on* The Simpsons *last night*") was used halfway through the second class of the day, and the Bingo money was handed off as part of the weekly awards ceremony. The next day, Jerry and I sat down at lunch and drew up new phrases for the coming weeks. *I'm glad you finally called on me* was one. *I'd like to refer back to what Jeremy just said* was another (there was nobody in the section named Jeremy). *I didn't read the case but . . .* would be a particularly tough one. *Could I please go to the bathroom now?* would be another challenge.

After the awards ceremony, I dashed off to the train station. Monday would be Columbus day, bringing the first long weekend of the year. I got through most of my cases on the ride home, as well as a short writing assignment for MC class.

This was our first graded exercise at HBS. It was based on a case we had read about the McDonald's restaurant chain's transition away from Styrofoam packaging.

By the time the train pulled into my station, there was little to trouble me over the long weekend, with the exception of a small assignment that I was saving for the ride home. I did very little over the next few days other than spend time with my family and my friends who were still in the area. This little break was very well timed, as it seemed that life would soon get very busy at HBS. The weekend's MC paper was the mere tip of the grading iceberg, and in the coming weeks we would inevitably see far more of the submerged behemoth that lay beneath it.

7

THE GRATUITOUS GOAL COUNT

ALONG WITH THE MC paper, our school's Columbus Day gift to its first-year class was a 350-page volume entitled *The Goal*. The book was assigned in addition to our normal weekend casework, as a supplement to the TOM curriculum. I finally cracked the cover of my copy a few minutes after my parents dropped me off at the Amtrak station for the journey back to Cambridge.

The book is an interesting attempt to introduce some basic industrial engineering concepts in the forum of a novel. The protagonist is the general manager of a wheezing, rust-belt factory. At the outset of his adventure, management informs him that his inefficient plant is slated for closure, a fate that can be averted only by extraordinary financial and operational improvements. Beset by conniving corporate rivals, marital problems, a disheartened staff, and the unfortunate name Rogo, he sets out to achieve the impossible. Aided by an almost supernatural Israeli physicist named Jonah, Rogo gradually gets on top of his circumstances. About sixty pages into the book, Jonah confirms a fact that Rogo has already begun to suspect on his own: that the goal of a business is to make money! Armed with this and other shattering insights from his mentor, Rogo slowly rights the situation.

I wasn't in the best of moods when I started reading the thing. The train was packed to the rafters with post-holiday passengers, forcing me to stand in the clattering netherworld between two cars throughout my journey. These circumstances aside, I was by no means happy about having a supplementary nuisance from the TOM faculty devour what might have been a contemplative (if uncomfortable) journey back to school.

Despite all this, I soon found myself enjoying that damned book immensely. It was a quick read, and the author managed to convey some valuable lessons in an engaging, understandable way. And although I found the soap opera surrounding Rogo's family situation to be trite at times, I couldn't help but grin when his wife came back to him. I was approaching the novel's climax when I heard a voice over my shoulder. "How's my buddy Rogo?" I turned to see a pretty young woman who looked vaguely familiar. "It's not such a bad book once it gets going," she continued. "We read it in TOM last year too." *Last year.* Clearly this was a second-year from HBS.

We chatted idly about school for the rest of the ride to Boston, which by then was almost over. Tina, the second-year, was rather fed up with HBS, and was looking forward to getting out. I asked her what her gripes were. "First off, the faculty. Given how much money we pay, you think they'd at least hire some experienced staff." Her section, she told me, had only two or three tenured professors in their entire first year. Of these, she only thought one was particularly good. She hadn't liked any of the younger professors.

"Now that you mention it," I mused, "we've only had one tenured professor for a graded class so far." This was Frank Cotton, in Marketing. Rosenthal in OB was in his third or fourth year, Toddson in FRMA was in her second, and Stanley in TOM was a rookie. As for MC, it seemed like most of the department was composed of part-timers who only taught one semester a year.

"Get used to it, it'll be more of the same in January," Tina warned. "My section got so screwed in terms of faculty that we practically rebelled."

Her other complaint about the school pertained to recruiting. "If you don't want to become a consultant or investment banker, you're pretty much on your own when it comes to finding a job," she warned. This statement concerned me, as I planned to explore beyond this narrow world. It also didn't ring entirely true, as I knew of several marketing and manufacturing-oriented firms that recruited on campus. "Yeah," she said when I asked about this. "They come, but not exactly in droves. Whether it's deliberate or not, the whole recruiting process funnels people into a few narrow directions."

"Funnels? How's that?"

"Think about it. When you first get here, a lot of people are right out of that consulting/banking track. For the most part, they're eager to try out something new, and most of them do over the summer. Then there's people like me, who don't come in with that background. We get herded into the summer interviewing racket, and generally end up in one of those fields, because they have the best-paying jobs, carry a lot of prestige, and hire a lot of people. Second year is different. Everyone'll tell you they want to work in a 'small organization,' 'take a line job,' 'develop trade expertise in a dynamic new industry,' or what have you.

"But getting off the beaten professional track takes a huge amount of discipline around here. It means spending weeks in the library, whether it's researching industries, identifying good companies, or figuring out which alumni to call. Not everybody has the time or the discipline to do this. Suddenly it's January, and the stampede is on for job interviews. People come out of the on-campus recruiting process with their McKinsey or Lehman Brothers offers, and suddenly they lose their stomach for turning over new stones. I heard all about this from my second-year friends last year, and it's already happening to us this year. Don't kid yourself; HBS is nothing but a prep school for two boutique industries."

The next day's edition of *Harbus* offered at least one explanation for the bias toward consulting and investment banking. Its lead article reviewed a survey carried out by the school's MBA Placement Office, which had covered thousands of graduates from the classes of '90, '91, and '92. The article focused on the two big issues of "Where Did They Go & How Much Are They Making?" A full three quarters of the class of '92, it said, had gone into nonmanufacturing industries, where they enjoyed an average base salary of $64,249, or less than 10 percent more than their counterparts in manufacturing. This small differential hardly bore out the common contention that manufacturing jobs didn't offer adequately competitive salaries to draw top MBAs. But there were a number of hidden factors involved.

First, the nonmanufacturing category included a wide range of industries. Salaries of the noble few who went to the public sector surely brought this group's mean earnings down. Average salaries in consulting, by far the most popular nonmanufacturing field, ranged from $72,500 to $80,000, depending on specialty. The survey also seemed to focus on base salaries rather than total compensation packages. Consulting and investment-banking firms typically offered signing and end-of-year bonuses that could push the total first-year take into the six-digit range. Also, many top consulting firms offered tuition reimbursement plans to returning employees. This alone could be worth close to $40,000.

Finally, graduates looked beyond the first year when evaluating compensation issues. Investment bankers, who started with lower base salaries than consultants and did not get tuition reimbursed, quickly moved onto steep financial trajectories. Even five years after the Crash, it was not unheard of for budding Wall Street superstars to clear half a million a year by their fifth reunions. Such prospects were not to be found at General Motors.

The career issues raised by the *Harbus* acquired a new immediacy on Tuesday, the appointed date of the Salomon Brothers' dinner. I was initially disappointed to hear we were expected to attend the event in business attire. It seemed to me that casual dress might inspire a more relaxed and convivial atmosphere, helping people get to know one another more easily. Hank, a guy in my section who worked three years on Wall Street, had a good laugh at my naïveté. "You better get one thing straight, Rob," he said. "Salomon Brothers is no OB case."

A table outside the restaurant's upstairs dining hall was covered with laser-printed name tags for Salomon's guests. I found mine; somehow they knew I went by Rob rather than Robert, a fact I hadn't pointed out in the letter I sent them. Inside were dozens of first-years clutching drinks and chatting in small groups, most of which were centered around Salomon representatives. I grabbed a beer and found some Section I people. We talked idly, and were eventually joined by an associate from Salomon. "So, how you folks doin' tonight?" he started. We cheerfully reported that we were A-Okay, thanks. He turned to the first person to his right, glancing briefly at his name tag. "Simon, huh? How's the first year treating you, Simon?"

He slowly worked his way around the group, engaging everyone in an abbreviated chat about HBS, the weather, the New England Patriots, or whatever else came up. When one person was talking to him, the rest of us would shut up and listen in rapt attention. The situation was stilted by nature, but everyone held up well. The Salomon guy deserved particular credit, as he surely went through this routine more than he cared to during recruiting season. After about an hour of this we drifted off to dinner. Each table had at least one senior and one junior Salomon person in among the students.

I was seated with Stanton, a managing director from the Domestic Corporate Finance group, as well as a recent HBS graduate named Minouli. They were both terrific fun to talk to, as were the other students (all from other sections) seated around us. Minouli startled me a few times by rattling off facts he remembered from my résumé. This impressed me, as the dinner tables were not assigned, and I had sat down with him more or less randomly. "You were a Fulbright scholar in Egypt, weren't you," he said at one point out of the blue. "There's a Fulbrighter from Salomon with us tonight; I'll make sure you meet him. We also have a guy who worked with your company in Poland once. I'm sure you have mutual friends." The man had certainly studied up on his guests.

As I had expected, Salomon got a good turnout. At least fifty students were on hand that evening, and a similar group was scheduled to attend a second dinner. Between meals, the open bar, and plane tickets for their people, Salomon shelled out a handsome sum for this get-acquainted stage of their summer recruiting. Subsequent phases would probably be higher-budget, if anything. I left with a very positive feeling for the firm, although I was somewhat alarmed by the amount of time the dinner took up. We were there for over four hours from start to finish, quite an investment on a three-case night. For students and companies alike, recruiting was clearly no small-scale commitment.

The next day continued in the investment banking theme, as FRMA class delved into its first annual report. General Mills's 1991 report to its shareholders made it painfully clear that a big gulf still divided our section in terms of accounting background.

Toddson started the class with an innocuous question. "Who'd like to tell us what they found out about General Mills from reading this thing?" A few hands shot into the air. Toddson called on a seasoned investment banker.

"Well, basically we've got an ideal LBO candidate," he started. "They're squeezing good margins out of a stable business that's a commodity game for some players, their operating cash flow's huge, the P/E's kinda low, and it looks like they're overspending on capex. They've levered up a bit since '82, but they could definitely handle more debt." About a dozen people nodded sagely at this outburst. Many others looked panicked.

"A bit early in the year to be showing off, isn't it?" Toddson reproached. The panicked segment of the class burst into the relieved laughter of vindication. "Who'd like to bring us back to terra firma," Toddson invited. The conversation resumed at a more fundamental level. The sage nodders started gazing off into space.

The discussion continued to ebb and flow in this manner for the rest of the class. It would briefly touch upon an esoteric topic, then somebody would call a time-out and ask what the hell was going on. What might have been a fun, free-ranging discussion for those more versed in accounting turned into a review of things they had known for years. And what might have been a solid introduction for those less familiar with accounting became an unnerving reminder that some of their sectionmates were way ahead of them. This was by no means Toddson's fault. It was simply impossible to satisfy the divergent needs of both constituencies in one class.

Sandra emerged from our classroom looking distracted and downcast about something.

"What are you so bubbly about?" I greeted her, half expecting a grouchy exposition on the FRMA curriculum's irrelevance to Wall Street veterans.

"Something I heard in there," she answered. "A couple of the guys were talking about what Phyllis said." Phyllis was one of the less accounting-wise students, and had made a somewhat off-base comment during the case discussion. "Then one of them laughed and said, 'you can bet if her name had been Philip she wouldn't be here.' It's like he thinks she only got in because she's a woman."

"Hoo boy."

"Some jerk, huh? I guess things like that should get me fuming mad, but they only seem to get me down."

We talked about this more over lunch. Sandra mentioned that this wasn't the first time she heard someone suggest that the admissions department accorded female candidates preferential treatment. "Nobody's ever accused me of being a 'diversity admit' or anything, but the subject still upsets me," she said.

"So you don't think there's any truth in it."

"Christ, I don't know. I don't think so." She paused. "At the beginning of the year, I used to feel somehow superior to people from less-traditional MBA backgrounds. You know, people who worked for hospitals, arts centers, nonprofit groups, that kind of thing. I felt like they were let in more to spice things up on campus than because their credentials qualified them to be here. Pretty snide attitude, huh?

"Well, it didn't take me long to realize a lot of those people were women. Not all of them, maybe not even most of them. But there was definitely a higher concentration of women in that group than there was among the investment bankers, for example. Now that I've been in class with these people since September, I've stopped being so snobby about them. I've seen how much they add to the section, and I understand the relevance of their backgrounds. And while I don't see them as Admissions Department charity cases any more, I know a lot of people still do. I don't like that attitude, but I understand it, because I used to have it myself."

I nodded, making room for Rick, who had just arrived with a tray.

Sandra continued. "Certain people look at that group and say hey, they're all diversity admits, and guess what, a lot of them are women, ergo, women are diversity admits. And that really bothers me. Those people were let in because they're just as qualified to be here as any management consultant or investment banker."

"So why are women more likely to come from those backgrounds?" Rick interjected. "Assuming, for the moment, that they are."

"I don't know. Some people think it's because women are too wimpy, by and large, to take life at McKinsey or Salomon Brothers. Well, that's ridiculous. I think there are actually a few societal reasons behind it. One is that it's just less acceptable for men to do things that are closer to their hearts. Men have to go slay dragons and close deals on Wall Street. A woman can get away with having a life. Not that I ever did," she added sardonically. She looked up at Rick. "Well, what do you think? Do you think the Admissions Department makes it easier for women to get in? Or for minorities?"

"I suppose it depends upon what you mean by the question," Rick replied. "Are you asking if the school deliberately builds some diversity into its classes? We all know it does. Are you asking if this might benefit women, or people with minority backgrounds? Of course it might. Just as it might benefit people from Venezuela, people from Wyoming, former journalists, people over thirty, engineers, women who were accountants, men who worked in broadcast media, or practically any other group you could think of.

"You could go to the extreme of saying that the only people who *aren't* favored are white American men from Ivy League schools who worked in consulting or investment banking. And I think some people actually believe that. But are they right? If you looked at the numbers, I bet you'd find that people from this group have an incredibly high hit rate for getting into business schools. A much higher rate than, say, African Americans, women, or foreign students as a group."

I thought about this and realized he was probably correct. Virtually everybody I knew from Bain had gotten into one of their top two business schools of choice, and a majority of them fit the white American male profile. From what my classmates had told me, it seemed that a similar situation prevailed at the other elite consulting firms. I was less certain about the investment banks, but imagined that they weren't much different. "So maybe those typical HBS types are the real beneficiaries of the quota system, to the extent there is one," Rick concluded.

Eventually our discussion moved to the less sensitive issue of our classes. With the exception of FRMA, we agreed, all were moving along at a reasonable clip. TOM was still down on the factory floor, and every case was covering new concepts. Jerry, I told them, had started the Gratuitous *Goal* Count, a tabulation of how many times *The Goal*'s name was dropped in class discussion. Citations of the book, he maintained, were made only by people who wanted to show off to Stanley that they'd actually read it. *The Goal* turned out to be a wildly popular work to mention; by Friday the count had topped fifteen.

Marketing had meanwhile moved from Price Policy to Product Policy. Cases focused on warranties, product features, brand name transitions, and other such topics. We continued to study a diversity of products, including automobiles, airlines, and industrial glue dispensers. OB, we all concurred, was definitely a little offbeat. One night in the middle of the week we had gathered in Burden Auditorium to watch the classic World War II film *Twelve O'Clock High*. We since used Frank Savage, its heroic protagonist, as a case study in 'leadership' (the differences and similarities between "leadership" and "management" had been the subject of our outside readings for the past week).

After lunch, Sandra and I headed over to the Cole Room at Baker Library. This was the nerve center of career planning and networking at HBS, and we decided it was time we figured out how it was set up. We found a free staff member moments after we arrived. "What areas are you interested in researching today?" she asked us helpfully.

"Ballerina market for me," Sandra answered. "Astronaut stuff for this guy."

The Cole Room staffer folded her arms and glowered at us like a cross librarian.

"Old joke around here, huh?" Sandra offered sheepishly.

"First-years, I can tell," our guide answered with a bemused grin. "We better start with the basics." She led us to the back of the room to start our tour. "A lot of you are here more to get a job than an education," she began, "so we try to stay plugged in."

"Plugged in" was an understatement. The place was loaded with files about the hundreds of companies that came to interview at HBS every year, as well as the countless others which solicited correspondence inquiries from HBS students. There was recruiting literature from organizations throughout the world, thousands of microfiched and hard-copy annual reports, and on-line electronic mediums that could access reams of data and articles on every major company on earth.

But the Cole Room's greatest resource was surely the alumni network. Over 27,000 alums had volunteered (and re-volunteered annually) to serve as career advisors to any HBS student who contacted them. They were listed and crosslisted by industry, company, geographic area, and function. The possibilities afforded by this data bank were staggering. It seemed that no journalist, no bureaucrat, no spy, king, or senator had a wider access to the world's business elite than the lowliest first-year at HBS. Sobered by this thought, Sandra went off to Shad, while I headed back to McCulloch to get started on the weekend's cases. The next two days would be busy, and I didn't want to be swamped with work on Sunday night.

My Saturday was partly taken up by a visit to a small Boston-based virtual reality company. I went as a member of the Volunteer Consulting Organization, a club that assembled groups of HBS students to help small businesses and charities. The VCO had put together a team to help the company attract venture capital financing for its R&D and working capital needs. The team was composed of Amos, a second-year student who had worked at the company over the summer, two other second-years, a first-year student from another section, and me. We met late Saturday afternoon as dusk was gathering. It was overcast and windy, the midautumn chill summoning grim images of Warsaw.

Twenty minutes after we had squeezed into Amos's car we were at an old factory in an aging industrial town. It was almost dark by now. The wind howled eerily as a clutch of crows circled above the menacing brick edifice, cawing like birds of prey. The setting conjured up clichéd images of nasty nineteenth-century capitalists wearing top hats and grinding the toiling masses underfoot. "Workers of the world, unite," I muttered as we mounted the steps of the towering relic.

We took an elevator to the second floor, where we were met by the small company's silver-haired founder. "Welcome to tomorrow," he said wryly as we pressed into the cramped laboratory. The place was a collage of lenses, mannequin heads, electronic components, and files.

Our team was introduced to telepresencing that evening. When it was my turn to try out the technology, Amos fitted a helmetlike device over my head. Moments later he flipped a switch, and a pair of Sony video cameras started feeding pictures into the helmet. While grainy, these images were wide-angled and three-dimensional, and gave me the eerie feeling that I was actually standing where the cameras were rather than across the room from them. The effect was all the more powerful when Amos started walking the camera around the lab.

When I got home that evening I was still disoriented from the experience. "Well, that's the perfect frame of mind for the Hong Kong!" said Carter, who crossed my path in front of McCulloch. While I was at the VR company, he had been off Doing Good. HBS was having its annual community service weekend, and each section had been assigned a couple of noble deeds. Most of Section I's volunteers were deployed to a nearby day care center, where they repainted a gymnasium. "Everyone had fun, but it was a bit low on the Save the World factor," Carter observed. Still, it could have been worse. Another guy from our section had recently helped out at a community carnival for underprivileged children. His specific role there had been to sit on a wooden stool while kids paid quarters to hurl heavy wet sponges at his head. Now *that* had a low Save the World factor.

Somehow I let Carter talk me into a bout of Scorpion Bowls at the Hong Kong, followed by an evening of pinball and mayhem at the Bow and Arrow, another Cambridge dive. It was late before we started on our way home. The next morning would bring the Head of the Charles, a Harvard-sponsored rowing regatta which drew hundreds of crews from around the world. Carter planned to rise with the sun and race with an alumni squad from his prep school. Luckily, it would be the sidelines for me.

A few hours later I was trudging back across the bridge in the morning light, marveling at the throngs that had descended upon Cambridge for the event. It was a beautiful day, and the banks of the Charles were awash with the colors of banners, blankets, and T-shirts. Virtually every major East Coast school sent crews and a complement of rowdy fans. For many of the college kids, the race was an excuse to start drinking in the single-digit hours of the morning. I had arranged to meet up with Sandra, Jerry, and his wife Melissa near Harvard Square. I found Sandra almost immediately, but it took us about five minutes to locate Jerry and Melissa in the crowd.

"There you are!" Jerry hollered when we finally joined them. "Tough to spot you. You damn kids all look alike these days!"

"*Kids?*" Sandra asked, in a tone of mock indignity.

"That's right," Jerry answered, affecting the wavering tone of an elderly man. "You twenty-somethings are too much to handle. Bunch of damn beatniks." We carried on like this until the joke was good and tired. Teasing Jerry about being one of the section's elders was by now a standard routine. A little while later, Sandra asked Jerry in seriousness if he found it difficult being on the high end of the HBS age spectrum.

"It does make me feel somewhat removed from the section," he replied, "because face it, there's some big differences between what you do for fun when you're twenty-four and single versus when you're thirty and married. And yeah, being thirty around here can make you feel sort of behind, if you let it. Because we'll all start from the same point when we graduate, regardless of our age or experience coming into school. I'll probably end up in a company with the same rank and salary as another new MBA five years younger than me. And that'll be the same rank and salary I would have had four years earlier if I hadn't signed up for another tour of duty in the army.

"A cynic could look at it and say those four extra years were a waste. But the more I think of it, the more the advantages I see to being a bit older. A big one is that I actually know why I came here. That's something a lot of the Ivy Leaguers who spent three years in some high-powered job haven't got. It's like you guys are preprogrammed, you have your lives mapped out for you. That's nice and all, and it'll be good to have a six-digit salary so early in life. But lots of people just don't have a clue about why they're here, other than that it was the next step on the ladder.

"The other thing is management. A person who spent two years at McKinsey has never managed people, period. Telling a secretary not to take a long lunch doesn't count. And at the end of the day, I have to think it's knowing the people side that makes the difference. Anybody can run the numbers. It's knowing how to operate in the fuzzier areas that makes an organization move."

The four of us had fun wandering about in the regatta's carnival-like atmosphere. We spent some time trying to figure out who was racing whom on the river, and eventually spotted what we thought was Carter's boat. Sandra and Melissa had only met briefly once before, and were soon getting along famously.

"Why don't we see more of you?" Sandra asked her as we sat down by the river for a lunch of hawker fare.

"Oh, I went to a few of your pub nights at the beginning of the year," Melissa answered. "But those can feel pretty strange if you're not a member of the section."

"Hell, they can feel pretty strange if you *are* a member," Jerry added. He recounted how he often felt alienated from his new peers during the opening weeks of the year. "If you hadn't worked in banking or consulting at some point, it was like you were from Mars," he concluded.

"And if you're just someone's wife, it's more like you're from Pluto. Especially if you're married to one of these Martians from the military," Melissa added, tousling her husband's hair.

"Did you feel like people from the section just ignored you?" I asked. "Do we act like complete snobs?" I felt an uncomfortable pang of guilt. It suddenly occurred to me that I had seen very little of the section members' "partners" since orientation.

Melissa thought for a moment. "I think it's actually indifference rather than deliberate snobbishness. It's like there's a social wall setting HBS people apart whenever there's a group of them together. Once someone you're talking to figures out that you're a grade school teacher with no aspirations to work at Goldman Sachs, they sort of run out of things to say. Next thing you know, you're in a corner with a couple other partners talking about how late your spouses stay at study groups. That gets old quick."

After lunch we continued on our meandering walk along the river. At one point, Sandra waylaid some kids flying a spectacular Chinese kite. She charmed them into giving her the reins, and within moments had the thing bobbing and weaving majestically above the Charles.

"You're a real pro," Jerry said admiringly when she was done.

"I love kites. I used to make them when I was a girl. Hell, I used to make them when I was in college. One of those hobbies we sacrifice for Wall Street." She turned to me. "A tip for the single boy. Kiting on Cape Cod is a quality first date. A bottle of Cabernet makes it really classy."

By four the day was hardly over, but Sandra, Jerry, and I

felt the tug of unopened cases and, of more concern, unwritten speeches. The new round of MC lecturettes was upon us, and this one would be graded. I had yet to choose a subject for mine.

When I got home, I gazed out at the McCulloch courtyard and tried to come up with a topic. This one was supposed to be a "persuasive" (as opposed to an "informative") speech. I knew Golden loved to see "energy" and "passion" in a speaker. He also liked it when somebody demonstrated "committedness" to a subject. But more than anything, he urged us all to "concretize" our points with examples and supporting evidence. So what concretizable subject excited energetic, committed passion from me? I glanced at my desktop and the haphazard pile of cases that covered it. On top was a reading assignment on the gripping subject of *Accounting for Plant, Property, Equipment, and Other Assets.*

That's it! I thought. FRMA! By then, Sandra and I had groused so frequently about the FRMA curriculum that pontificating about how it should be changed was almost second nature to me.

The next day's lunchtime chatter centered not on speeches, but on *BusinessWeek*'s bi-annual ranking of business schools. The survey had come out over the weekend, and Harvard only placed third for the second time in a row. Northwestern finished on top, where it had been since 1988. The University of Chicago placed second. HBS GETS A III trumpeted the headline in *The Harbus.* Somebody at our table had a copy of the magazine, and it was quickly passed around. Wharton and Stanford, HBS's principal rivals in the eyes of many of its students, had fared even worse, getting the number-4 and number-7 rankings respectively. Everybody had a good look at the survey, but few took it very seriously.

People argued that HBS was number one in the "things that really mattered," like average graduating salary ($84,960, presumably inclusive of signing and other bonuses); average number of job offers at graduation (3.5); lowest percentage of graduating students without job offers (3 percent); and highest percentage of graduating students with six-digit salaries (30 percent). Stanford was a close runner-up in the salary competition, but nobody could touch us in the job offer categories.

The attitude that coming out on top in these areas vindicated HBS and made it the "real" number-one business school was prevalent throughout our class. It showed how right the woman in the Cole Room had been in saying that many of us were here more to get jobs than educations. There was also a certain elegant rationalization that could be made from these statistics. By becoming an American MBA student, you implicitly bought into the authority of the free market. And since the Harvard MBA achieved the best statistical results in the job market, it was, in a sense, the top degree.

The survey areas in which HBS fell down pertained to fuzzier, organizational-behaviorlike areas, which were tougher to quantify with dollar values. Areas like "teaching" and "curriculum" got lower marks. HBS pulled an embarrassing thirty-fifth-place finish (out of thirty-six schools surveyed) in administration responsiveness. Nobody was surprised by this particular ranking. By now, almost everybody had an archive of pet stories about incompetent, unyielding, or condescending treatment from administrative functionaries. Petty fees, inane rules, and dithering about things like printer use in exams were cited as proof of administrative mediocrity.

After lunch I spent a few minutes flipping through the notes I'd made for my MC speech. I was scheduled to speak on Thursday afternoon along with about fifteen other people. The following week, we would listen to another group give their speeches. I was beginning to feel apprehensive about the MC curriculum. The course was starting to look like a three-month evaluative exercise. We were scheduled to progress from one graded project to another (both speeches and papers), with little if any class time between them. There would be two weeks of speeches in small groups, a plenary session to discuss speaking or writing skills, and then either a paper assignment or another set of speeches.

Students who didn't find time to visit Golden to review their papers or videotapes would therefore get next to no instruction in the art of Management Communication. HBS would never propose to teach TOM or Marketing by just giving a series of midterms and a final exam, but this was effectively its approach to MC. I toyed with the idea of making my speech a plea to change the MC curriculum, but decided to stick with the safer topic of FRMA.

Two nights before I was to speak, a weird rumor started circulating about something that happened in an OB class. At study group, Spencer, who had recently been elected social chair of his section and was by now plugged into everything on campus, had the whole story. For weeks, we had been getting little End of Class Notes (ECNs) after every OB session. Most of these summarized recent research on a subject related to the day's discussion. The OB faculty distributed these to expose us to a wide range of scholarship without having to assign us thousands of pages of primary text. A few days earlier, they had decided to squelch a particular ECN for a variety of reasons. But by some administrative foul-up, the censored ECN (which, as the nineteenth ECN of the year, was referred to as ECN-19) was accidentally delivered to one of the sections.

The ECN reviewed a 1975 book entitled *The Social Psychology of Bargaining and Negotiation*, which discussed, among other things, the ways different ethnic and gender groups responded to negotiating situations. The ECN reported that the book grouped African Americans and women with "low risk-takers" and "abstract thinkers." These tendencies, the ECN said, made people from these groups more likely to fare well in negotiations than white males, who were grouped with "high risk takers" and "concrete thinkers." The ECN was authored by Bob Rosenthal, our own OB professor.

It wasn't long before a furor was brewing on campus. Some felt that by characterizing women and African Americans at all, the note was inherently racist and sexist. I found this interpretation just a bit alarmist. After all, Rosenthal hadn't done the research himself, but was rather summarizing another publication. Still, having seen neither the ECN nor the original book, I decided to withhold judgment. The next afternoon Rick came by with a copy of the notorious ECN. It had been placed in his pigeonhole (and presumably those of all the other African American students) by an anonymous party.

I read it quickly. It indeed attributed the controversial generalizations to the book, but the qualities ascribed to women and African Americans were portrayed as neutral traits, not managerial inadequacies. I also saw that Rosenthal had used phrases like "tend, on average" rather than painting gross stereotypes of the groups in question. It was clear that the issues raised by the ECN were far too sensitive and involved to adequately explore in a two-page handout. But to characterize Rosenthal or the OB department as racist because it existed was overreactive. Unless one was ready to advocate book burning, I felt there was nothing wrong with Rosenthal having read and summarized the book. The OB department had then exercised good judgment in choosing not to distribute the ECN; in the absence of class time to discuss and debate the issues it raised, handing it out risked problems of the type that had now surfaced.

I found the cover sheet that was distributed along with the ECN to Rick and the other students to be disturbing. "As Women, African-Americans, and other minorities in general," the anonymous missive read, "we must always strive hard to eradicate discrimination at every turn, no matter how subtle, no matter how blatant. It is a contradiction, to say the least, that at one moment we watch an uplifting speech by Martin Luther King, Jr., in Ethics and then, another moment, find that some faculty still subscribe to those beliefs that all of us have worked so hard to erase. . . ." This implicit association of Rosenthal with the segregationist sheriffs of the 1950s was outlandish to me. I asked Rick what he thought about the matter.

"Well, it might be a case of people crying wolf, but I'm suspending judgment until I can find someone who read the original book," he said. "If Rosenthal was making a faithful report of what he read, then who can fault him? But if it turns out he was reading this crap into a book that made a totally different argument, I'd be concerned."

He was especially concerned about the characterization of his own ethnic group as risk averse. "I think that's a particularly unfortunate message to communicate to the HBS community," he said. "It goes back to what we were talking about at the beginning of the year, when I told you why I decided to come here. A lot of African American students here grew up in hard economic situations. And when somebody comes up from a situation like that, gets a good job, and then leaves it during a recession to take out a $50,000 loan and get an MBA, they're taking a huge risk. They're taking a bigger risk than people who come here from privileged backgrounds, who have broad financial safety nets of last resort from their families.

"And fiscal issues aside, simply being from a community where people are fully familiar with the MBA and its attendant benefits makes coming here less risky. Business school was familiar territory to you. You hadn't been through it yourself, but your father, your uncle, or your best friend's older brother had. You could think of a hundred examples of what having an MBA had done for somebody you knew well. As a result, you weren't mortgaging your future for an intangible. And I'm sure you had your family behind you. A lot of the black students at HBS are from very different situations, and they put a lot more on the line to come here. So now we have this note telling us that we tend to be risk averse, when just by being here we're probably the opposite. That doesn't help anybody."

Our section was fairly divided over the ECN. Many people felt that characterizing Rosenthal as racist and sexist was unfair. But a significant group thought that if he wasn't biased, the ECN had demonstrated a lack of good judgment. Another common anti-Rosenthal theme touched on Rick's worry; that the ECN had not been an accurate summary of the original book. One of the book's coauthors argued this to *The Wall Street Journal*, which reported the incident on the front page of its Marketplace section.

Sandra was particularly frustrated about the incident. One of her concerns focused on the whole accuracy issue. "From what I hear, he really had to fish through that book to come away with the conclusions he did," she said one afternoon as we were heading to Shad. This, she felt, indicated that Rosenthal's agenda was not entirely benign.

Furthermore, she disputed the argument that the ECN's perspective was not necessarily that of the broader faculty. "They give us those End of Class Notes to expose us to research and ideas that we don't have time to cover in class. There's a big body of knowledge out there, and they're forced to present it to us in little two-page summaries. When you have a lot of important things to cover in a tiny amount of space, you don't waste time on stuff you think is nonsense. Those ECNs are meant to be frameworks for understanding the world, not introductions to debatable points." For this reason, she felt that any idea that made it to the ECN stage only did so with the faculty's tacit endorsement. That ECN-19 was not ultimately designated for distribution was irrelevant.

But what upset Sandra the most was the reaction of some of her fellow students. "It blows my mind that so many people don't see why this is a big deal. People who are perfectly on the ball when it comes to business, classes, or careers, but who *just don't get it* when it comes to this one." More annoyingly still, many of those very people were convinced that it was Sandra who just didn't get it. "We were talking about the ECN over lunch yesterday, and this one guy called me a femi-nazi. Me! As if I'm some kind of knee-jerk orthodox feminist! That really hurt."

For another group, perhaps the largest one, the ECN wasn't much of an issue at all. "The whole thing's a circus," Jerry contended. "I got too much to worry about with this idiot MC speech to lose much sleep over it."

8

DAYS OF
RECKONING

SANDRA WAS NOT fond of MC. Commanding and Baker-bound in every other course, she found MC assignments to be either excruciating (writing) or terrifying (giving speeches). Her phobia about speech making mystified me, as she was a frequent and articulate participant in class discussions. "There's just something I don't like about delivering prepared comments," she whispered through tightly clenched teeth as she waited her turn to do just that.

Sandra and I were among the people scheduled to give graded speeches that afternoon. We were holding our whispered conversation as a woman from our section stood in the Pit, delivering a lecturette on the merits of a hypothetical bond issue. Sandra was next, so I tried to calm her with a little arithmetic I had done. "Look. This class is for five units of credit, just like FRMA and OB. TOM and Marketing are eight-unit classes. After Christmas we'll take over forty units of credit, and the following year we've got close to eighty. And this speech is only *one fifth* of your MC grade! That means it's just *a hundred and sixtieth* of your total HBS grade! So what's there to worry about?"

Sandra stopped panicking for a moment and laughed. "Rob, you are such a dork! Did you really figure all that out?" Now that hurt. I thought my calculations were pretty clever. "I don't care about my *grade*," she explained. "I just hate speaking in public!" Moments later, she got up and made a knockout speech about a merger deal she had worked on. Returning to her seat, she whispered that she'd been ready to fly into a nervous fit throughout it. This made her performance all the more impressive. "Look, if I didn't have a poker face, I wouldn't be here," she explained. Golden called my name. "Good luck," she said as I stood up. "*A hundred and sixtieth* of your damned GPA's on the line!"

I got through my speech without much trouble. Invaluable as the section system was, I argued it was a mistake to think everyone in a section had to be together for every class at all times. After all, we were split into smaller groups for MC projects. Why not do the same in FRMA? Unlike most things taught at HBS, accounting was a well-defined field with a specific base of knowledge that every businessperson should know. Some of us came to HBS with this base knowledge intact, while some of us did not. Forcing both groups to take accounting together benefited neither. To help the less initiated, FRMA spent a good deal of time on the basics. To placate the experts, the basics weren't discussed thoroughly enough to set them firmly in the heads of the beginners.

My proposal was to start the year with an accounting placement test to identify the students who were less familiar with accounting. These people could then spend the semester in a thorough basic accounting course, which would largely be taught in a lecture-textbook format. Blasphemous as it may sound, I argued, there were certain things that the case method wasn't ideally suited to. A rigorous introduction to a broad, detailed art like accounting was one of them. Harvard's enslavement to teaching by cases at all times did its students a disservice in situations like this. It was true that splitting sections into two for FRMA would partly violate the spirit of the section system. But as we would still have eleven of the twelve first-year courses together, this would hardly constitute a dangerous subversion of Harvard's fundamental standards.

It felt very good to get the speech done with. Still, there was no time to wallow in relief, as the long-dreaded TOM midterm was by now looming at the end of the week. And this was a far more serious proposition than any MC speech. It would be a nine-hour test of endurance, running from eight to five on

Friday. A take-home exam, it would consist of a single case and a series of questions. The case would be an integrative study touching on most of the concepts the course had explored thus far. Tyler and my other second-year friends had warned me that a common pitfall was to get paralyzed by the numbers. This could cause the test-taker to leave insufficient time for writing, which was a mortal error. Under no circumstances, I had heard, should one begin writing any later than two-thirty or three.

The next week was overshadowed by the approaching midterm. A few of the student clubs, such as the Women's Student Association (WSA) and the Manufacturing and Technology Management Club (MTM), held review sessions for interested students. I hadn't originally planned to attend any, but at a study group session, I decided it wouldn't be a bad idea to go to one. Spencer and George, both industrial engineers by training, reported that they had found the WSA session to be well worth the time. "The things are chaos, but you should probably go," was Spencer's review.

I wasn't sure what he meant by "chaos" until I got to the appointed classroom five minutes before the start of the Manufacturing and Technology Management club's session. Perhaps 300 people, almost half of the first-year class, were packed into a room meant for 90. An MTM functionary was frantically trying to collect a $5.00 admission fee from any attendee who wasn't a member of his club. The organizers were running low on their typewritten study guides, which prompted a panicked run of the remaining supply. After about fifteen minutes of this anarchy, somebody hollered that the session would move to Burden Auditorium as there were now too many people on hand for the classroom to hold.

Once it got rolling, the session was useful. The speakers (all second-years who had presumably passed the test the year before) gave hints on how to organize time, what points to bring up, and what pitfalls to avoid. After the session ended I drifted over to Baker Library. Model answers to previous years' tests were on reserve for us to ponder and emulate. While none of the cases used in the old tests were unreasonably hard, all were extremely broad, covering most of the concepts explored in the course. The model answers were exam essays written by students who had scored well on the tests. It was useful to see what had passed as topflight answers, but also a little frightening. These essays were good.

As I was giving the model answers a final perusal, Sandra came up to say hello. We chatted about the upcoming exam, and she mentioned that the review session she attended had been particularly useful.

I nodded in agreement. "But it's funny," I added, "I didn't see you there this afternoon." This actually wasn't funny at all; almost half of the first-year class had been in Burden for the MTM review.

"That's because I wasn't there this afternoon. I went to the Women's Student Association's review instead."

This surprised me, as I remembered how Sandra had avoided this organization back when we were signing up for clubs. Groups like the WSA, she had worried, might be viewed as crutches for people too nervous to face the rigors of HBS alone. I asked her about this.

"I've kind of changed my mind about the WSA," was her surprising answer. "First of all, the academic reviews are there for everybody, so going to one doesn't make a woman look like a charity case." This was true. By all reports, the audience at their TOM review had included substantially more men than women. "And beyond that, I'm realizing that women have more unique concerns around here than I originally thought."

"Such as?"

"I don't know, lots of things. Remember what we were talking about a while ago? How some people seem to think women are here only to add diversity to the class?" I nodded. "That kind of frustrates me. Also, what about our cases?"

"What about them?"

"Well, how many female protagonists do you remember from them?" I drew a blank. "Now this is a weird issue. I heard some people griping about it at the beginning of the year, and at that point I thought it was ridiculous. I mean, gender is usually irrelevant in our cases. It's a marketing problem, a manufacturing problem, or whatever, and the protagonist is just a name that crops up every two or three pages. But I started to change my mind after we looked at Mary Kay in OB."

This had been a couple of weeks before. Instead of a case, we were assigned a photocopied magazine article to read about the feisty cosmetics entrepreneur. Much of the subsequent class was given to watching a *60 Minutes* segment about her organization. This included scenes from a company conference, which featured footage of adult women parading about in bunny ears, singing spirited ditties, and carrying on like hyperactive adolescents.

"First of all, it bugs me that one of the few classes that focused on women in a corporate setting featured a videotape that made them look like a bunch of bimbos," Sandra continued. "But what really got me was that the school didn't bother writing a case. I mean, Mary Kay is the most accomplished entrepreneur we've studied so far. She's a good role model for any of us, men or women. And all they gave us on her was a seven-year-old magazine article and an insipid *60 Minutes* segment."

Sandra went on to cite the treatment of some of Mary Kay's male counterparts in the OB curriculum. Jan Carlzon, a Scandinavian airline executive, had merited a thirty-eight-page case study. John Reed, the Citibank executive, was the subject of two cases totaling twenty-six pages. Sir John Harvey-Jones, a British chemical executive, had been the subject of both a case and two lengthy videos, which we watched outside of class time. And just that week, Harold Geneen, the one-time autocratic CEO of I.T.T., had been examined in an endless forty-three-page case.

"So all of this means you're changing your view of the WSA?" I asked her.

"I think I'm getting there," she answered.

Aside from the midterm, the rest of the week was spiced up by the remaining embers of the ECN controversy. News and opinions about the incident dominated the pages of *The Harbus* on Monday. A particularly vehement letter attacked the anti-Rosenthal manifesto that Rick had found in his box. At issue wasn't its content, but the anonymity of its authors. "A corollary of freedom of expression," read the letter to *The Harbus*, "is that one should take responsibility for one's own speech and writing. To shirk that responsibility is to descend to a primitive intellectual terrorism through which we feel free to slur the good name of another, without even allowing them knowledge of the identity of their assailants." It went on to argue that "An anonymous note of this nature is little better than a nuisance call from the thought police."

The ECN question was also given a full treatment in OB class. The department was so concerned about the incident that it rapidly produced a full-fledged case centered around it. This was immediately appended to our curriculum. Because Rosenthal was personally so involved in the issue, he had decided to invite Sam Lubbock, our Ethics professor, to lead the section's discussion of the case. Throughout the class, Rosenthal sat on the side, answering the questions that were occasionally addressed to him. The session wasn't as contentious as I had expected. Discussion centered more upon the general issue of stereotyping than on Rosenthal's memo. A few pointed remarks referred directly to him, including one from a man who had read the original book and argued that Rosenthal had done a sloppy job of summarizing it. But for the most part, conversation was nonconfrontational and subdued.

It was also remarkably one-sided. People who had earlier expressed an antagonism to Rosenthal's shriller critics were almost universally silent in class. Jerry was in this group, so I raised the subject with him after class. "C'mon, it's just not worth it," he said. "You step outside the party line on this issue, and the next thing you know someone'll be stuffing your box with notes calling you a fascist. I've decided to keep my mouth shut on subjects like this. I'll save my energy for talking about cycle times in TOM."

Indeed, TOM and its upcoming exam soon eclipsed the ECN issue for almost everybody else as well. I was careful not to kill myself studying for the test, but still put in more hours than I'd expected. Conventional wisdom had it that exam time was the most relaxed period at HBS. With no cases to worry about, there was nothing to do but study for tests. And the nature of HBS tests (open notes, open book, open computer) made most studying redundant. But at least for this first exam, the conventional wisdom did not hold. Even with nine hours to take the test, nobody wanted to waste time flipping through folders looking for formulas. The night before the exam, our campus was as quiet as a meadow smothered in freshly fallen snow.

At 8:00 A.M. on Friday, Section I was packed into the Pit of its classroom. Soon the signal was given to grab a test and get moving. I got mine, charged off to Kresge, bought two cups of coffee, and raced up to my room. The case was entitled *Lehigh*

Valley Industries (LVI). LVI produced forged parts, and was plagued with the ills that were so common to companies in TOM cases. Long lead times, inventory control problems, bad process designs, a poor factory layout, an ill-conceived manufacturing philosophy—LVI had it all. I read the case carefully, underlining its key points in four colors of ink.

At nine-fifty the phone rang. I looked at it mutely. We were on our honor not to talk to other students during the test. Who could it be? It rang three more times, then the answering machine kicked in. It was my old roommate from Warsaw, who was making her fourth attempt to reach me by phone. Oh, why not, I thought. I picked up the phone.

"Howdy!"

"Screening your calls, huh?"

"Naw, I'm actually taking my first midterm right now," I drawled, trying to affect a tone of reckless bravado.

My old roommate expressed the requisite amazement at my cavalier willingness to talk on the phone at such a time. "I should probably let you go . . ." she started.

I looked at the clock. *Hell, I had seven hours left!* "Nah, don't worry about it. The test doesn't look too awful and we haven't talked in weeks."

After we finished chatting, I called the TOM faculty hotline. There was a diagram of the plant's process flow in the case. I wanted a few extra copies of it to work on, but wasn't sure if we were permitted to do photocopying during the test. "Go for it," said the professor on the other end after I explained my quandary.

It felt good to stretch my legs, and campus was so quiet! I walked over to Baker Library at a leisurely pace, made some copies of the floor diagram, and strolled back to my room.

Ten-forty. I turned on my computer and started to write:

LVI's Easton plant, a technically advanced producer of forged parts, faces daunting managerial challenges due to changes in the competitive environment, its parent company's LBO-related debt, and its own substantial growth. To surmount these challenges and forge a future of growth and stability, the plant must adopt a new manufacturing philosophy as well as implement significant operational changes.

I am such a hero! I thought. 10:40 and I'm already writing! I glanced idly at my clock, wondering when I'd knock off for a relaxed lunch. At this rate I'll be at Shad by two o'clock, I thought smugly.

I looked back at my first paragraph. ". . . *forge* a future of growth and stability . . ." Hoping Stanley would forgive this accidental, yet egregious pun, I returned to my work.

I wasn't at Shad at two o'clock, nor at any other time that day.

I didn't end up getting any lunch either. I cranked along at a steady pace from ten-forty until well into the afternoon. I began printing my exam only a few minutes before five, and found myself charging across the Aldrich lawn with the rest of my class in order to get the damn thing in on time. In the end, there was no denying that I could have used the extra hour I had squandered during my midmorning break. I was a bit angry with myself about this, but soon forgot about it. *It was over!* And it was Friday. Time to unwind.

Section I had a keg over in one of the dorms. Most people were gleeful to have the ordeal over, but a few, like Carter, just looked weary and shell-shocked. I didn't stay at the party for long. On occasions like these, I often sought the company of Alistair and George's crowd. Theirs was a far rowdier section than mine, and George was hosting their post-TOM party. I cajoled Rick and Jerry into defecting from our section for the evening, and we headed over. The scene of our staid study group sessions was packed with drunken first-years by the time we banged on the door. A few minutes later we were followed by the section's TOM professor, who was greeted with a noisy cheer. The guy was immediately handed a beer and swept into a chug-off with three of his students. He lost, but only narrowly. Much as I liked my own section's TOM professor, I couldn't ever imagine him pulling that one off. Granted, he was a devout Mormon.

Jerry thanked me energetically for dragging him to George's celebration. "It's pretty rare for me to get out like this," he said.

This was true; by now, Jerry had dropped from the mainstream social scene almost as completely as his wife. Of course, this was no coincidence; given that Melissa felt a certain social wall between herself and the section, it was unsurprising that they spent little time at section functions. "But this doesn't mean we don't see people from school," Jerry pointed out. He told us that a certain underground partners' world had developed in the ranks of the married, engaged, and seriously dating. "We see other couples from the section all the time. We have dinner parties, we play tennis, we do things. It's like a parallel universe to you single folks."

We talked about this for a while, and agreed that it was regrettable the section was fragmenting on partnered/unpartnered lines so quickly. Jerry said that even if Melissa and her compatriots felt fully integrated with the rest of us, much of the section's social life was slanted toward single people anyway. "What are the section's organized activities? Meeting in bars after dinner, for the most part," he pointed out.

Jerry wished we would have more event-oriented get-togethers, like dinners, dancing, movies, or even bowling. Melissa would probably find such evenings more appealing, and he wasn't about to go to the more typical section functions without her. "You'd be amazed at how little you see of each other when one person's living student hours and the other one's making an honest living," he said. "I don't usually get home from study group before 11:00. And by then, she's sound asleep; she gets up at 5:45 every morning. Much as I like hanging out with the section, I'll tend to bag something that's going to pull me away from her."

Rick, who had rejoined us in the middle of this conversation, mentioned that most of his social life also lay beyond Section I. While he attended many of our formally organized functions, he rarely joined in on the impromptu dinners or nights on the town that often took place. "Ever since September, I've tended to spend most of my social time with other black students on campus," he explained.

He didn't find this situation to be unhealthy or somehow imposed on him. Rather, he viewed it as an unsurprising social outcome. "People who share common backgrounds just tend to bond more. The Germans like to spend time together. So do the married folks. The dynamic's not any different with us."

We discussed this partial social segregation on campus, then drifted toward the subject of racial tension. Despite the anxieties raised by the ECN-19 incident, Rick said he didn't think this was a major problem. Still, certain students struck him as being awfully naïve about racial issues. "A lot of people around here lose sight of the fact that folks like me operate in two worlds," he explained. "On the one hand, we're in the Ivy League–MBA–Wall Street environment. But on the other hand, a lot of us came here from somewhere very different. A person who meets me in the HBS world might forget that I'm not immersed in it at all times. When I go out with the section, I sometimes look around and see that I'm the only black person in the bar. And most of the people I'm with are completely unconscious of that fact. They don't even realize there might be something uncomfortable about it. But if I took one of you to a black club, you can bet I'd be sensitized to the fact you might feel awkward."

Rick said that generally, the lives of black students at HBS differed little from those of other students. One exception to this was in the realm of dating. "I know all the guys around here like to bitch about how bad the ratio is, and how hard it is to meet women on campus." He nodded at Jerry. "The single guys, that is. But think of how it is for us! First of all, there are maybe forty black students in each class. With the ratio at HBS, that translates into around fifteen women. Now how many of these ladies are married, and how many have boyfriends? There's no more interracial dating around here than there is anywhere else, so you can see that we're looking at a pretty small group of eligibles."

The next day was Halloween, perhaps an appropriate day for the world's top financiers to arrive at the Harvard Business School campus. It was time for the annual Finance Club Career Fair, and all the major investment banks and big commercial players like Citibank were there. Downstairs at Kresge was a primping throng of palm-pressing, job-happy students. Company tables were set up throughout the cafeteria area. I grabbed a few brochures and signed a few guest lists, but soon gave up on talking to any of the company representatives. Most firms had only three or four people on hand, a presence that was quickly overwhelmed by the hordes of attendees.

As I was starting to leave, I spied a hole in the crowd around the J. P. Morgan table. Why not, I thought, I may as well talk to at least one company. I parked myself next to a young woman wearing a Morgan badge and tuned into her conversation. She was talking to one guy, a first-year with I-banking experience by the sounds of it, as a second guy listened attentively. I put on my best fixated-with-the-conversation face and dutifully waited my turn. The first guy left after a couple of minutes, and the second guy started with his questions.

As he was wrapping up, I felt a body pressing against me. Funny, I thought; Kresge was crowded, but this felt like being on a Bombay bus at rush hour. I turned around. Behind me, some clown with an obsequious grin was trying to lunge into the conversation. As the student in front of me finished, this joker cut around me and planted himself squarely in front of the Morgan rep. "Hi there, ma'am!" he blurted. "I've heard some terrific things about J. P. Morgan, and I have a few questions I'd like to ask!" He spied a student handing out Morgan brochures behind her; presumably someone who had interned at the bank over the summer. "Oh, hi there Sam!" said the aggressive dork. Sam tried his best to ignore him.

The interloper continued. "Like Sam, I'm a former military officer, and I think the leadership skills and analytic background one acquires in the service can be invaluable in the investment banking environment." The woman from Morgan politely fielded his questions, which seemed to have no end. About five minutes into his monopoly of her attention, she caught my eye and gave me a helpless shrug. You want to swim with the sharks, you better be aggressive, she seemed to be telling me. As the minutes wore on, I decided that I didn't have the stomach for this game, so I picked up a pamphlet and left.

The evening was an energetic one around campus, and many Halloween parties raged. This was unsurprising. With the first two graded hurdles of our HBS careers at last behind us, everyone in the first-year class had a certain amount of steam to blow off. Unfortunately, there was little time to relax once Sunday morning came, as the Marketing midterm was to start in only four days. In honor of this impending trial, I decided to try an experiment with the night's marketing assignment. A number of people in our section had taken to typing up their notes on every case and bringing them to class. I viewed this as a fairly extreme practice, but decided to try it at least once. Around seven I sat down with *The Procter & Gamble Com-*

pany: Lenor Refill Package. This had been a midterm once, and was assigned to show us what kind of case we might face on Thursday. Like the old TOM exams it was comprehensive. It touched on prices, products, distribution, and a variety of other marketing-related issues. About twenty minutes after I started outlining my analysis on the computer, I knew I'd made a big mistake. I was typing out my every little insight and opinion, and meticulously reorganizing the whole morass every five minutes. At this rate it would take forever to finish! Unwilling to quit what I had started, I doggedly saw my experiment through, wrapping it up almost two hours later. I raced off to study group fifteen minutes late, vowing to never type another outline again.

I arrived at the next morning's class a bit early, and watched Cotton begin what was fondly known as his Death March. By now, most professors cold called without warning. But Cotton, God bless him, still drifted over to his victims to tell them of their status about a minute before class started. This was a decent-minded policy; it gave people a chance to decline a cold call without embarrassing themselves in front of the entire section. It also let the section's voyeurs watch the day's cold callee shift into panic mode moments before the start of each class.

Cotton was heading my way, I noted dully. I looked up at Jerry, who sat in the Sky Deck behind me, and idly wondered if his number had come up. As a relatively frequent participant in class discussions, I generally felt safe from cold calls. Whereas professors had cold called more or less randomly at the beginning of the year, by now they almost exclusively picked on people who didn't speak often in class.

Cotton was coming closer. Cotton was closing in. Cotton was in my face. "Mornin', Rob," he said affably. "How would you like to start us off today?"

I glanced at the neurotically detailed outline of my thoughts about Lenor. "I think I could do that."

Moments later I began one of the most interminable openings in Section I history. Before I had even worked through two thirds of my outline, I realized that I was approaching the twenty-minute mark. *Time to shut up.* I glanced at my first and last typed outline, which I had cursed so roundly the night before. *What timing!*

A few people took issue with some of my points, but the
damage they inflicted on my analysis didn't seem mortal. Afterward, Carter walked up to me shaking his head. "Man, are you
always that well prepared?" he asked.

"Of course," I replied casually. "Aren't you?" When it
looked like he actually believed this, I quickly told him about
the fortunate timing of my excessive preparation and Cotton's
cold call.

"Some people have all the luck," he said, sadly shaking his
head. "If I could just bring myself to open my mouth in class
I'd be feeling pretty good." Unfortunately, this was no exaggeration. A few weeks before, Carter had briefly seemed to be
beating the demons that held his tongue in Aldrich Hall. But
as quickly as this remission began, it faded. I asked him what
happened.

"I guess I kind of rallied back when FRMA started," he
recalled. "If there's one thing I know it's accounting, so I managed to make a few good points in that class. I even got my
mouth open in Marketing and TOM once or twice. But speaking still made me nervous, so I decided to take a breather after
about a week of this. I just didn't raise my hand at all for maybe
three days. And this turned out to be an easy way to get through
class. No butterflies about speaking, and no frustration about
not getting called on when I raised my hand.

"Before I knew it, a week or two had gone by like this. And
by then, I'd gotten back to my old inferiority complex about
talking in class. It's amazing how quickly this happened. I just
kind of tricked myself into thinking that almost everybody who
spoke had some unique and valuable insight. I was too self-
conscious to speak just to hear my own voice, so I only raised
my hand when I *really* had something to add. This turned out
to be maybe once or twice a class, and you know the numbers
well enough to know this meant I never got called on.

"I guess that's where I've been ever since. Occasionally I
say something, but it usually turns out to be a stupid chip shot
that makes me even more self-conscious. So every day I just sit
there with my hands at my side. It's like being in a dream, when
you're sliding toward the edge of something, and you just can't
stop yourself. You could stop sliding just by screaming, but you
can't bring yourself to utter a word. Pretty bleak, huh?"

Bleak indeed. And unfortunately, stage fright was only half

of Carter's problem. The other half, he said, was that he just didn't get most of Marketing and a lot of TOM. He recently brought himself to seek some help in redressing this. Like Hans, he made appointments to see our professors, but ultimately found this unsatisfying. "The reality is, you just can't get into their offices for long enough to do much more than shmooze a bit. It's definitely not their fault; they've got ninety of us to deal with and there's only so many hours in the week. But the best I could come up with was an occasional fifteen-minute appointment, and that wasn't enough to bring me back from the abyss."

Carter's next stop was the on-campus peer tutoring system. This was a network that connected troubled first-years with seasoned second-years who had been nominated by their first-year teachers to tutor certain subjects. An on-campus office provided Carter with a list of certified Marketing, TOM, and OB tutors. He was told that tutoring would cost $10 per hour. The school would pick up the tab for his first ten hours of tutoring, and he would have to pay his tutors directly after that.

"When I first heard of this I thought, wow, what a neat system! It really says a lot that so many second-years give up their time for token wages to help out people like me." Carter was right; it was a neat system and it did say a lot about the time-pressed second-years who participated in it. Unfortunately, this was one market in which demand often exceeded supply. "Most of the tutors can only squeeze in three or four people a week, and they tend to see the same people throughout the semester," Carter explained. "By the time I called down the lists, almost everybody I talked to had been fully booked since the second week of school," Evidently, Carter wasn't the only person anguishing about his academic position in the first-year class. He was just less organized in his panicking than some of his peers.

He managed to get a few appointments with tutors when they had cancellations. But while these meetings were helpful, they alone were not enough to right his situation. "So now I'm back to my old strategy of ultra-excessive overpreparation," he concluded gloomily as he headed home to a long afternoon of just that.

Later that day I ran into Tyler at Shad. We caught up for a while, and I told him about my cold call in Marketing. "It really caught me off guard, given that I've participated a lot in class so far," I added.

"Well then it was probably what we call a wake-up call," he informed me. "Every so often, professors cold call people who've been contributing pretty regularly, just to make it clear to the section that nobody's safe."

Tyler's theory seemed accurate, because on the next day Cotton cold called Sandra, one of the most vocal and articulate people in the room. The case was a crusher dealing with all of the big themes of the course. Sandra outlasted my opening by at least five minutes. After she was done, Cotton called on William Simmons, who unleashed the longest noncold-call comment of the year. Cowed by the approaching midterm, we were all taking Marketing very, very seriously.

Meanwhile, the pressure from TOM had mercifully diminished. That week marked the beginning of what became known as the kinder, gentler TOM. The first case after the midterm, entitled *Gunfire at Sea: A Case Study of Innovation*, was a breezy, qualitative discussion of nineteenth-century naval artillery. Gone were cycle times, bottlenecks, throughput, and those endless numerical exhibits. From now on, TOM would focus on industrial strategy and personnel organization. It was nice to shift gears. Despite Stanley's inspired teaching, the old subjects had become rather tired.

After class, Sandra walked up to Jerry as he and I were leaving for Shad. "Howdy, Captain Jerry," she greeted him. "High time that military background came in handy, huh?" He had made a particularly astute comment in the *Gunfire at Sea* class.

Jerry responded with an uncharacteristic flash of temper. "Surprised to see that someone who didn't come out of Morgan Stanley actually had some relevant work experience?" he asked sarcastically.

Sandra, who had meant no harm by her comment, cringed. "Easy, boy," she reproached. "Didn't know about the raw nerve."

Jerry relented. "Sorry, Sandra. Sore subject." He explained himself. "At the beginning of the year, it bugged me how some of the Princeton-Morgan Stanley types acted. It's like they were too busy being impressed with each other to give us normal folks the time of day. Even now, I run into some people who can't understand why there are so many military people here.

It's like they think we all got in through some kind of affirmative action plan."

"That's obnoxious," Sandra said, by now feeling thoroughly chastised.

"No doubt," Jerry agreed. "Particularly because when I think back on the application, it's almost hard for me to see how a *non*-military person would have dealt with it. I mean, Harvard says they're trying to groom general managers, and those essays really bore that out. Think about it; they asked us about our leadership experiences, about our ethical dilemmas, that kind of thing. I'm sure I had more meat in my answers than some hotshot who was fourteen months out of college when he started his application. Anyhow, I'll see you folks. Gotta vote."

"Oh no," Sandra muttered as Jerry hurried off. "The election!" She pulled out her calendar, wondering how she would squeeze one more chore into an already cluttered schedule. But like most of our classmates, Sandra eventually figured out how to heed the call of civic duty, and helped the country select the man who would govern it for the next four years. It was a good year for the Democrats, the party that a *Harbus* straw poll had indicated that HBS students preferred by a significant margin.

The campus's reaction to the election's outcome was most understated. Despite the fact that their candidate won, most students spent the day and evening quietly going about their business. After all, it was a three-case night, and a thirty-hour midterm was less than two days off. The atmosphere at a sister school across the river could not have contrasted more sharply. I had two good friends who were first-years at the John F. Kennedy School of Government, Harvard's graduate school of public policy. They invited me to a "small election party" in the Forum, their main common area.

I got there just as the final returns were coming in. The place looked like a cross between a New Year's party and a football rally. Dangling into the atrium from an upper floor were sweeping thermometerlike scrolls. Caricatures of various candidates clung to these at heights indicating their relative performance.

The room was thronging with "K-school" students toasting the election, hugging one another, and whooping with joy. Whenever the wide-screen TVs announced a Democratic victory, the crowd roared with triumph. When a race went to the GOP, the room echoed with hisses of scorn. I found Hannah, one of the people who invited me.

"Quite a bipartisan crowd you've got here!"

"I think a lot of people are applauding their job prospects, really," she joked. Harvard academics, particularly those from the Kennedy School, had traditionally enjoyed generous representation in Democratic administrations. "What's happening on your side of the river?"

"Well, nothing quite approaching this scale . . ." I hadn't actually heard of anything, aside from a small section gathering in front of the tube in McCulloch's lounge. "People just don't have much time for this sort of thing."

"For this sort of *thing*?" Hannah gave me an incredulous look. "This is the biggest changing of the guard since grade school!"

She had me on that one. Still, our school's reaction to the election was hardly a whisper compared to the hubbub likely to surround McKinsey's first day of interviews. After all, tomorrow we'd have TOM, FRMA, and OB, and there were cases to prepare. It was easy to forget there was an outside world at all. Thinking of this reminded me of something from a couple of years back. It was January 17, 1991. I was working late at Bain, proofreading overhead slides for some partner to present at a routine meeting with a client. About an hour earlier, allied forces had started bombing Baghdad.

Going home early was out of the question; war or no war, there was a client meeting the next morning. Naïvely, I thought it might be possible to slip downstairs for fifteen minutes to watch the president's televised address to the nation in a neighborhood bar. Nothing doing, my manager told me. Miles needs this stuff in St. Louis tomorrow. I made it home long after midnight, too weary to watch the news for more than a few minutes. It was then that I suspected there was something uncomfortably surreal about Bain, about the Lemming March that drove people at all levels (after all, my manager was there too) to lose perspective to this insane degree.

Granted, the election-night situation at HBS that night was not quite as bizarre as this. Elections were more common and predictable events than wars, and besides, there were good reasons to be obsessed about school. Wednesday's cases aside, we were all girding for the rather unique trial of a day-and-a-half "group" midterm in Marketing class. A few days before, our section had been randomly divided into four-person teams. After classes on Thursday a case would be handed out, and each team would have until late Friday afternoon to crack it and write it up.

I didn't know my teammates very well, but was optimistic about our prospects. Hank and Don were both former investment bankers. This was a plus, as Cotton was known to appreciate quantitative analysis. Stephanie, the team's sole woman, had worked for a state politician. Together, she and I could probably nail down the qualitative end.

Our team decided to meet during the afternoon before the test to agree on a strategy for approaching it. This meeting was brief and focused. The key to doing well, we agreed, was to manage the process as effectively as the output. Given the intensity of our task, success would depend as much on good OB skills as on marketing wizardry. Our plan was to spend three hours reading the exam after receiving it. Then we would convene at Au Bon Pain and break the work into four equal pieces. To force a quick consensus, we would strictly limit this meeting to one hour. Everyone would then take their assignment and spend the next few hours rigorously analyzing it and outlining their conclusions.

Early in the evening we would reconvene at Hank's to eat dinner, watch *The Simpsons*, and review the outlines. By ten we would return home to type up our pieces, synthesizing the points that came out in the outline review. Everybody would hopefully be asleep by 1:00 A.M. and well-rested by nine the next morning, when we would meet again. We would then theoretically spend the next eight hours merging the four parts together and fine-tuning them.

The next day, the first-year class received a case entitled *Chipman-Union, Inc.* Hardly glamorous in subject matter, it concerned the licensing of the Odor Eaters name to a hosiery manufacturer for a line of odor-resistant socks. We met three hours later as planned. I had gotten through the case quickly, which gave me time to work up a tentative outline of our report. The group bought into this outline with minor changes, and we quickly divided up the work. Hank and Don got the quantitative chores of analyzing product line profitabilities and cash flows, as well as reviewing price points and discount policies. Stephanie took on the more political issues pertaining to Chipman-Union's sales force and their relationship with wholesale customers. I volunteered to survey alternatives to the Odor Eaters launch and concoct a possible communications campaign.

"Good lord," Hank marveled as the first meeting wrapped up slightly ahead of schedule. "It's actually going like we planned."

"Don't worry, we've got more than a day left to screw up," cautioned Don.

That night, Hank drove by campus and ferried us out to his place. Just as planned, we ordered food, began discussing the outlines, and broke briefly to watch *The Simpsons*.

A few minor disputes about our four individual outlines were resolved with an agreed-upon mechanism; majority vote ruled, and the view of the outline's author held sway in a tie. By ten-thirty we were on our way home, a clear sign of solid OB process control. Many other teams had structured their time very differently, meeting straight through the afternoon and evening with very little time apart. We had considered this approach, but feared it would result in only one or two people working at any given time. Our system was meant to prevent this waste of our human resources. And by exposing us to one another in small doses, it also reduced our risk of getting on each other's nerves.

This turned out to be a wise approach. Stephanie's roommate had a team that met nonstop throughout the entire exam period (unfortunately for Stephanie, their meeting place was her apartment). They ended up having a bitterly contentious time of it, and expended more energy wrangling over details than producing analysis. A group that met in my suite's lounge also opted for the marathon meeting approach, and spent countless hours spinning their wheels together.

· The next morning we were back at Hank's, and within a couple of hours had signed off on one another's written segments. Being more literarily inclined, I took on the task of organizing and editing the text. Stephanie quality-checked and proofed my output, while Don and Hank cranked out numbers. By three o'clock, Stephanie and I had generated a solid report.

But hard as we worked on it, our essay's text was outshone

by its accompanying numerical exhibits. The mind boggles at what two former Wall Street analysts can accomplish in five solid hours of running numbers. The only real challenge Hank and Don encountered was getting their printer to print small enough to squeeze everything into the three-page limit. From a logistics plan that would make a TOM professor weep with pride to a sensitivity analysis that would cow a Baker Scholar, it was all there. Our only worry was that the report, which was supposed to be under 2,000 words ("Any report exceeding these restrictions will not be accepted by your instructor," our guidelines warned), weighed in at 3,087. "Don't worry about it; every syllable's priceless," was Hank's verdict at four.

Shad was packed after the tests were handed in at 5:00, and the beer flowed liberally. Everyone on our team was in a great mood, as the last day and a half had given us all a terrific feeling of accomplishment. Many, if not most of our sectionmates felt equally good about the experience.

Some people had gotten awfully creative with their exhibits, crafting prototypes of Michael Jordan promotions and the like. There were also some horror stories. In one section, a student reportedly arranged a blind date for the night of the exam. He snuck off during his group's two-hour dinner break, not returning until the near-dawn hours. As penance, he offered to write his team's entire report. They left him to it until early the next afternoon, when he handed them an inarticulate, rambling document that hardly touched on the case's central issues. The ensuing panic almost yielded a corpse.

That night our section rented a trolley car to ferry us around downtown Boston's hot spots. Unfortunately, there was a two-hour lull between the Shad celebration and the start of this escapade. By the time we got going, the three beers I'd downed at 5:00 weighed upon me like a leaden overcoat. Between "hot spots" I fell into a deep slumber on the trolley. When somebody woke me up at the next stop, I decided to call it an early night.

The morning brought the Marketing Club's Career Fair. After my unhappy experience at the Finance Club's fair, I had little interest in attending. The week's near-lethal dose of marketing put any doubts about this to rest, and I slept until the thing was almost over. The people who went made out like

Robert Reid

bandits from the consumer product companies' reps, who were handing out packaged goods like candy on Halloween. One woman came back to McCulloch so weighted down with food that she went on a rampage, giving away her loot like Santa Claus. I got a box of dried Kraft Macaroni and Cheese. At last, something at HBS had come without a price tag.

9

CARTER DROPS THE H-BOMB

THE SECOND WEEK of November was something of a watershed. The first two months of school had been a time of socialization and acclimatization. We learned the ropes, joined clubs, developed as a section, and figured out how to cope with our school's unique pedagogy. At the end of this period we met the twin challenges of the TOM and Marketing midterm marathons. Having now made the journey from novice to initiate, we had our first real encounters with two issues that would dominate the remainder of our time at HBS: academic performance and recruiting.

Monday's *Harbus* included the first of many pullout guides to company presentations on campus. With the exception of the Salomon dinners in October, recruiters had largely been held at bay until then. In an effort to keep our minds on classes for at least a couple of months, the school didn't permit on-campus job presentations directed at first-years until after the Marketing exam. But now, the dam holding back a tide of recruiters burst. Over sixty companies were scheduled to present on campus during the next eight business days, and dozens more would follow in the weeks thereafter. Many other companies would hold off-campus meetings in nearby hotels. The master schedule in *The Harbus* looked like a TV listing. Over twenty companies ran full-page or two-page spreads in the newspaper, and many others ran smaller announcements.

As recruiting geared up, we were also getting the first substantive indicators of our academic standing. Until then, the lone graded MC speech was our only window on this important subject. This changed on Monday, when we received interim assessments of our class participation in Marketing. Everybody was placed into one of five evaluation categories, ranging from "very strong" to "significant problems." The people who ranked in the bottom 20 percent of the section in the class participation game were also given official notices alerting them of their status. These notices (known as warnings) would ultimately be distributed in several of our other first-year classes.

While Carter wasn't ranked in the "significant problems" category, he was issued a warning. I knew of nobody else who received one of these unhappy notices; those who did were understandably tight-lipped about their status, confiding only in their closer friends, if anybody. Included with our grades were short personal notes from Cotton. In mine he was encouraging, and listed the cases on which he thought I had made good comments.

On that day we were also given our MC papers on McDonald's Styrofoam packaging. I did fine on mine which pleased me, as I probably hadn't given as much time to the assignment as I should have. Some people were far less happy, both with the time they invested in the paper and with the marks they received on it. Sandra spent hours on the assignment, and was rewarded with only a 3 − on a scale of 1 to 5. She showed me her paper, a mass of red marks from Golden's pen. "I know I can't write, but I'm not going to learn how to from this," she complained.

"You should make an appointment with Golden to go over it," I suggested.

"Sure, I plan to. But a half hour of looking at a bunch of little mistakes won't turn me into Tom Wolfe!"

Sandra's complaint was a common one. Like FRMA, MC directed one curriculum at people with a wide range of abilities, and pleased almost no one in the process. For people who knew how to write and give speeches well, the course was little more than an affirmation of their capabilities. For those who didn't, it provided far too little instruction to overcome their deficiencies.

The biggest day for interim grading came at the end of the week, when we received both our class-participation feedback and our midterm grades in TOM. Jerry got an 88 on the test, which was among the highest grades in the class. He later told me that this mark silenced a few lingering doubts he harbored (but never voiced) about the relevance of his military background to business school. I didn't hear how anybody else in the section did on the test. There was an unspoken taboo on widely broadcasting one's results, be they good or bad.

The excitement surrounding our interim grades was muted somewhat by the opening hubbub of recruiting season. The first weeks of this period were dominated by the company presentations whose announcements now cluttered *The Harbus*. Monday was the first day of on-campus presentations, and I made it to two of the ten that were scheduled. I began with Salomon Brothers. I went because I had enjoyed their dinner, and hoped to see some of the people I met at it. Minouli, the associate who sat at my table, was on hand. So was Jack, the guy who had once worked with my company in Warsaw.

I sat in the audience next to Carter, who had managed to forget about his agony over classes long enough to begin pursuing his dream of a summer job on Wall Street. We were astounded to see that a couple of students had donned suits after class just for this informal meeting. "Now there's a hardcore nerd," Carter noted, pointing at one of the overly dressed attendees. "If I ever come back to recruit here after graduation, I'm gonna shoot down anyone obnoxious enough to come to a presentation looking like that."

Salomon's lead speaker was a senior-level banker who gave a masterful survey of the state of the capital markets and the forces affecting the investment banking industry. "The guy's sharp," I said when he was done. Carter just nodded in mute awe; he was thoroughly blown away. As the room started to empty, we headed up to its Sky Deck, where Carter had spied Jerry. "I didn't know you were interested in banking," I observed when we caught up to him.

Jerry shook his head. "I'm just here out of curiosity. At least for the summer, it's gonna be management consulting for me."

"That's emphatic," I said. This was an unusual degree of focus so early in the year.

Jerry explained that he thought working in consulting was the best way he could avoid narrowing his postgraduation options to a single industry. "Let's say I decide to work in brand management this summer," he said, by way of example. "And let's say I don't like it. What happens next fall when recruiting starts? Everyone'll look at me and say, 'Hey, here we've got a military guy who's done nothing but marketing.' And guess what, now nobody but P&G will talk to me! But consulting's different. It's broad enough that it won't shut many doors next year. And while I'm at it, I can pick up some general business credentials that the army didn't give me."

In addition to the countless on-campus presentations, several firms were also hosting recruiting events in nearby hotels and restaurants. Later that week, Rick and I went to one of these. It was hosted by the Sales and Trading group at Morgan Stanley, and was held at a hotel in Cambridge. The atmosphere at off-campus receptions was quite formal, and business attire was mandatory rather than laughable. As we left the hotel, Rick and I discussed the presentation, which we both had found eye-opening.

"Before I got here," Rick told me, "I didn't have much firsthand exposure to banking, consulting, marketing, or a lot of these other fields. The only recruiters I spoke to or even *heard* about at my college were engineering firms. We had our own little hierarchy of prestigious companies to work for, but it was focused more on firms like United Technologies, GE, and McDonnell Douglas. I hardly knew a thing about Morgan Stanley until four months ago."

Rick's early conviction that he would return to United Technologies after graduation was by now waning. He definitely planned to experiment with something new over the summer, and was increasingly open to the notion that whatever he did might draw him back after graduation. He hadn't yet narrowed his summer interests, but he had some ideas. "To begin with, Wall Street and consulting are logical things to consider at least. They sure have a big draw around here, and it's with good reason. I might also look at some of the marketing firms. Some of my friends from college ended up in the marketing arms of their companies, and they all seem to like it."

When we got back to campus, we headed over to a wine-tasting party that one of our section's budding enologists was hosting. Because it actually attracted members with "partners," this turned out to be one of the most successful section events of the semester. The husbands, wives, girlfriends, and boy-friends of several section members were on hand, and a few unpartnered people had gone so far as to bring dates. This was surprising, as dating was not yet a widespread practice with the first-year class. Single people who were in long-standing relationships when they came to school had generally main-tained them, while those who arrived without attachments had done little to acquire them. Frantic schedules inhibited new relationships with people outside of the business school, and most people were still cautious about dating internally.

Despite this, a few people had managed to work a little romance into their lives. Certain guys had already taken to flourishing their HBS credentials at local nightspots. Carter had an adventure along those lines a few days before, when he was finally giving himself a night off in the wake of our midterms. He related the details to Sandra, Jerry, and me over a glass of Section I's finest. He was out with a few guys from the section at The Boathouse. Located right across the river from the business school, this bar was a time-honored haunt of HBS students.

"The place was just crawling with Wellesley women," Carter recalled. "We talked to a group of them for about five minutes, then Larry dropped the H-bomb and it was all over."

"Dropping the H-bomb" was a euphemism for telling a young woman, particularly one from Wellesley, that you were studying at Harvard's MBA program.

"Now I've got enough phone numbers to last me a month," Carter concluded proudly.

Sandra smiled and shook her head gently. "Boys will be boys," she chided. Carter winked at her and trundled off in pursuit of another wine bottle. "See?" she said to Jerry and me teasingly, "I can be perfectly tolerant. And to think someone called me a femi-nazi because I got angry over that ECN-19 hoopla."

"You mean this Wellesley connection really doesn't bother you?" I asked. Carter's escapade was not an isolated incident; by now several short-lived liaisons were said to have flared be-tween our classmates and students several years their junior from the famous women's college.

"No, how could it? I dated older men when I was at Yale, so why should I have any problems with seeing the flip side of that a few years later?" She gazed at the ceiling with mock wistfulness. "I just wish things came so easily for the women around here."

"You mean you want to date an undergraduate?" Jerry asked. This just couldn't be.

"No, of course not! But I wouldn't mind dating *somebody*." Sandra had broken up with a long-term boyfriend two months before coming to Harvard, and was now one of the section's bachelorettes. "It's a pretty stilted dating scene for women around here. I mean, if a guy meets someone at The Boathouse, at a party, or wherever else, the fact he's from HBS is a huge asset. But try that if you're a woman! Unless the guy you're talking to has gone to the business school or someplace similar himself, you can bet he'll find HBS women completely intimidating."

"That's funny," I said. "A lot of guys think the women are better off because the ratio on campus is so skewed in your favor."

"That might be true, but who's got the nerve to take advantage of it? People talk around here, they gossip as much as they did in high school. And I suppose that's natural, given that most of us live practically on top of each other. But if you're a woman in a situation like this, you have to be insanely cautious. We all knew women who had promiscuous reputations in college, and we all saw how people talked about them. That's bad enough when you're in your late teens, but it's a whole different story when you're starting to build your professional network. If a woman goes out with somebody at HBS, she better be damn sure it's going to turn into something steady. Because if she has a few relationships that just turn out to be flings, 800 of her future peers in the business world might start viewing her as some kind of whore."

"Ouch."

"Yeah, I'll say. So women have to be cautious around here. And even if we aren't," she added, sending a gaze of mock yearning in Carter's direction, "it's hard to compete with all those youngsters from Wellesley."

Jerry turned to me. "And how about you," he asked. "Sandra makes it sound like a land of opportunity out there for HBS men. So how long 'til you turn up here with some young momma-cat from the outside?"

"Momma-cat?" Sandra interjected, a look of mock outrage on her face.

"Western slang," Jerry explained. He returned his gaze to me. "Well?"

"Hell, I don't know, ask me after midterms," I offered. Things had been so frantic that the thought of dating had hardly crossed my mind since September. But the outside world suddenly seemed rich with possibilities. H-bombs. Momma-cats. My, yes.

Throughout the week after the wine-tasting soiree, the atmosphere in class seemed somewhat more relaxed than usual (perhaps the consequences of a postenological haze?). One day in FRMA, some people were feeling positively disruptive. Early in the session, Toddson directed a question at Fernando, one of the section's Latin Americans. By now Fernando had distinguished himself as quite a singer. He performed at a Shad talent night a couple of weeks before, and had more recently serenaded a number of Section I women at one of our parties. As Toddson approached Fernando's seat to hear his answer, somebody in the Sky Deck muttered "Sing!"

This caught Toddson off guard. "What?" she asked, trying to figure out who had spoken.

"Not you," came a voice from the other side of the room, "Fernando!"

"Sing! Sing!" someone else hollered. Soon the entire section joined in. "Sing! Sing! Sing!" People started thumping their desktops in unison as they chanted; it sounded like a Turkish prison riot.

Toddson, always the good sport, sat down beside Fernando. "You heard 'em, 'Nando. Sing!" she commanded. Fernando rose to the occasion, and wowed the section with a lilting Latin lullaby. His performance was rewarded with a thunderous applause. After that, everyone was in a punchy, upbeat mood, and the rest of FRMA went painlessly.

At lunch I ran into a friend of mine whose section sat in the room immediately above ours. "What the hell was going on today?" he demanded. "It sounded like a rugby match down there!" He was hardly one to talk. His own sectionmates had long since taken to pounding their fists on their desks at the slightest provocation. This would always cause a dull rumbling down in our room, giving the frequent impression that we were meeting under a subway station. "Oh, it was nothing," I told him. "Just FRMA."

It was Thursday, so a few of us sat down with Carter to plan out the next afternoon's awards session. Fernando, our most obvious candidate, would receive the If She Understood the Words, You'd Be Getting a Three award. Another guy was slated for the Wisconsin Must Be Filled with Gymnasts award. This was for saying that the managers of Milwaukee's Harley-Davidson Company were "all walking around with their heads up their butts" when they lost the small-bike market to the Japanese. A woman who secretively did her knitting during class was slated for the We're All Lucky Your Hobby Isn't Bowling award.

After lunch I worked out, then joined Sandra at a long-hyped presentation. Early in the week, Kraft had slipped boxes of their famous macaroni and cheese into everyone's pigeon-hole to publicize their recruiting efforts. This was smart, as the recruiting season's first week was not the easiest time for a marketing firm to make its pitch. At that point, many first-years were still a bit starstruck over the investment banks and (particularly) the consulting firms they had been hearing about all year. This probably reduced the campus's receptiveness to the charms of other industries.

About eighty people turned up for the Kraft presentation; not a bad showing. The free loot for attendees was off the scale. Outside they had little packages of crackers and neon-orange cheese. Inside it was even better. On every seat was a handsome Kraft-General Foods canvas bag with a matching T-shirt. The bags were stuffed with salad dressing, marshmallows, parmesan cheese, barbecue sauce, Fudgies, and still more macaroni and cheese. It was a good take, but partly useless for us dormies; without access to a grill, the most we could do with the barbecue sauce was eat it with a spoon.

The presentation began. The team from Chicago knew how to play to a consultant-happy crowd, and used all the right buzzwords. Kraft, they told us, was a "Meritocracy." It was "Entrepreneurial." "Dynamic." All went well until they started the video, which featured clips of people describing their summer-employment experiences with the firm. The first person to speak was a well-dressed and distinguished-looking young man. "The most *important* project I worked on," he said without a trace of irony, "was a Handi-Pak Fun Kit for marshmallows" (or some name close to that effect). The audience, filled with students who had been seduced by other companies' tales of high finance, corporate restructuring, and saving Russia, erupted with laughter. SO MUCH FOR THE SEXINESS OF PACKAGED PRODUCT MARKETING, Sandra wrote on the back of my hand.

Afterward she told me that while she felt the presentation had smacked of big-company bureaucracy, it hadn't diminished her interest in getting a marketing job for the summer. "I already knew I wanted to work for a small, entrepreneurial company instead of a big consumer products firm anyway," she explained. Because such companies didn't recruit in droves on campus, she knew she'd have to "work the network" extensively in her job search. She was now a frequent visitor to the Cole Room, where she could access information on the over 27,000 alumni who were willing to provide career counseling to any HBS student who called.

I asked her how the process worked. "It's governed by this weird sort of etiquette," she reported. "You're not allowed to ask the alums you contact about getting jobs with their companies, but if they broach the subject it's okay to talk about it. Otherwise you have to couch your questions in terms of where you might find work in the industry, or how different companies are positioned."

Sandra was happy to discover that most alums were helpful and approachable. "By the time I get off the phone with someone, they've usually given me the names of a half dozen other people to contact. But of course, this makes the process a big time commitment. I spend entire afternoons by my telephone, either calling people or waiting for them to call me back. This takes a lot more energy than mailing off a few résumés to companies that actively recruit here.

"Another problem is that I sometimes get dizzy over how much is out there. Narrowing the field down to who you want to work for is confusing enough when you start with the few hundred companies that interview on campus. But when you go through the alumni network, your starting point is the whole world!"

The weekend brought a dizzying recruiting event to the rest of us in the Management Consulting Club's annual Career Fair, which was held in a nearby hotel. I arrived about an hour before it was scheduled to end, after the crowds had thinned. I drifted about, talking to representatives from the firms that interested me. I was curious about Deloitte and Touche. As the consulting arm of a Big Six accounting firm, they were snootily viewed by some as a second-tier operation. But I had run into some of their people in Eastern Europe, and had been very impressed with the quality of their work. I picked up some literature, signed my name to their guest list, and moved on.

The McKinsey table still had a substantial crowd in its orbit. The people manning it were frazzled by now, but kept up a brave front. They had been swamped all day, as McKinsey, in a lot of people's minds, was simply the hottest thing going. Coming from Bain, I couldn't help but be impressed with the company's sheer size. After McKinsey, Bain was about tied with BCG as the second largest strategy-only consulting firm. But McKinsey had to be four or five times the size of either of its rivals. Whereas Bain had three U.S. offices, McKinsey had fourteen, covering even such smaller markets as San José, Minneapolis, and Cleveland. When I was working there, much of Bain's internal rhetoric had been McKinsey-obsessed hype, portraying the rivalry as a Coke-Pepsi thing. In reality it was probably closer to a Coke-RC thing. On instinct I grabbed a pamphlet, signed my name, and moved on.

In the hotel's lobby I ran into Hans, who was lugging an armful of information booklets from the fair. "Howdy, Hans," I greeted him. "Gonna be a consultant this summer?"

"Oh no, I don't think so," he responded cheerfully. "I am here mainly to see what it is that people have been talking about all year." Management consulting had been a popular topic since September.

"So what are you planning to do?"

"Well, this is a rather difficult question," Hans replied. "When I came here, I thought I might take the summer off and bicycle around America. But now I realize this is not the HBS way." I suppressed a grin. Hans was right, of course. "Then I thought it would be nice to work for one of the large European industrial companies, so I wrote letters to many of them. I am particularly interested in Airbus, and the company which is making the Volkswagen cars."

"And how's that going?"

"Regrettably, not well. Most of these companies are unfamiliar with the needs of MBA students, and don't have suitable summer programs in place. Still, I am trying."

In addition to the consulting fair, the weekend was punctuated with the start of our second big group project at HBS. The section had again been split into random teams, this time for an MC assignment. Each team was given the business plan of a real start-up company, from which they were to craft a persuasive sales pitch for potential equity investors. About half the teams had presented during the previous week, right after the Marketing final. This was a nightmare for them, as it only allowed a few days' preparation after the test. But our group had it even worse, as our presentation was scheduled to end seventeen hours before the start of the final examination in OB. It would have been nice to have a bit more time to prepare for this, our first final exam at HBS.

MC speeches had the power to make most of us profoundly nervous. This was silly, as we spoke in front of one another (without the benefit of extended preparation) every day. Despite this, my group, like most, was a little anxious. I ended up with the role of CEO of our "company," which meant I would speak twice during our twenty-five minute presentation. We were to represent a company called Master Software, a developer of utilities for computer operating systems. We spent much of both Saturday and Sunday practicing.

Our rehearsals continued into the following week. Between this unusual burst of MC-related work and the recruiting presentations, I was finding less and less time for cases. Luckily, I was now virtually immune to cold calls in Marketing, which made it easier to get through (it was exceedingly rare for a professor to cold call a student more than once). I still read the Marketing cases and ran some numbers, but generally spent less time on them than I used to. Sometimes I truncated my preparation for other classes as well. But this was a dangerous toss of the dice.

More and more people were indulging in this sort of cold-call brinkmanship, something which was sure to result in a fiery wipeout. This finally happened one morning in Marketing. At the start of class, Cotton went through his normal death march, and stopped in front of Carter.

Unfortunately, Carter chose not to exercise his option to pass on Cotton's cold call in private, and agreed to open a case he couldn't possibly have read. Cotton called the class to order, and moments later Carter began his opening with a quick obser-

vation about the case. Cotton went over to the board and dutifully wrote down Carter's point, then expectantly returned his
gaze to him. By then, Carter was flipping silently through some
exhibits. This continued for ten seconds. Twenty seconds.
Thirty. I began to shift nervously in my seat. *Say something,
dammit!* I wanted to scream.

Carter continued to flip unhappily through his case. Everybody turned their gaze to the board, to their notes, to their feet.
It wasn't long before Cotton put a stop to it. "Would you like
to wrap it up there, Carter?" he asked gently. Carter nodded
and the hands shot up.

That night I related this story to my study group. Nobody
had seen so bad a wipeout in their sections, although Spencer
mentioned that somebody had once passed when cold called in
TOM. Our meeting soon degenerated, as it often did, into a
rambling bull session about almost everything but the evening's
cases. I mentioned Kraft's Marshmallow Handi-Pak Fun Kits,
which got a good laugh. While we all agreed that jobs in consumer product marketing had their appeal, we also feared they
might entail predictable, regimented, and corporate lifestyles.
On top of this they brought the risk of spending one's working
week dealing with trivialities like Handi-Pak Fun Kits. Alistair
mentioned a guy he once met who spent a summer working on
Miss Piggy Cakes. This somehow lacked the glamour one ideally
hoped for in a summer job.

While we all had clear notions of what we did not want to
do that summer, we were low on ideas of what we did want.
Alistair and Spencer wanted to do "something in high tech."
This sounded interesting to me, as did venture capital, international development, investment banking, and perhaps the film
industry. Gary was a bit more focused; he definitely wanted to
spend a summer on the corporate finance side of a big Wall
Street firm, but was still looking at consulting, and wouldn't rule
out venture capital. George was the most focused; he wanted a
manufacturing-related job in his native Georgia.

There was a good deal of discussion that night about the
Gold List, an 84-page directory which listed all the firms that
would hold formal, on-campus recruiting for summer jobs. Well
over 100 companies were already scheduled to come through,
and many more were sure to sign up once their summer needs
became clear. We agreed that this was pretty amazing when you

thought about it. There perhaps wasn't another school in the world that could pull in so many recruiters looking for summer hires.

Eventually the conversation turned to MC presentations. Gary had a particularly funny story on this subject. A group in his section was assigned to pitch a textile firm's business plan, and scripted an ambitiously elaborate presentation. Unknown to their professor, they recruited a number of outside students to model their company's clothes. They also managed to procure a spotlight and a smoke machine. Their idea was to cut the lights in the middle of the presentation and march the models in under a billow of smoke.

At the front of their classroom was a set of doors opening onto a small foyer, where another set of doors led to the outside. This foyer was rather like the narrow, darkened anteroom that separates a movie theater from its lobby. It was in this little room that the MC group set up their fancy props. They figured the confined space would fill up quickly with smoke, which would then tumble neatly into the classroom when the doors opened. As the first presenter began to speak, the smoke machine went to work.

A few minutes into the second speaker's patter, someone from the audience noticed that smoke was pouring into the classroom. Panic spread. The terrified professor ran from the room, fire alarms went off, and the audience, presenters, and models erupted in uncontrollable hysterics. Once order was finally restored, the professor saw very little humor in the incident. Everyone in my MC group took heart when I related this story to them the next morning. Even if our afternoon presentation wasn't a home run, it couldn't possibly go that badly.

I had planned to go home to practice my CEO rap as soon as TOM ended. But as class was concluding, we were all urged to stick around for a few minutes, as some people from Old Section I wanted to pass a "genuine Section I relic" on to us. Moments later, a second-year student came in and gave us a little HBS history lesson.

It was 1962, he told us. JFK was president, the economy was robust, and the business school was primed to expand. In September the program grew from seven sections to nine, rolling back the alphabetic frontier from Section G to Section I.

Among the men of my section's maiden class was James Dixon Robinson III, who later became CEO of American Express. Robinson was thrilled to be part of HBS history, and was eager to make a lasting mark on this brand-new section. But his excitement soon turned to dismay. Class discussion, which he expected to be thrilling and stimulating, was turning out to be boring and pedantic.

Fortunately, four of his sectionmates were old friends from his prep school days at Exeter. Jim summoned them all to a weekend emergency session at his wooded New Hampshire retreat. They didn't speak to God out there, but they must have had a chat with Moses, because when they returned to Harvard on Monday morning they were armed with "The Ten Commandments of Section I."

"Be Punctual!" their commandments thundered. "Be Insightful and Articulate When Speaking!"

Also in that class was Richard Hampton Jenrette, future cofounder of the aggressive investment bank Donaldson, Lufkin, and Jenrette, and future CEO of the Equitable. Jenrette was less than impressed with the Robinson gang's revelations. "What a bunch of dorks!" he muttered darkly. It wasn't long before he and his cronies wandered into the forest as well. The Moses they found was a kinder, gentler sort. "When in Town, Come to Class," his commandments suggested softly. "Class Takes Up an Eighth of the Day, so Give It an Eighth of Your Attention."

A grim rivalry quickly developed as the two camps proselytized their conflicting commandments to the section. Robinson didn't like Jenrette's flip attitude, and didn't appreciate his purloining of the commandments concept. Jenrette's list of complaints about Robinson was considerably longer. He hated that Exeter snootiness. Those damnable tweed smoking jackets. That aristocratic drawl. But most of all, he hated the clubs. Because Robinson, a big golfer, was always hustling to or from the links, and often brought his golf clubs to class. Early in the year he developed the imperious habit of occasionally passing clubs to members of the section after they spoke. Expansive comments which drove class discussion forward were rewarded with the hard-driving three wood. Mediocre insights which barely justified the speaker's lung power were awarded with the nine iron. These lesser "nine iron comments" were soon known to the section as "chip shots," the golfing term for a short, easy whack to the ball.

It was not surprising that Robinson often awarded Jenrette and his disciples with the demeaning nine iron. It was even less surprising when that very club vanished from Robinson's bag toward the end of the year. Robinson was livid. He stopped bringing his clubs to class, but by then the use of golfing terms to describe class comments had spread to all the first-year sections. The staying power of the Robinsonian jargon was evidenced by the fact that thirty years later, students still used the term *chip shot* to describe an unadventurous remark in class.

Now this was a thrill, I thought. Like most people, I had been using this term all year. Little had I known that it first came into usage in *my* section!

The saga continued. Legend had it that Robinson never found his heisted club. A few months after he glumly bought its replacement, it was September again, and an eager group of new students assembled in Aldrich Hall. They were the new Section I. A few weeks into their first semester, an extremely relaxed-looking second-year student strolled in to make an announcement. It was Dick Jenrette. He told the story of the nine iron, then solemnly passed the abducted club on to a new student who was appropriately named Chip.

The following year, Chip passed it on to Skip, who passed it on to Kip, and then on and on it went. And today, this particularly relaxed-looking second-year, also named Chip, was here to carry on the tradition. With a great flourish he produced the nine iron, which he gave to us to pass on to our sectionmate Trip (who unfortunately blew his allocated fifteen minutes of fame by being out of the room for that momentous hand-off). For the first (and certainly last) time in my life, I caught myself wishing my parents had named *me* Trip. When Chip left, our section was brimming with excitement. A genuine Section I relic! And what a story!

The saga of Robinson's nine-iron put me in an exuberant mood for our MC presentation. Everybody on the team ended up doing fine; it was neither a home run on the scale of my previous team's Marketing midterm nor a disaster like the smoke-machine debacle. The one unpleasant surprise came during the question-and-answer session. A group of students who had presented during the previous week were assigned to play the part of "investors" and ask us questions. We had done the same a week before after another group's presentation. In that role we had been careful to raise only innocuous, non-threatening issues that were easily answered making the presenters look good.

Two people in our "investor group," however, had nothing like this in mind. Every question they directed at us was tricky, hostile, and loaded with phrases like "how can you expect us to believe . . ." When the episode was over, our group was fuming. Who did those two think they were? We joked about "sharkish" in-class comments all the time, but it was rare to see such aggressive behavior. Perhaps this pair thought that by tearing us down, they'd enhance their own group's chance of getting a good grade (like everything, MC was scored on a forced curve). Whatever the motives behind it, theirs was an unwise approach. Because whereas MC would end in a few weeks, the five of us would be their sectionmates for the rest of the year, and we would all need to get along.

There was no time to kick back and celebrate the end of our little public trial, as the OB final was scheduled for the next morning. The silly printer situation had not changed; HBS still had neither a mechanism nor a policy for printing exams after tests. Partly in response to this, the OB department scheduled an extra hour of exam time and made their test a take-home affair. As with the TOM exam, we could print it in our rooms.

I decided to treat myself to a short stroll around campus before heading back to McCulloch and my exam preparations. As I was passing by Morgan Hall I spotted Carter, who was just exiting the building. "Meeting with somebody about my laryngitis," he explained when I caught his eye. One of our professors, he preferred not to say who, had called him in. The professor asked Carter to try to speak up more in class, gently warning him that his grade might be negatively impacted otherwise. They spent the remainder of the appointment constructively discussing how he might achieve this.

"It was a good meeting," Carter concluded. "It's nice to find substance behind the rhetoric about professors caring about us on an individual level."

"Hey, do you want to get together for dinner or something tonight?" I suggested. It seemed that Carter could perhaps use some upbeat company on the night before this first big final.

"Thanks, but I've already made plans to eat with a friend of mine at Siam Garden," he said. "Something about Thai food relaxes me."

"Hey, whatever works."

We wished each other luck on the exam and headed home to get ready for it.

I spent a good deal of time studying that night. As I flipped through my OB binder, it made me smile to see how my preparation habits had changed over the semester. My first OB cases were accompanied by pages of detailed notes, outlines of openings, and answers to the study questions. By the third week, this had dropped off to a few scrawled lines. Midway through October, it was rare for me to take any notes at all. OB had been very relaxed; Rosenthal stopped cold calling early in the year, and discussions were so qualitative and capricious that preparing extensive comments never made sense.

The exam was an odd one. We weren't even given a case, but rather a 10-page, four-month-old article from *Fortune* magazine about IBM's need for a new chief executive officer. On the last page was a clue as to why it might have been chosen as our exam; the writer quoted John Kotter, HBS professor and architect of the OB curriculum, at length. Gee, what a coincidence I thought cynically when I saw this.

Attached to the article were five questions in ten parts. They were all rather fuzzy and qualitative in nature. *Of all the people we have studied in the course, who comes closest to the person you think IBM needs as the next CEO? Why?* read one. *What general advice would you give the new CEO?* read another. Having learned my lesson from the TOM midterm, I immediately went into overdrive and didn't slow down until I finished the thing.

That evening, as Cambridge braced itself for the next day's home football game against Yale, Section I had a German-Korean party hosted by two students from those countries. Not surprisingly, the exam was a hot topic of discussion. A good deal of cynicism stemmed from the fact that we were given an article that quoted Kotter so prominently. "It's like they're trying to prove they have some kind of legitimacy after all," groused Jerry, who had derided the course since the beginning of the year.

Hans had a more serious criticism of the exam. "It seems unfair to foreign students that they gave us a magazine article

to read, particularly after three months of giving only cases,"
he said. "The language used in American magazine articles is
very informal, so parts of it were difficult to understand. I spent
perhaps two and a half hours just reading it, leaving little time
to formulate my responses."

Another big topic that night was the section's new golf
club. Somebody had done some checking, and discovered that
Jenrette was from the class of '57, and Robinson was from the
class of '61. Not only were they not contemporaries at HBS, but
there was no evidence that either man had been in Section I.
Telling elaborate tall tales to younger students, it seemed, was
as hallowed a school tradition as lofting chip shots in Marketing
class.

"I sure feel like a sucker," Sandra said upon learning of
this, shaking her head in admiration of our deceptive second-
year cohorts.

"Look on the bright side; we'll be able to do the same to
the first-years next year," I pointed out. "Care for some of
Korea's finest?" I gestured at a platter of Korean chicken and
rice.

Sandra shook her head smiling. "I'm sticking to the German fare tonight. I'm all Asia'd out—had Thai food last night
at Siam Garden."

Siam Garden? This sounded awfully familiar.

"Oh yeah? Go with anybody I know?"

"Yeah, well. Just a friend," she answered evasively.

Hmmmm. "How was it?"

"Pretty good. We're gonna get together again on the Monday after Thanksgiving." There were no classes scheduled for
that day. A number of people planned to come back on Sunday
night and spend the extra vacation time collecting their wits
and getting mentally prepared for the rest of our finals, which
would start about a week and a half later. "I'll tell you how it
goes."

The next morning, my estimation of Harvard's avarice hit
a new low. The whole thing started around ten, when I drove
out of the parking lot to meet some people for brunch. I headed
back a little after eleven. The Harvard-Yale football game was
about to kick off right across the street, which made for a good
deal of traffic around the business school. When I finally made
my way to the lot's gate, I encountered a parking attendant who

imperiously waved me away. I pointed at my parking permit, but he just scowled. "Lot's full," he sniffed, then continued his waving.

Now this was impossible. Even on school days, when every professor, off-campus student, and administrator was around, there were plenty of spots to be found. I eventually talked my way past the attendant and got to the guard booth, where I got a fuller story. "There's a football game today," said a petulant man as if talking to an imbecile. "How the hell do you expect to find parking an hour before the game?"

"I expect to find parking because I paid $550 to park here," I answered. This went back and forth for about ten minutes. It turned out that Harvard wasn't content just to charge its students unconscionable rates to park their cars in a thief-infested lot. When the opportunity arose to rent those spots again, the school zealously seized the day. The lot was now full of road-tripping Yalies, who were happy to pay top dollar for the spot of anybody foolish enough to pop off to run an errand on game day. Any unlucky student returning to the lot was left to search for nonexistent parking in a city swamped by visitors for its biggest athletic event of the year.

Through dogged and at times obnoxious persistence, I ultimately prevailed upon the attendants to relocate a barbecue grill so that I could park. Not long after I got to the game it started to rain, so I took off with some fellow Stanford alums for a Boston bar which was featuring the Stanford-Berkeley game on its many television sets. By kickoff time, the place was packed with alumni of both schools. I ran into a number of people I hadn't known were in Boston, and had the dual satisfaction of seeing both Stanford and Harvard trounce their perennial rivals that day. The glow this brought went far to eclipse the morning's frustration at the parking gate. Still, it was hard to completely banish the incident from my mind. This, the computer printer debacle, the endless little rules, all of it made the second-to-last ranking our administration got in the *BusinessWeek* poll seem generous.

On Monday we got our Marketing exams back. Our report received a terrific mark, which made us all very happy. After class I caught up with Carter as he was heading over to check his mail. He was looking rather downcast. "0 for 2 on the midterm front," he greeted me.

"Uh-oh."

"Somehow our group just never clicked, and I guess it showed. We ended up with a pathetic grade. And that's bad news for me, because I also tanked on the TOM midterm." He shook his head sadly. "I don't blame myself for the marketing midterm. Our group just didn't work out, and it's nobody's fault. But as for TOM, well, I just can't keep up the pace in an exam after four or five hours. If I don't start opening my mouth more in class I'll really be hosed."

"Any big Thanksgiving plans?" I asked, hoping to change the subject to a less depressing topic.

"Just going home to see the folks," he said. "Except," he brightened somewhat, "I actually have a date lined up for Monday."

"The Monday after Thanksgiving?" I asked. Carter nodded. First Siam Garden, now this, I thought. This can't be a coincidence.

"By the way, do you have any bright ideas of where I could take her?" Carter asked. "I've been so buried in the books, I hardly know what there is to do around here. We're planning to spend the whole afternoon together."

If ever there was a friend in need of a boost, this is he, I realized. I thought back to something Sandra told me on Head of the Charles day. "I know it's a bit cold this time of year," I said, "but kiting on Cape Cod is always a quality date. And a bottle of Cabernet would make it really classy."

"I think I might try that," Carter said, his academic woes briefly forgotten.

My own Thanksgiving plans were a bit less dramatic. I went back to Connecticut to spend the break with my family and old friends. I tried hard to forget about my academic life while at home, which was easy as there was plenty to do. At the top of my agenda was to peruse the Gold List and decide where I wanted to interview. I also had to think about extending my job search to companies that weren't on the list. This would be time-consuming, but was my most realistic shot at finding high tech or venture capital work, two fields which had started to appeal to me.

It only took a couple of hours to scan the Gold List and make a preliminary selection of the companies that interested me. I decided to postpone the chore of writing cover letters until Christmas, as I felt I'd be better able to do a careful job over the longer vacation. The rest of the break was a welcome period of relaxing and catching up with people. For years I had been living far enough away that going home on Thanksgiving was out of the question. The new state of affairs was easy to get used to.

10

THE BIG PUSH

THE WEEK AFTER Thanksgiving passed quickly, and was tinged with anticipation surrounding the coming weekend. Friday night would bring the long-trumpeted Holidazzle, HBS's black-tie Christmas formal. No cheesy affair, it was guaranteed to blow the European Club's autumn ball clean out of the water. The event was to be held in a downtown Boston hotel. It would kick off with a large cocktail party for all attendees, followed by dinners for each section in separate dining rooms. After dinner, the sections would put on talent shows for their own entertainment, then reconvene downstairs for the dance itself.

Holidazzle morning dawned clear and cold. Our classes zipped by, and soon it was time to don our formal wear and head over to Boston. I arrived at the hotel early, as Spencer had rented a suite where a group of us could hang out before and after the main event. It was all adding up to a big night.

Our section dinner was well attended, with many showing up with partners or dates. Every table was amply provisioned by a small army of waiters, and by nine o'clock the air was heavy with wine and song. I noticed that Carter and Sandra found seats next to one another, a likely sign that the Monday after-noon they had shared went well.

Sandra cornered me right before dessert and confirmed

176

my suppositions. "Thanks for making the kite suggestion to Carter. It was a great day."

"Is he as handy with the things as you are?"

Sandra laughed. "Hardly. At one point he managed to get the string tangled up in his coat. Don't ask me how, I've never seen anything like it. Anyway, this big wind came up and he almost got dragged out to sea!"

I laughed. With Carter, this was easy to picture. "So it's going well," I said. Sandra smiled and nodded. "Any plans to come out of the closet with it?"

"No, not yet. Anybody onto us?"

I shook my head. "Not that I know of. But if I start hearing rumors I'll warn you."

The section talent show began right after dessert. The skits went well enough, although certain performances were impaired by the copious amounts of wine consumed by their participants. Eventually we adjourned and headed for the elevators. The other sections were already downstairs, and the second-years (most of whom had dined outside of the hotel) were arriving in force.

The event enjoyed near-perfect attendance from our class, and pulled in a healthy majority of second-years. With all the husbands, wives, and dates, this made for a crowd of perhaps two thousand. If the European Club's ball had been reminiscent of a high school prom, the Holidazzle more closely approximated a fraternity formal. While insobriety was not universal that evening, it was by no means uncommon. Many of us were anxious to blow off some steam after the long semester, and came ready to act several years younger than our ages. Needless to say, not everyone was wowed by this state of affairs. Some people, particularly those with guests, were downright unimpressed.

While he enjoyed having a beer with his friends as much as anybody, Jerry was not pleased with the Holidazzle. "Melissa and I aren't prudes, but it didn't exactly amount to our ideal night out," he later told me. "It was the first time I'd talked her into coming to a full-fledged section event since orientation. And guess what, she thinks we're all a bunch of lushes!"

Hans also found the whole event rather unsettling. "All of that drinking, shouting, and cursing," he later told me, shaking his head in woe. "You can surely find that and more in Munich on a good night. But at a graduate-school outing from an elite university? Never."

Despite the long evening, I was showered and shaved by nine o'clock the next morning. John Sculley, CEO of Apple Computer, was scheduled to speak, and I wasn't about to miss it. There were plenty of empty seats in Burden Auditorium when I arrived. Still, there was a respectable turnout given that this was the single toughest morning of the year to draw a crowd at HBS. Sculley was one of a number of speakers, the rest of whom were professors at HBS or MIT's Sloan School of Management. The symposium's subject was "The Dawn of a $3.5-Trillion Communications Mega-Industry: Information Access, Processing and Distribution in a Digital World." For me, it proved to be an even bigger event than its grandiose title implied.

The speakers supported a common theme. The world was changing faster than ever, they argued. Advances in the silicon microcosm would soon unleash technologies that could transform society. Nobody made this argument more persuasively than Sculley himself. While he wasn't a flamboyant speaker, his style and his message were compelling. His central thesis was that digital technology was forcing several massive industries into convergence. By the turn of the century, the boundaries between the computer, telecommunications, entertainment, and consumer electronics industries would blur and perhaps even disappear. The resulting "digital information industry" could become the biggest economic sector in human history.

Even in my sleepy, post-Holidazzle state, Sculley's message resonated clearly. The mainstream press was rife with articles about bizarre combinations of companies forming multimedia consortiums. Now I realized that this could be just the field for me. The technologies Sculley discussed and their potential applications were truly fascinating. I was also interested in the industries they touched upon and sprang from. What could be more intriguing than the cross-pollination of Silicon Valley, Madison Avenue, and Hollywood?

As I headed home for a lengthy nap, my feelings about HBS hit a new high. Where else could you go to so remarkable a party, then crawl to a fifth-row seat to see a great speech by so prominent a CEO? Maybe at Stanford, I thought (and there you'd get a tan with the bargain), but nowhere else came to mind.

The next morning my volunteer consulting team met to discuss its project with the virtual reality company. By then, our project was wrapping up. We had provided the company with a good deal of analysis concerning its markets, competitors, and finances. We now hoped to polish this up and hand it off before Christmas break.

Amos, our team's leader, was by then readying to deepen his understanding of the nascent virtual reality industry through a field-study project with four other second-years. Field studies were very popular with last-semester HBS students, and typically centered on research of a company or industry. Many were the first steps to launching new companies. Amos's project potentially fell in this latter category. He and his colleagues had some exciting concepts for VR products, and planned to develop their ideas further while still in the relatively low-risk position of being HBS students.

After my exposure to Amos's entrepreneurial enthusiasm, it was hard to refocus on the relatively mundane world of corporate recruiting presentations. But Monday was a red letter day for these events, so I made the transition. McKinsey and Goldman Sachs, arguably the Mercedes and BMW of recruiting at HBS, made their big pitches that afternoon. McKinsey was so confident of a healthy turnout that it ran four simultaneous presentations in different rooms. This approach worked well in my view. There were about sixty people at the presentation Section I students were asked to attend, a small enough group to allow audience members to ask questions and interact with the speakers.

Goldman took a more standard approach, simply booking the biggest meeting room available. Their draw completely eclipsed that of any other investment bank. In contrast to the fancy videotapes and visual props of other recruiters, Goldman set a Spartan tone. The stage boasted only a simple podium, subtle floor lighting, and a massive banner sporting those magic names, *Goldman, Sachs*. Wall Street's late eighties heyday may have been over, but Goldman still had a singular aura.

Their exterior of polished aloofness was lightened somewhat by the fellow who introduced the keynote speaker. "What can I say about this man," he began. "How can I possibly describe him?" The precise descriptor may have eluded him, but he took several cracks at coming up with it. Before he let the guy speak, he characterized him as his father, priest, rabbi, coach, brother, icon, beacon, and friend. This may just have been some bonus-time obsequiousness, but it certainly raised our expectations. The man he introduced wasn't exactly the messiah, but did have a certain patrician air. He spoke at length about Life, the importance of the career decisions in front of us, and the core values of Goldman Sachs.

At about this time a number of companies, mainly banks and consulting firms, were hosting evenings similar to Salomon's get-acquainted dinner. Almost all were invitational affairs, and each firm had its own way of generating guest lists. Résumé books, sign-in lists from recruiting presentations and career fairs, and club membership rosters were all popular resources. A few firms conscripted former employees who were now on campus to feed them the names of talented people in their sections. Somehow, this practice struck me as improper. If it became widespread, it could well taint relationships between sectionmates (*Boy, Rob just made the stupidest comment, but I better not attack him because he used to work for Bain, and I'd sure like an interview with them . . .*)

Wednesday night was a dinner doubleheader for me. I had received invitations from both Lehman Brothers, an investment bank, and Deloitte and Touche, a consulting firm. I decided to join the Lehman people for cocktails, and then connect with Deloitte and Touche. Although Lehman invited only a small group that night, the atmosphere was less relaxed than it had been at October's Salomon dinner; with interviews only two months off, people were getting self-conscious.

Something I saw that evening showed me just how stilted the atmosphere could get at these things. Something had put a certain senior Lehmanite into an extremely contrary mood. Like most of his colleagues, he stood at the epicenter of a small knot of students. I walked up to this group as he was heatedly refuting something one of them had said. The conversation then turned to Eastern Europe. He bitterly disagreed with a Polish woman who said that Poland had less ethnic trouble than most of its neighbors (he was wrong). He then attacked someone for saying that Goldman Sachs's recent assignments in Russia were very high profile (they were). He argued vitriolically that Hungary's population was five million, not ten million as someone suggested (wrong again).

Finally, one guy whom he had abused particularly badly got a chance to reply. "Tomorrow," he started humbly, "the chairman of J. P. Morgan will be speaking at Harvard Business School. If you could be in the audience, what question would you ask him?" The grumpy Lehmanite warmed to his one-time whipping boy, and launched into a cutting pontification about Morgan's strategy and structure. The student, who in normal circumstances might have stormed off by now, stood on, obediently nodding at every word.

The Deloitte and Touche dinner was a more relaxed affair. It was also much larger; perhaps a hundred students were on hand. It started with the requisite cocktail party, followed by dinner in several small dining rooms. I ate with a cross section of students, consultants, and partners from the firm, and really liked the group. Deloitte and Touche may not have been the first choice of the most prestige-hungry students, but refreshingly, nobody from the firm seemed troubled by this. They had a large and stable business, were very good at what they did, and probably enjoyed more balanced lives than their counterparts at the fast-track strategy firms.

One senior consultant summed up their attitude nicely. "Look," he said, "we're not McKinsey, and people who want McKinsey wouldn't really fit in here. We don't just fly at 30,000 feet, doing top-level strategy overviews. If you like drawing circles and triangles on charts, this isn't the place for you. We do good operational work, and we can talk to the guys on the shop floor. We like to get into the trenches and add value straight to the bottom line." I liked this guy and his attitude, and decided to submit my résumé.

While I had received some modest attention from recruiters, other people were positively swamped with invitations. Hans was a particularly hot property at that time. "Virtually every consulting firm and investment bank has invited me for dinner," he said one day as we were leaving FRMA. "I couldn't possibly go to all of these things!"

"You must have quite a résumé," Sandra said encouragingly.

"I do, and I know precisely the line on it which is so impressive. It is the one which is listing my home country! Every European student on campus has received these attentions."

This indeed appeared to be the case, as most of the international students were as busy with recruiting receptions as Hans himself. The big consulting and banking firms typically had special events for Europeans to which Americans were not invited. Some firms were almost pathologically competitive when it came to staging these things. The Boston Consulting Group for example, reportedly flew *every one* of its European partners to Boston for their international recruiting dinner at HBS.

"Still, I'm sure they're all crazy about you," Sandra insisted. "Who interests you the most? The consulting firms? The banks?"

"Oh, none of them really," Hans replied, almost dismissively. "My plan has always been to get a job with a big European industrial concern. It was these sorts of companies that I dealt with as a banker, and I am most eager to see what one is like from the inside." This, I remembered, closely echoed what he told me at the management consulting career fair.

Academically, life was a bit less inspiring than this. The semester had by now simply lasted a couple of weeks too long. TOM and Marketing, which accounted for the bulk of each week's class time, were verging on monotony. Marketing had progressed through several modules by now, exploring all major aspects of "the marketing mix" and "the marketing process." But the similarities between the forty-odd cases we studied were starting to eclipse the variety of the subject matter. Case melted into case in a bland sameness; a dozen pages of text, a dozen numerical exhibits, some detailed analysis, and a few spread sheets to crunch. I enjoyed Cotton's capable teaching and his increasingly easy, humorous manner. But still, I'd had enough of Marketing for one year.

My feelings about TOM were similar, but clouded further by another frustration. It now seemed like an eternity since Stanley had last called on me. I initially responded to this by vigorously overpreparing my TOM cases. This, I reasoned, would give me more ideas to raise my hand about, thereby increasing my chances of actually getting called. But the airtime drought continued, and my frustration heightened.

The problem, I felt, was that Stanley now had a core group

of people he liked to hear from every day. This, of course, came partly at the expense of the rest of us. That he'd rather have somebody speak for the sixth time in three days than hear from me for the first time in weeks was upsetting. But though I sometimes felt unjustly condemned to silence, I didn't think there was anything deliberate or malicious about Stanley's calling patterns. By now he had his opinions about who was worth hearing from, and probably felt obliged to call on them in order to get the best discussion he could out of the section. Still, it hurt a bit that I wasn't one of the people he focused on.

Sandra and I discussed this one night as we were having a quick meal in Kresge. She said she sometimes felt the same frustration that I did in TOM. But, she argued, with ninety-one people in the room, every professor would inevitably leave at least a few students feeling neglected.

"Anyhow, as a woman, I feel like the section got a pretty decent draw of professors," she concluded.

"How's that?" I asked.

"Well, none of them seem to be biased. And that's important when so much of your grade is subjectively determined." She went on to cite an anecdote she heard from a friend in another section. One of her friend's professors had only cold called two women throughout the entire semester. Since his course included roughly forty classes, this could not have been a statistical fluke. Worse, the cases he had women open were two of the least quantitative ones in the curriculum. "It's as if he thinks women are incapable of running numbers," Sandra concluded. "If any of our professors were like that, it would infuriate me."

Even as certain classes were becoming frustrating, I found an unexpected savior in the form of Cindy Toddson and FRMA. The knowledge gap between students in the class had by now narrowed. This didn't alter my views on the curriculum; the change had come at the expense of the students who were more wise to accounting spending several weeks treading water. But we were now on a more level playing field, and the quality of discussion had improved markedly.

And even on those days when class did move slowly, FRMA was usually pretty fun to attend. Toddson's energetic demeanor livened up even the drabbest cases, and her sessions were always relaxed and humorous. And when things got *really* boring, you could always harass her about what she wrote on the board. Because although she was a dynamo—a Ph.D. in Business Administration, a professorship at HBS, a quick wit, keen intellect, and a riveting presence—*the woman couldn't spell*: Obsolesense. Absorbtion. Busines. Allocasion. Inditement. Ussage. We called her on all of them. If she had lacked human flaws, she would have been terrifying; this tiny oasis of incompetence endeared her to the section.

But charming as most of us felt she was, there were those who occasionally found Toddson unnerving. Among them was Hans. He once had a particularly memorable run-in with her over his old nemesis, abbreviations. As a former banker, he was usually quite at ease in FRMA. But on this day he was baffled. The topic was debt, and the acronym of the day was FV, for Face Value. Unfortunately, Hans had already forced himself to learn, in a previous FRMA class, that FV stood for *Future* Value. Worse, Cindy's V wasn't easy to decipher. Mightn't that be a U? Baffled, Hans nervously raised his hand. Cindy acknowledged him.

"I'm sorry Cindy, but what is this on the board?"

Cindy, who was irritated with the section for its rather lackluster performance that day, was brusque. "It's a big board, Hans. What're you talking about? Help me out here." The room twittered softly with laughter.

Hans adjusted and readjusted his owlish glasses and struggled to keep his composure. "F-U," he said, pointing at the center of the board. "F-U!" The section erupted into guffaws, Cindy made a characteristically sardonic remark, and Hans looked like he wanted to hop the next flight to Vienna. But despite his discomfort, he figured out that it was a V on the board, divined that F-U was some sort of colloquial insult, and pressed on. "Okay, so it's a *wee*. Just what is this eff-wee? I thought that eff-wee meant future walue. Now it means face walue!"

This was the first time I heard Hans make that distinctively Germanic switch of a w for a v. Clearly the man was on edge. He was mute in FRMA for several days after that.

It was a pity Hans got so rattled, because it was time to collect our nerves for the last big push. OB was already finished, and FRMA would stretch into January, which left three classes that would wrap up soon. Monday was the deadline for our final papers in MC, Thursday would be our Marketing final, and Friday would bring the TOM exam and the start of vacation. Our study group meanwhile had one additional hurdle to contend with; in one week, Alistair would be married, and the Friday before exams was slated for his bachelor party.

The weather couldn't have been more wretched for that big event. Several inches of snow had fallen on the ground during the afternoon. The snow turned to rain around dusk, just as the temperature paradoxically dropped. Snow, slush, water, and ice mingled promiscuously in the streets as an evil wind whistled through the cloudy, moonless sky. It was a truly dark and stormy night.

The evening began for some of us at a cozy apartment in the Back Bay, where Madeleine, a Stanford woman now at Harvard Medical School, was having a Christmas party. Spencer and I told Alistair to meet us there. Spencer, meanwhile, had a nasty trick up his sleeve. A few days before, he had acquired a bowling ball and somehow drilled a hole straight through it. On the way to Madeleine's, we stopped at a hardware store, where we acquired a length of chain and two padlocks. When we got to the party, it was in full swing. There were students from the medical school and the law school, as well as a number of people from our Stanford class. Madeleine's apartment was warm, snug, and awash in holiday cheer. At about eight o'clock, Spencer and I surrounded Alistair. It was time to take him away from all this.

We hustled him outside as the tempest raged. "What's that?" Alistair asked, looking suspiciously at the clanking Macy's bag Spencer was struggling to carry.

"Sweaters, dude!" Spencer gasped, shoving him into a waiting cab.

The taxi drove us across town to a steak house, where Alistair's dad and about twenty of our friends were waiting. Throughout dinner, the waitress brought rounds of shots; vodka for Alistair and (unbeknownst to him) water for the rest of us. "You guys are machines!" Alistair marveled as we downed round after round without trouble. He was especially impressed with his father, who unflinchingly polished off three doubles in the space of five minutes.

The ball and chain came out after dinner, just before Alistair's dad headed home. The ball was chained to Alistair's ankle, and he dutifully set to lugging it around for the balance of the evening. At the end of the night, Spencer reluctantly unlocked it, leaving Alistair unencumbered for finals week.

The days leading up to our exams were mercifully low on work. Very little studying could be done for either TOM or Marketing, because by December, you could either crack one of those cases or you couldn't. My own preparation consisted mainly of organizing notes for easy access during the open-book exams. We meanwhile had cases to do for both Monday and Tuesday. On Wednesday we also had a full complement of classes, but the time was divided between filling out course evaluation forms and having final review sessions with our professors.

It was sad to say good-bye to the people who had taught us all semester. We bought each of them gifts, as was traditional at the school. My favorite gift was Stanley's. We all signed and then framed a copy of *Donner and Company*, our first TOM case and his first case as an HBS professor.

He gave the section a farewell address that had people talking for weeks afterward. He urged us to always keep a good balance in life, to never let our family, friends, or faith get eclipsed by our careers. He reminded us of the importance of remaining humble, regardless of how much success we might achieve in our professional lives. And he stressed the fundamental position that our own ethical principles should always occupy in our public and private lives. Few people could deliver such a talk without sounding trite or ingenuine, but most felt Stanley's sincerity was beyond question, and few were unmoved by his words. Over the months he had forged a tremendous bond of trust and respect with the section, and his intellectual and spiritual credibility could not have been higher.

Unlike their colleagues in the OB department, the TOM and Marketing faculties were unmoved by Harvard's absence of a test printing policy. Their exams would be in-class, proctored affairs, and sections would have to rely on their own resources and ingenuity to print them. The administration generously decided to allow the use of laser printers in exam rooms after all.

Section I computer users were told to take the Marketing exam in Baker Library's main room. I arrived about ten minutes before the test began, and the place was already packed with students from several sections. I paced the length of the gymna-sium-sized room, but couldn't find a seat anywhere. I finally spied an empty spot at a crowded table and pounced on it. Baker was jammed as I had never seen it. Hundreds of us sat before our humming little Powerbooks, as countless tons of books, notes, and old cases crowded the tables and spilled onto the floor.

A small detachment of teaching assistants handed out ex-ams, and a little after nine the signal was given to commence. When I finished reading the case, I set it down, befuddled. The Marketing department had certainly made an odd choice with this one. Entitled *Tyler Abrasives*, it focused on a producer of "bonded, coated, and loose" industrial abrasives. The case dealt mainly with international marketing strategy, a subject we had barely touched upon during the year. And unlike most of our cases, its exhibits contained few if any processable numbers. Either that or I was completely missing the point of the thing. After worrying about this for a few minutes, I buckled down to my writing. Soon Baker was echoing with the clatter of thou-sands of tiny keys.

Before I knew it our time was up, and the farce of printing began. I wandered about aimlessly in the now-chaotic library, looking for one of the Section I people who had generously loaned a printer to the cause. I eventually joined a long line behind an Apple printer. Bored, I turned to the woman in front of me. "Call me crazy," I deadpanned, "but that seemed a lot more like a Marketing case than a TOM case!"

Fear, uncertainty, and doubt bloomed briefly in the line. "You mean this *wasn't* the Marketing exam?" asked a panicky student who had overheard me.

Just then, a collective groan issued forth from our side of the library. All the printers had stopped. As Karen Trumble predicted months before, our laser printers had indeed blown a fuse. Somebody relocated our printer to a socket near the men's room, and I eventually printed my exam, signed my name to the back, and handed it in. By then the testing period had ended more than an hour before.

People reacted to this test much differently from the way they had to its midyear predecessors. I never discussed the contents of the TOM midterm with anybody; the subject was tacitly off limits, as none of us wanted to hear about the insights we had failed to make ourselves. But by now, people were far bolder. The test's central issues were a hot topic at lunch, and it seemed that I had, in fact, missed several things. Depressed, I went to Shad and drowned my sorrows on the Stairmaster.

Our section had a slightly better draw on Friday, and got to take the TOM exam in an Aldrich classroom. The test's case concerned a GE dishwasher plant, and was typical of the cases we had done since the midterm. I felt good about my essay, and even managed to get it printed in less than a half hour.

At that point it was a sprint to the airport. In two hours I was scheduled to fly out to Los Angeles for Alistair's wedding, and I still had yet to pack. I hurriedly slapped a suitcase together and raced across campus to meet Sandra. She was scheduled to fly out at the same time as I was, and we decided to cab together.

As I was charging toward her dorm, I came across Carter. He was looking a bit dejected, despite the impending vacation. I asked him what was going on.

"Man, I just tanked on those finals. Didn't have all the cylinders firing."

"Come on, it couldn't have been that bad."

"Yeah, we'll see," was his pessimistic response. "With my class participation I really needed to kick ass just to keep my head above water, and I know I didn't do that."

"Hey, Sandra and I are heading to the airport right now," I said, hoping to distract him from his worries. "Want to come?"

Carter brightened visibly at the mention of Sandra's name, although he said he couldn't make it; his own flight left about an hour after ours, and he still had a good deal of packing to do. "Besides," he added, "I'm heading down to DC in a few days to hang out with her and meet the family." Meet the family? I thought. This was getting serious.

Sandra's door was open when I arrived, and her bags were everywhere. "Sandra, what are you *thinking*?" I asked. Her luggage would have challenged a camel.

"I'm thinking it's nice to have such a good friend in my hour of need," she quipped, tossing me a tennis racket and two duffel bags.

We staggered downstairs and caught a cab. "Logan Airport, and fast!" I said breathlessly.

Sandra grabbed my wrist and looked at my watch. "Oh, quit panicking, Rob, we're not *that* late. Driver, pull over!" We stopped next to a convenience store. Sandra was off like a shot, and before I knew it, she was back in the cab with a six-pack of Molson's and some skinny paper bags to hide them in. "The last two weeks were just too much," she explained as she opened one for me, "and I've hardly had a beer since Thanksgiving. To TOM!" We toasted the class and drank, the driver regarding us suspiciously through his mirror.

Both of our flights were delayed by the holiday rush, so we sat down in an *airport ice cream shop* to finish the beers. Our next toast, of course, was to Carter. Our third was to the opening he had blown so spectacularly in Marketing. "Poor old Carter!" Sandra said, shaking her head. "That wasn't his finest moment. But he handled it well. I've heard some pretty scary stories about bad openings in other sections."

"Such as?"

"Well, a guy in my study group told me about this woman who had a disaster like Carter's a few days ago. She spent the next seventy minutes *sobbing*. Right in class! I mean, tears." Maybe it was the giddy sense of freedom brought on by the conclusion of exams and the start of vacation. Or maybe it was just the fact that we were about to start on our third round of beers. Whatever it was, we both somehow found the image of this to be unbearably funny. "Heard of anything else like that?" Sandra prompted me after we stopped chuckling.

So I told her a tale I had heard from somebody in another section. "This professor cold called someone who hadn't spoken for days. So the guy got this deer-in-the-headlights look, then started to talk. He was really articulate, but was completely bogged down in the details of some minor subject. Suddenly everybody realized that he'd just opened to the middle of the case and started *reading* the thing, word for word. He went on for three or four minutes before the professor finally shut him down." This put us both into another bout of hysterics.

By now, it seemed we were entering the war story mode. Almost everybody occasionally indulged in this manner of releasing tension, whether in study groups or with a few friends in the off-hours. Chuckling over the year's legendary in-class disasters somehow made the HBS experience seem less threatening and more amusing. And it certainly made one's own memorable blunders seem less unique and academically crippling.

"By the way," Sandra said, changing the subject. "Was that Rachel woman scary or what??"

"Hell, yeah," I agreed, opening us another round. A few days before, Sandra and I sat down at lunch with a guy we knew from another section. He was seated with several of his friends, one of whom was Rachel, a woman neither Sandra nor I had met before. Within five minutes of meeting us, Rachel told us (and the rest of the table) how she was on the verge of tears at the end of every day, how HBS had turned her into an emotional basket case, how TOM had her confused to the point of lunacy.

"It's people like that who end up on clock towers with M-16s," Sandra observed, almost making me choke on my beer with laughter.

By now, we must have been quite a sight. Here you've got a feisty little blonde with some swarthy guy who hasn't shaved in two days. They're drinking out of paper bags in an airport ice cream shop, for Chrissake, and by the looks of things, this isn't their first round. Young, troubled, and somewhat unbalanced, we suddenly looked more like something out of a David Lynch movie than a McKinsey recruiting poster. They should put us on the cover of *BusinessWeek*, I thought, and spice it up with a sensationalistic headline. THE FACE OF TOMORROW'S CORPORATE ELITE: OUR FUTURE HELD HOSTAGE! it would say.

"Aright, d'you wanna know the *best* one," Sandra was saying. "It's second-hand information so take it with a big grain of salt."

I nodded, and she told me a story that dated back a few years. Right after she graduated college, a friend of hers had moved to Boston to live with her fiancé, an HBS man. She affiliated with a club that provided support and social activities for the husbands, wives, and lovers of HBS students. One night, this club had hosted a special evening, in which a psychologist came to answer members' questions. Sandra's friend gave her a full report. The atmosphere at the meeting, she said, was very somber. The attendees were mostly young women, and they had an unsurprising litany of complaints. "My husband never spends time with me," said one.

"He's always stressed out," said another.

"He's always so grouchy," said a third.

Finally, a woman on the verge of hysterics stood up. "My

husband," she sobbed, "he doesn't have sex with me anymore!" A wave of sympathetic nods rippled through the crowd.

Now here was an ugly story. I knew of a few cases of HBS-induced insomnia, but impotency?

Eventually our flights were called. I was asleep before my plane left the ground, and hardly moved until I got to Los Angeles.

11

THE VACATION
THAT WASN'T

MY FLIGHT DISPATCHED me to Los Angeles almost three hours after my scheduled arrival, torpedoing any delusions I had about going out that night. It was almost two in the morning before I pulled up to my friend Kent's apartment. Despite the late hour (sunrise Boston time), we stayed up for a while catching up. But before long, my post-TOM torpor gained the upper hand and delivered me to a deep and dreamless sleep.

The next day was given to the hubbub of the approaching wedding. The afternoon brought a barbecue at a beautiful beach club somewhere near Pacific Palisades. L.A. was going through a cold snap in the hills, but it was warm and sunny by the ocean. People were casually playing volleyball in shorts and T-shirts as Boston slogged through the throes of a new ice age. That night, Alistair married Emily, a woman I had worked for in both San Francisco and Warsaw. Emily graduated from HBS a few years before, and was now vicariously enduring the school for a second time through her soon-to-be husband. Love conquers all. The wedding and reception were wonderful, and in no time I was back at LAX for my return journey.

It was midnight before I got to McCulloch, and I groggily chose to postpone the long haul to Connecticut. The next morning I decided to pass by the Cole Room before heading home.

I hadn't visited the place since my first exploratory foray, and Rick said it had a number of resources I should check out before starting my job hunt. I was beginning to feel rather behind on this front; a handful of people had already started sending résumés to Gold List companies, and many more had done some preliminary Cole Room digging. The place was usually humming, but now that vacation had started, I figured it would be free of its usual crowds.

I was sadly mistaken. Although Christmas break was already four days old, the place was as packed as I'd ever seen it. Christmas itself was only three days away. *Don't these people have anything better to do over vacation?* I marveled. There was literally no place for me to put down my notebook, let alone sit and do research. I glanced halfheartedly through some pamphlets about Apple and Microsoft, then left. It would be better to come back after vacation, when the siren song of cases would hopefully draw some of this throng away.

So I got home on Tuesday afternoon. Already I was feeling the bite of the vacation's impending end, as in only twelve days school would reconvene with a three-case day. The balance of the holiday blurred by. My parents were leaving the house we'd lived in since I was a baby, and there were the contents of an attic, basement, and countless closets to dispatch to moving boxes or garbage cans. All told, moving was a depressing proposition. Although I graduated high school eight years before and had lived far away ever since, I still liked being in my town for Christmas. It was nice to see the people I grew up with, and I liked the feel of my bed and my old house. It was sad going through the local holiday rituals for the last time. My parents weren't actually moving very far away (about eighty miles north, and still in Connecticut). But they would be distant enough that my old hometown would become inaccessible except on the longest of vacations.

While all this was going on, there was still the small matter of the Gold List to attend to. The chore of considering companies and then writing cover letters, so blithely deferred at Thanksgiving, could no longer be ignored. Of the hundred or so companies on the list, maybe half fell into the broad categories of consulting or finance. The others were grouped into perhaps a dozen and a half diverse industry classifications. I began my survey with the investment banks. I had read volumes about Wall Street over the past several years, and my friends who had worked there had loved and hated the business in roughly equal proportions. My father also spent much of his working life in finance, and had long encouraged me to at least consider the industry. Together, all of this piqued my interest considerably.

I had already decided to apply to at least a couple of the leading banks. Because regardless of how it turned out, I strongly believed that a summer in investment banking would never be wasted. New York's financial community was inarguably one of the most powerful forces in the international political economy, and Wall Street's late-eighties' boom was a defining period in American social history. A few months of seeing the Street's dynamics and culture firsthand would therefore be fascinating. It could even prove to be a materially valuable education if I ever worked off enough HBS-related debt to have investable funds of my own. And of course, there was also a significant chance that I'd enjoy the business enough to want to continue with it after graduation.

Most of the larger banks conducted summer recruiting for at least two distinct areas: Corporate Finance, and Sales & Trading. Corporate Finance groups worked directly with the world's giant companies, structuring deals and underwriting massive issues of corporate debt and equity. It was this side of the business that saw the crushing eighty- to one-hundred-hour work weeks that Wall Street was so notorious for. Summer jobs in Corporate Finance were known to be professionally enriching but physically draining affairs.

Sales & Trading groups dominated the day-to-day flow of stocks, bonds, and their derivatives. Traders were the legendary split-second decision makers of Wall Street. Together with the sales people and the hybrid sales traders, they provided liquidity to the international capital markets. Internships in Sales & Trading were said to be almost farcically relaxed. Summer associates lacked training and licensing, and couldn't be entrusted with multimillion dollar transactions. Accordingly, they spent most of their time quietly observing the fulltime force at work. I had heard the experience described as enthralling and boring with equal frequency.

I flipped through some job descriptions I had picked up at the Cole Room. A position in Morgan Stanley's Sales & Trading group had an alluringly international bent: "Interns will work for 10 weeks. If they are hired for Tokyo, they will split their summer between Tokyo and New York; if they are hired for London, they will split their summer between London and New York; but if they are hired for long-term placement in Hong Kong, they will most likely spend their entire summer in New York." Salomon Brothers' description of their Corporate Finance position was extremely concise: "The Summer Associate Program provides a realistic intro. to the firm and work experience comparable to that of a fulltime associate. After an initial two-day orientation, summer associates are assigned to particular projects assisting managing directors, directors, and vice presidents in servicing our clients' needs."

I spent some time mulling over the differences between Corporate Finance and Sales & Trading. Corporate Finance would surely be interesting, but I was skeptical about my long-term ability to keep up with the job's frantic panic and pace. Also, the ongoing, daily involvement with the global markets that Sales & Trading offered would be intriguing. I therefore decided to focus most of my search on this side. But should I apply for a Corporate Finance position anywhere? I was still somewhat naïve about the industry, and learning about both sides through the forum of interviewing probably made sense.

I decided that to even consider logging the hours required in Corporate Finance, I'd have to be very comfortable with the people I'd be working with. Over the months, the Corporate Finance recruiters I'd clicked with the best were from Salomon Brothers. Salomon had made a sincere effort to reorient itself in the wake of the bond scandal, and its people were genuinely enthused about their organization. The firm's internal structure and work ethic also seemed to be unusually unfettered and entrepreneurial. Salomon, then, was the place I felt best about applying to for Corporate Finance.

As for Sales & Trading, I decided to send letters to Morgan Stanley and Goldman Sachs. These were premier firms, and their on-campus presentations had impressed me. That was it then; only three firms. Had I been completely focused on Wall Street I would have contacted perhaps a dozen more. But I planned to pursue a time-consuming off-campus job search in high tech, and was leery of diverting my attention to Wall Street firms I was less familiar with.

I was initially tempted not to send off résumés to any consulting firms at all. I'd spent my whole professional life in that field, and it made sense to break away during this "experimental" summer. Furthermore, most of the consulting job descriptions I came across were too vague to be inspiring. McKinsey: "A summer associate position with McKinsey & Company, Inc., provides the opportunity to work with talented colleagues in a stimulating, professional environment and to solve problems of concern to the top management of leading organizations worldwide. . . ." Monitor: "Summer consultants, along with a case team, creatively apply state-of-the-art conceptual frameworks to the client's business. . . ." Corporate Decisions, Inc: "Consultants work with clients' management to develop creative, fact-based analytical concepts to recommend and implement strategic business decisions having potential to improve long-term performance. . . ." Clearly, the author of our fuzzy OB reading had found some adherents.

But despite my hesitations, consulting still had its appeal. I could conceivably land a summer job in an office with projects in media, telecommunications or high tech. This would allow me to learn about these converging industries while in a setting I already knew I liked. With this in mind, I sent résumés to McKinsey (how could I resist?) and Deloitte & Touche. I chose these firms because they were quite large and had well-developed industry "practice areas." This, I reasoned, increased the odds that certain offices within their systems would have summer projects in the industries that interested me. For example, the San Francisco offices of both firms had substantial high tech practices. If I ended up at either of them, I could almost surely get onto a high tech project if I wanted to. In a smaller firm, the industrial composition of a particular office's project base would likely be more haphazard and unpredictable at any given time.

The jobs in nonservice industries were more diverse and in some cases more appealing. I was quite interested in the few high tech companies which were coming to campus. Among them were Microsoft and Apple. I also sent a résumé to Sony, as they were involved in at least one of the mysterious multimedia conglomerates springing up in Silicon Valley. Unfortunately, crafting an appropriate cover letter for Sony was difficult, as their job description was an incomprehensible jumble:

JOB DUTIES AND RESPONSIBILITIES:
Part 1: Understanding Sony's business strategies and global operations through meeting with executives and plant visits. Part 2: Being assigned to a project/product of a business group and a) finding facts on assigned project and analyzing the market; b) coordinating activities between divisions; c) formulating the project strategy; d) submitting a final report.

The Sony listing also mentioned that people with engineering degrees and experience in "electronics, computers, and manufacturing" would be preferred. This spelled trouble for me. My nontechnical, nonmarketing background would be a hurdle at the other companies as well. Microsoft sought people with "experience in marketing, sales, systems engineering, or development." Intel, the microprocessor titan, was looking for an "MBA with marketing emphasis, technical undergraduate degree, three-plus years' experience in the software industry." Apple never got around to sending in a summer job description, but was presumably looking for similarly qualified people.

On a whim, I sent a résumé to Merck, the pharmaceuticals company. Ranked by a *Fortune* magazine survey as the Most Admired Company in America for several years running, Merck had always fascinated me. I also sent one to the Strategic Planning unit at American Express. Amex was in the throes of a serious reorientation, which would probably make the group an interesting place to work. I also knew of a former manager from Bain's San Francisco office who had recently taken a job with them. While demanding to work for, he was said to be an outstanding mentor, and I had always regretted not having a chance to be on one of his teams.

After sending my cover letters off on the day after Christmas, I returned to the frantic task of squeezing my life into orderly numbered boxes. Leaving one's childhood home is an underrated rite of passage in our society. Bidding my old bedroom farewell before racing back to campus was as poignant a moment as any graduation or departure had been. For the first time in my life, I felt genuinely rootless. A top-floor cubicle in McCulloch and a seat in Section I's Warning Track were now my most familiar anchors. And one of these was about to vanish from my life as surely and finally as my old backyard.

12

MY FALL FROM THE WARNING TRACK

As I DROVE BACK to campus, I was plagued by trepidation. I wasn't worried about returning to classes and the pressure-laden pace of the academic week. I wasn't concerned about seeing my first-semester grades, which would be handed back in a matter of days. I wasn't apprehensive about facing on-campus job interviews, which would commence in less than two months. Rather, I was anxious—no, panicked—about my seat. Back in December, the administration had shown every sign of following through on a long-standing threat to randomly redistribute our seats in January. The one rule to this indiscriminate process would be that no one would remain in the same deck. This made me nervous. While I had only one chance to trade up (Sky Deck), there were three decks to which I could feasibly tumble. I didn't need a doctorate in statistics to be cowed by these odds.

When I got back to campus, I decided to wander around and stretch my legs a bit. After a while I strolled by Aldrich Hall, which loomed dark and menacing against the midnight sky. The new seating chart, I knew, would be posted outside our classroom, but Aldrich was surely locked at this hour. I tugged idly on the front door's cold brass handle. *Open!* Inside it was dark as a bottomless chasm. Even with a flashlight, navigating these opaque corridors would be a treacherous proposition. No seating assignment was worth mucking about down there (I could see the headlines already: IDIOT STUDENT VANISHES WHILE WANDERING ALDRICH AT MIDNIGHT—BOSTON INDIFFERENT).

I was tearing up my room, searching for a flashlight when Rick stopped by to welcome me back to school. Moments later, he saved me the effort of exploring Aldrich's dark and surely dangerous recesses. "You can bag the flashlight," he told me. "I was over there this afternoon. You got Center Garden Deck."

A quick detour to our classroom before breakfast confirmed these grim tidings. Center Garden Deck it was. Fewer notes would now be passed. More attention would now be paid. My consolation (and it was a big one) was that my neighbors were terrific. To my right was a guy I really liked from my MC presentation group. To my left was Craig, a regular on the Section I pub night circuit. Sandra was right in front of me, and Carter and Jerry were behind me in the Power Deck. Also behind me was Barrett, HBS's first blind student. To the section, he was known as someone who had overcome a tremendous physical challenge to excel in a trying academic environment. To those who sat near him in the fall, he was also known as a canny wit whose under-the-breath commentary could make even a tedious class fly by. Garden Deck might be bearable after all.

The morning kicked off with a new class called Managerial Economics. From the syllabus and course description, it seemed that ME would survey a grab bag of microeconomics and statistical tools. Our professor, Tim Flanders, was a first-time teacher. His debut case concerned a small construction firm whose sole supplier had just announced a substantial price increase. At issue was whether the firm should hike its own prices, change suppliers, or respond in another manner. A key lesson was that a business can sometimes raise prices, lose customers and revenues in the process, and still make more money. The case also showed how one company's actions can influence the behavior of its customers, suppliers, and competitors. These were all commonsensical points, but the case suggested certain quantitative approaches that were new to a lot of us.

Flanders struck me as a thoroughly good-spirited person. He got his MBA from Yale, a program known for its strong public policy bent. He later spent some time working at

Greenpeace, an unusual credential for an HBS professor. He was also said to be a very accomplished guitarist. He had the excitement one expects from a first-time teacher, and a gift for rendering ideas in a visual manner which greatly enhanced his effectiveness.

As the day unfolded, I grudgingly accepted the reality of my new seat. I also acknowledged that it could have been worse; the seating lottery's treatment of some other people bordered on cruel. Sandra, for one, was dealt a particularly harsh fate; her Garden Deck seat (lousy to begin with) was swapped for one in Center Worm Deck (inarguably the room's least desirable address). It wasn't long before a Top Ten list commemorating her awful luck made its way to me:

SANDRA'S TOP 10 RATIONALIZATIONS OF WHY HER NEW SEAT'S NOT SO BAD:

10. New seat is closer to apartment than most others.

9. Bill Clinton used to sit in Worm Deck.

8. Flanders has great ankles.

7. Professor might get mad if I fall asleep, but class-mates will never know.

I added: NOT CURRENTLY AFRAID OF HEIGHTS, BUT SHOULD THIS CHANGE, SEAT IS PERFECT and sent it along.

Our other new class that day was Human Resources Management (HRM), which would be taught by Karen Trumble, our section chair. A number of people, tired of being chided about attendance and disheartened by the ongoing printer debacle, had expressed reservations about having her as a professor. I was personally looking forward to her teaching. After all, the woman had a demonstrated ability to elicit controversy from our section. And in a qualitative course like HRM, this could only add to the content of discussion.

Trumble's first case concerned Hewlett Packard. HP was portrayed as having a warm and accommodating corporate culture, one which now had to adapt to a rapidly changing business environment. When the class ended, I felt like the course was off to a good start. The discussion was lively and contentious, and it was good to have at least one class in the schedule that wasn't overtly quantitative. My one complaint about Trumble's teaching style was that she tended to cut people off in midsentence when she wanted to add to what they were saying. But because I sometime suffer from this tendency myself, I was not one to hold it against her.

All told, it was great to swap in some new courses. My general optimism about classes was shared by everyone in my study group. Spencer also had Flanders for ME, and agreed that he showed promise. He also had some interesting intelligence on the man. Evidently, he hadn't just been a low-level whale counter while at Greenpeace. For two years, Flanders had directed the organization's New England operations, and had been one of its top people. An untraditional HBS background indeed.

After class I caught up with Carter, and asked him how his holiday visit with "Mr. and Mrs. Sandra" went.

"Beautifully," he answered with a satisfied smile, "but the whole trip went by much too fast."

Tuesday was the first of many days of final judgment. At the end of our last class ninety-one little white envelopes were distributed containing our final grades in OB. I clutched mine anxiously. Sure, I didn't care about grades, but then what accounted for the flutter in my chest and the pit in my stomach? I ripped the envelope open like a kid with a Christmas present. There it was in the middle of the tiny page: I.

Yes!!! Roman numeral uno! What was that word next to it? "Section." Section I. Well, I knew that. Better check again. At the top of the page I found another I. And this one was my grade. I traipsed out of the room. I'm practically a Baker Scholar, I thought. A few moments later I regained my connection with reality, but still felt pretty good. OB had been a real question mark for me, as it was the one course in which there had been no interim performance feedback (not counting Bob Rosenthal's reproachful note at the beginning of the year). This made my grade a particularly pleasant surprise.

We were told that we could get more information about our grades from Rosenthal's assistant in Morgan Hall, so Rick and I headed over after lunch. I found that by some unknowable methodology, I had scored a 49 out of 60 in "class participation." I did a bit better than this on the exam. Because it counted for 60 percent of our final grades, it was the exam that really drove everybody's standing in the course.

I now felt like flipping through my test to see what kind of commentary Rosenthal had written in the margins. But doing this wasn't just a matter of asking for it and taking it home, as the status of graded final exams was governed by one of the most arcane of HBS's many Byzantine rules. With a professor's clearance, you could see and physically touch your exam. But under no circumstances were you allowed to walk out of the building with it.

There were many theories about this odd regulation's genesis. One had it that it was meant to prevent students from comparing exams and then griping about inequitable grading. Another centered on an improbable tale about a professor who left hundreds of graded exams on an airplane. The new rule was promulgated, this legend went, to make sure that no test ever left the Boston area again. Whatever the reason, we could only inspect our exams while under the watchful gaze of Rosenthal's assistant. And we had to be quick about it, as all exams were ultimately destined for the furnace, sometimes as soon as one semester after they were written. When it came to grades, HBS never left a paper trail.

The next day brought our first section-chair meeting with Karen Trumble since the vacation. Many of these episodes had been drawn out and uneventful, but this one was a bit different. It began with a characteristically uncharted discussion about what we had learned at HBS. We launched comment after disconnected comment for perhaps ten minutes, but suddenly, somebody made a meaningful point. He said the school really had surprised him. Anticipating a class full of Machiavellian cutthroats, he instead found a community of ninety-one supportive people.

At that another guy raised his hand to agree, saying that he'd struggled mightily with two of our first semester courses, but had pulled through because so many people in the section had made time to help him. Then a woman who had recently suffered through a family crisis said that the section's support had made a big difference to her when she was coping with it.

At that point, another guy chimed in. "You always hear that everybody at HBS is a total butthead," he pointed out. "So

how come there aren't any buttheads here? Are HBS people
not really buttheads after all? Or do we all just become buttheads after graduation?" While he might have put it less bluntly,
the guy had an important point. HBS students weren't exactly
known as being the most benign people in the world, yet somehow the nine sections had become (trite as it may sound) like
families. The family analogy was drawn by a few people, and we
basked momentarily in the warmth of a collective Section I feel-
good glow.

This didn't last long, as there was regrettably one matter
of business left to discuss. Recruiting season was fast approaching, and Trumble was obliged to saddle us with an unam-
biguous reminder from the administration. "Folks," she began,
"remember that under no circumstances are you to miss classes
for recruiting activities. Harvard has strict rules about this. The
recruiters understand them, and you should understand them
too."

This sparked a decidedly un-feel-good debate. One guy
argued that we all paid plenty of money to come to HBS, largely
because we wanted to graduate to good jobs. "So how can you
tell me I don't have the right to pursue a job in the manner I
see fit? *I'm* the one paying the bills around here, and I'm *twenty-
eight years old*, for Chrissake!"

Trumble countered, declaring that in the absence of illness
or family emergency we all had a "moral obligation" to come to
every session of every class. If we wanted to break this covenant,
we would have to accept the consequences for our grades (and
also, presumably, a greatly diminished status in the Hereafter).
Trumble was surely bound as our section chair to toe the party
line on this issue. However, many felt that dressing Harvard's
uncompromising attendance policies in the guise of a moral
edict was taking it a little far.

It was perhaps not surprising that recruiting had become
such an emotionally charged issue, as it was starting to loom
large in our lives. Some people were still struggling to get their
last résumés and cover letters off to Gold List companies before
January 15, the submission deadline for most firms. Meanwhile,
responses were trickling back to the people who mailed out
letters over vacation. I had already been invited to meet with
McKinsey—a nonfeat, as they granted interviews to literally

every HBS first-year that requested one. I was also invited to meet with Goldman Sachs's Equity Sales unit, a group that was a bit tougher to get a meeting with.

Toward the end of the week I received a letter from the Boston Consulting Group's Australian practice soliciting my résumé, as well as a dinner invitation from the company's central recruiting office. I hadn't planned to interview with BCG, but decided I might as well. Australia could be fun, even though it would be winter there in June. I skipped their dinner—I'd roomed with a BCG employee in San Francisco, and didn't need to invest an evening to hear what they were about.

A few days into the semester, HBS provided us all with a welcome distraction from the growing pressures of summer recruiting. Over a four-day period, we all took part in a team-based computer game known as WISE ("Worldwide International Simulation Exercise"). The sections were again randomly divided into small teams, and a few hours before the game commenced, the first-year class convened in Burden Auditorium to hear the WISE gospel. A faculty member who had been running the game for years was on hand to tell us how to proceed.

Each of our teams, he said, comprised a "company." Each company would now compete with five others in an "industry." To succeed, companies would have to develop and implement good manufacturing, marketing, and financial strategies. The game would take place over seven moves (submitted on computer disk), each of which would require a host of decisions touching on all aspects of our companies' operations. There would be no random external events, and each company would begin with precisely the same resources and infrastructure.

As in the Marketing exam, team dynamics and delegation skills would clearly be as critical to success in this pursuit as analytical acumen. There were simply too many decisions embedded in each move for one person to make them all. Teams prone to cooperation and constructive dialogue would therefore run circles around those inclined toward meanspirited argumentation. The professor shared an anecdote that illustrated this from the game's early years. He was administering it to one of HBS's special programs for senior executives. One day, he ran into a participant who was stormily exiting the program's residence hall with his suitcases in hand. "I will not spend one more moment with that group of *irrational bastards* you put me with," the executive raged. "I'm moving to the Ritz!"

My own team was devoid of *irrational bastards,* which was fortunate, as a weekend of sulking at the Ritz was not in anybody's budget. We first convened on Thursday evening, which was devoted to a practice move. There were two items in our manufacturing portfolio to consider, creatively named Product 1 and Product 2. Product 1 was a mass-market good, Product 2 was its high-end derivative. Questions quickly piled up. How should we allocate manufacturing capacity between the products? How much should be spent on advertising? Should we ship some Product 1 to South America? If so, should we use surface or air carriers? And since this was just a practice move, shouldn't we avoid doing anything that would telegraph our real intentions to our competitors?

Eventually we came up with a complete practice move which we transferred to disk. When we got the results back the following morning, we discovered that we'd made some serious blunders. The most significant of these was our failure to notice a huge stockpile of inventory sitting in Europe. Oops. Our five competitors had crushed us, but we learned a lot about the game's mechanics as a result. We attacked our first "real" move with renewed zeal.

The first decision we had to make in this move was whether to build factories in Europe and South America. "Ve shoot create no capacity in Souss America," opined Detlev, an Eastern European who had long since taken to Western capitalism like a duck to water.

"Ooh no, under no circumstances!" agreed Mario, a South American. He spent a few years working in an American bank's debt restructuring group, and was less than bullish about his home continent's WISE prospects. Consensus was reached quickly; we would spurn the South American market entirely, but add capacity in both North America and Europe. Production and marketing would be focused on the high-priced and profitable Product 2.

Excitement rippled through our group when results of the first move came back. All five of our competitors were building factories in South America, but only one was building in Europe. "Zey vill slug it out in Ecuador vile we slowly move toward

European domination," predicted Detlev, reflecting everybody's smug sentiments.

Our enthusiasm began to erode late in the afternoon. The European market simply wasn't as big as early projections had indicated, and we had overbuilt. Our inventory was now ballooning in both Europe and North America, just as cheap South American product was beginning to flood the world market. This situation deteriorated steadily. Because the game's algorithm did not permit sudden reductions in company employment (a restriction which was divorced from the real world it sought to model), we were unable to significantly decrease our output. Our optimistic, first-quarter building binge consequently plagued us throughout the game.

By Monday we had a lock on fifth place, ahead of only one hapless firm that had been on a path of steady self-destruction since the first move. We tried everything to reverse our fortunes. We shifted our product mix, put inventory on slow boats to Europe, "dumped" in South America, underpriced, overadvertised, and experimented with anything else that came to mind. From a starting point of calm rationality, we had become entirely reactive, recklessly slamming from strategic guardrail to strategic guardrail. By Monday afternoon, our interest in the exercise had completely dissipated. We spent most of the time between moves poring over the next day's cases rather than refining our strategy. Detlev alone maintained his dogged persistence, and worked through the last couple of moves almost solo while the rest of us did our best to put the trauma of WISE behind us.

It was all over early Monday evening, and the section convened for a "WISE Game Wrap-Up, Debriefing, and Good-Natured Mocking of the Losing Teams." We placed fifth as expected, our one honor being that we never had a stockout. Given that we finished the game with enough inventory to comfortably meet the entire world's Product 1 and Product 2 needs for months, this was unsurprising. Overall, WISE was an intriguing exercise. It illustrated the importance of cash flow, the difference between profit and contribution, the effects of certain actions upon competitor behavior, and many other issues.

WISE was technically part of the ME curriculum, but there was little integration of the game with the following week's cases.

This was unfortunate, but then again ME was starting to bog down in general. Class discussions, many of us felt, had come to be excessively tied to the cases. Even when the numbers and principles under consideration were fairly self-evident, we would often spend the entire eighty minutes poring over their details with numbing thoroughness. This situation seemed to afflict the entire department, as everybody in my study group had similar complaints about ME.

To be fair, we as students were often to blame for the occasional sluggishness of the class. Momentary lapses of self-control often resulted in OB- or Marketing-style chip shots at times when they just weren't appropriate. One class that typified this pattern came early in the course. We were discussing a situation concerning a woman who was moving to San Francisco. Her van was too small to carry all her possessions, so she measured their dimensions and assigned dollar values to each of them. Certain smaller items, like portraits, had high assigned values because of their sentimental worth. Other items, like her mattress, took up a lot of space but were also quite expensive. What methodology should she use in deciding what to bring? How should size, weight, cost and emotional value be traded off as she applied her limited resource (the van) to the items she wanted to transport?

It is difficult to imagine a scenario more unabashedly hypothetical than this one. Flanders was using it to introduce us to resource allocation analysis, not to describe an actual managerial situation à la Marketing or OB. The discussion began. "How can she assign dollar amounts to things with sentimental value?" complained one man. "What if the portraits are of someone who's ill? If that person dies, the portraits could become much more valuable to her."

Flanders patiently explained that although this was a good point, the case was meant to illustrate some specific analytic techniques. If we could suspend our disbelief about the items' dollar values for a few minutes, he would be happy to revisit such softer issues later.

He called on another student. "She could always just buy another mattress when she gets to San Francisco," was his insight. "Mattresses are essentially commodity goods. Most cities have outlets where they can be purchased at substantial discounts."

Flanders smiled good-naturedly and asked the class if any-body would like to respond to this. Surely, *anyone* he picked would bring the class back to the subject at hand. He chose a woman who was eagerly pumping her hand in the air. I looked back and saw Carter and Jerry exchange a worried look; she could sometimes be trouble. "That was a really good point!" she said to the mattress expert. "I'd like to build on it a bit." She proceeded to share a story her husband told her about buying a mattress in New York City in the early 1980s.

Flanders himself was ME's saving grace by then. He was witty and warm, and had quickly established a good rapport with the section. And at those times when things did get confus-ing, his exhaustive explanations usually saved the day. His knack for portraying perplexing concepts in a compelling visual manner was priceless. From Linear Programming to Critical Fractile Analysis, he could boil almost anything down to a few multicolored overhead charts that were worth the proverbial megabyte of words.

And at times, ME was downright entertaining. One day brought a "Probability Assessment Exercise," in which we tried to guess how the first-year class had responded to a survey handed out earlier in the month. The actual survey results told volumes about the high expectations many of us had from life. On the average, people estimated that they would personally earn $80,000 in the first year after graduation. This was more or less consistent with data from recent years. But optimism about the intermediate future was rampant. On the average, people from our class reckoned that they would pull down $510,000 a year by our tenth reunion.

We were even more bullish about our academic prospects. Over 75 percent of us expected to graduate in the top half of the class, something which would inevitably lead to roughly two hundred long faces come June of '94. Certain other statistics indicated that despite our diversity, we were not exactly a repre-sentative cross-section of American society (even after adjusting for our considerable international contingent). The survey showed that 42 percent of us drank imported beers more often than their domestic rivals, which sharply contrasted with the fact that only 3 percent of all beer consumed in the United States was of foreign origin.

Meanwhile, HRM was still going well. By now we were

focusing on labor unions. The company cultures we examined while exploring this subject were polar opposites of Hewlett Packard's gushy gentleness. One evening we were assigned to watch a particularly compelling film about 1984's North America-wide strike against GM. The documentary focused on Canadian labor leader Bob White, and his efforts to divorce his constituents' wage packages from those of their counterparts across the border. White was a winsome demagogue who interlaced his tirades with innumerable derivatives of the word "fuck." The documentary showed his brilliant politicking in all its gritty glory, and was a triumph of verisimilitude. Classes were similarly feisty (although generally devoid of White-style expletives). While Trumble's abrupt manner still put some people off, none could deny that she drew powerful opinions out of the section.

My only concern about HRM was that an inordinate proportion of its material was quite dated. I casually flipped through the first five weeks' cases and found that only about a third of them were set in the last ten years. Particularly problematic was the course's *Note on Why Employees Join Unions*. Although a notation in the upper right corner of its front page indicated that it had been revised in November of 1992, the appendage of this deceptive date was probably the only change made at the time. A 1981 copyright at the bottom of the page was a more honest reflection of the note's timeliness, as nothing cited in its fifteen footnotes or twenty-two bibliographic references was published after 1980. At one point the text mentioned that "Whether or not the upcoming decade will be for clerical workers what the 1930s were for industrial workers remains to be seen." Given that the "upcoming decade" was by now long over, it was regrettable that the HRM faculty had not yet updated its survey of this important and fast-changing subject.

By now the tension surrounding the summer job search had crept up yet another notch. Hell Weekend, the four-day period in which over a hundred companies would descend upon campus, was now just six weeks off. The official deadlines for sending in résumés were upon us, and the procrastinators among us were now scrambling to loft their last-minute bids for interviews. Occasionally you'd see a frazzled student heading toward the post office with dozens of envelopes in hand. Visions like these could terrify people who had been more restrained in their interview solicitations. *I only submitted twelve résumés, but Melanie's sending off about thirty right now, so maybe I ought to revisit the Gold List and come up with another eighteen companies that I wouldn't mind working for . . .*

A lot of people dampened the edginess surrounding Hell Weekend with a significantly more cavalier attitude toward schoolwork. For many people cracking cases was much easier than it used to be, and when time was tight, minimal standards for class preparation could be met with dispatch. Our study group convened less and less, and our occasional meetings became largely social events.

It wasn't long before more relaxed standards were imported to the classroom as well. When people weren't interested in the discussion, they simply clocked out. The section's note volume must have quintupled over the previous semester, and the proportion of people doing crossword puzzles, reading magazines, or doing the next day's cases under their desks increased similarly. One guy claimed to have done his taxes in three consecutive ME classes. And on at least one Friday afternoon, a flask of bourbon circulated furtively through part of Right Field during HRM.

Such exotic distractions aside, much of the section found its preferred antidote to boredom in the erudite pages of *The Wall Street Journal.* This was, of course, a less risky fetish than slugging liquor in the peripheral view of a woman who forbade bagels and candy bars from her classroom. Still, in-class *Journal* aficionados faced their own challenges. In the lower decks, it was almost impossible to turn the paper's noisily bulky pages without alerting our attentive professors. A former Sky Deck resident devised a resourceful solution to this problem. In his old elevated seat, he could browse through the *Journal* at will without attracting unwanted attention. He continued to do this at his new address with the aid of a Bowie knife that he brought to class every day. Now instead of turning a page when he was done with it, he quietly sliced it off.

I was grateful for the more relaxed academic tone, as I was now involved in an independent job search that occasionally detracted from my studies. Of the handful of high tech companies coming to campus, only a few offered work in the areas of "convergence" that John Sculley had discussed in his lecture. If I wanted to become involved in these areas myself, it seemed that I would have to create my own opportunities.

I started my research simply by trying to develop a fuller understanding of the computer and telecommunications industries. An ignorance about these would be an insurmountable handicap if I ever landed an interview with someone involved in interactive media. *Well, I don't know much about computers or telecom, but Sculley says they're gonna be the same business some day, and I'd sure like to learn more about this over the summer.* Somehow, this and five months of Harvard were unlikely to impress anyone. To avoid such embarrassments, I spent a lot of time in the Cole Room, digging through annual reports and scanning recent literature on anything related to the amorphous digital information industry.

Luckily, the second weekend after Christmas provided a timely break from this and other demanding distractions. Monday was Martin Luther King Day, and the first-year class celebrated with a large-scale skiing exodus to Montreal. Almost 200 of us boarded buses for the northward journey on Friday afternoon. Michal, a good friend of mine from Warsaw, was now a first-year in McGill University's MBA program. We collaborated in bringing Section I and some of his classmates together for a Saturday evening gathering in a sprawling student center.

The party was a hit, as people from the two programs actually mingled and got to know one another. A new rugby rivalry was born at the event, as well as at least one short-lived international romance. Talking to the McGill people drove home how different our programs were. They had two seventy-person sections to our nine ninety-person sections. Whereas we learned everything through cases, they had a healthy dose of lectures combined with a narrower selection of cases (they, for example, had eight Marketing cases to our forty).

These distinctions were strictly pedagogical, and both teaching approaches were probably well-suited to the needs of MBA students. The more significant difference between the programs was in their marketing of themselves to the corporate world. McGill, it turned out, didn't have a formal, on-campus summer job interviewing process at all. Companies only came looking for second-years, and even then they came in slim numbers. Demanding as the Gold List (and its attendant chores) was, it was nice to have it out there.

The more I thought of this, the more striking I found it. McGill had one of the better programs in North America, and the students I met there could certainly have cut it at HBS or any other school (actually, most of them would have been a lot of fun to have around). But the contrast between the corporate wooing that went on in Boston and Montreal could not have been sharper. One lesson was clear from this; much as we all liked to gripe about HBS, there was no denying that the place worked some strong magic on our behalf.

13

ADDRESSING THE CITIZENRY

ALTHOUGH WE HAD all assiduously avoided discussing the subject in Montreal, grading became a hot issue upon our return to Boston. On Tuesday we received our final marks in TOM, Marketing, and MC. Most of us had become impatient for these, as we had finished with exams more than a month before. Still, Harvard regulations required that we wait until the *end* of the day before seeing how we'd done. This was meant to shield the quality of class discussion from people's reactions to their results. Find out about that 3 in MC in the morning, and you're liable to waste valuable class time in a traumatized stupor. Find out about it in the afternoon, and you'll have plenty of time to see a therapist, wallow in angst, and read your cases before class the next morning.

After HRM wrapped up, the little white envelopes appeared again. I felt a familiar gnawing in the pit of my stomach as I reminded myself that I did *not* care what I'd ended up with. I took my envelope, placed it in my pocket, affected a deliberately nonchalant stance, and ambled toward the door. I was about halfway there when I broke down and ripped it open. Two more 1s and a 2, the 2 being in TOM.

While I was relieved by the contents of my envelope, some of my friends were downright alarmed by what they found in theirs. Among the people I knew well enough to discuss the issue with, Carter and Hans had received more than one 3. Neither was surprised by this. Carter, for one, had long harbored grave suppositions about his performance. He ended up with 3s in Marketing and OB, and his 2 in TOM was an awfully close call. With 13 of his 26 graded credits now in the 3 category, Carter had genuine cause to worry about "hitting the screen." This was a euphemism for going before the Academic Performance Committee, a body which reviewed the status of every student who got 3s in thirty-two or more of their seventy first-year course credits.

The fate of those who hit the screen was decided by the committee during the summer between the first and second year. People who could argue convincingly that their performance would improve were allowed to return on probationary status. Those who didn't were asked to leave the program, usually with a proviso that they could petition to return after some time away.

Although he hadn't done much better than Carter, Hans was generally pleased with his grades. While he wasn't thrilled about the 3s he got in MC and OB, they didn't surprise him. He was the first to acknowledge that his English-language speaking and writing skills weren't on a par with those of his classmates. And after struggling so mightily with the magazine article used in its final, he had low expectations from OB as well.

The good news was that he got 2s in TOM and Marketing, and was clearly at no risk in FRMA. Hans found his grade in TOM to be particularly astonishing. "A 2 from Stanley," he marveled over lunch one day. "I felt for certain I would do poorly in that course!" With two 3s on his record, Hans, like Carter, now had to be cautious. Still, his grades were much more of a relief than a disappointment to him.

As soon as I got used to my grades, I hiked over to the plush faculty digs in Morgan. It was time to get rolling on the summer job search again. In addition to high tech and Sales & Trading, I had a third interest, more or less at right angles to the first two, in international development. This was a notoriously difficult field to find work in as a first-year. The summer selection process at the World Bank was said to be arduous and contact-driven. And beyond this organization, I had only a vague idea of where an MBA might find summer work at all.

When I complained of this to Tyler, he had, as usual, a good recommendation. "Go find your section's BGIE professor," he suggested. "Most of those guys are really plugged into the development world." This made sense, as I knew BGIE ("Business, Government, and the International Economy," pronounced "Big E") would be an internationally oriented course. Scheduled to start after FRMA ended, it would analyze how different countries, rather than companies, coped with the world. It would also be a vehicle for exploring the broad issues of development, balance of payment accounting, and competitive advantage between nations.

I passed through Morgan Hall's atrium, repressed an urge to genuflect at the spectacular Tethys mosaic, and found my way to Nick Patterson's office. Patterson would be our section's BGIE professor, and had gotten adulatory reviews from a number of second-years that I'd spoken to. I knocked on his door. "Come in!"

The man inside was a compact fellow sporting wire-rimmed spectacles. In his vest pocket ticked an old-fashioned railroad pocket watch. Within moments we established that it was Sam Lubbock, my Ethics professor, that I should really talk to about development. Patterson, it turned out, specialized in American history, whereas Lubbock taught a second-year course entitled Managing in Developing Countries, and was quite an expert on the subject.

The business of our meeting now settled, Patterson pulled me into a wide-ranging discussion that lasted for the better part of an hour. He told me he had just finished reading an outstanding piece of research on Hitler and Stalin. We discussed this gruesome pair for a while, then got to talking about Boris Yeltsin, Lech Walesa, Huey Long, Sonny Bono, the value of Coca-Cola's trademark, the expense of admission to Disney World, sea lions, MTV, and the late President Hoover. Eventually it was time to leave. What a guy, I thought as I drifted off to Shad for a workout. Though I hadn't learned much about international development, I had figured out that BGIE would be terrific fun, and this was good news.

Carter was emerging from the locker room as I arrived.

"What was the guy like?" he asked, after I mentioned that I'd met Patterson. I told him about his pocket watch, old-fashioned vest, and academic credentials. "Pretty atypical background for a professor here," Carter observed, referring to his American History specialization.

I agreed and headed off to change. Then I started to think. Atypical? Carter was right, but who among our professors was typical? Our whale-loving, guitar-strumming ME professor? Our towering, wizardly entrepreneur of a TOM professor? Our witty, commanding, twenty-something FRMA professor? If they all broke the mold of the HBS faculty (and indeed they did), who did that leave to *fit* the mold?

The next day I followed up on Patterson's suggestion and passed by Lubbock's office. Lubbock told me that he'd pieced together a substantial global network simply by teaching Managing in Developing Countries for so many years. Countless MDC alums had gone off to the developing world to work for multilateral organizations, international companies, governments, and small local businesses. Many of them now wrote him periodically to describe their work, their organizations, and the professional challenges presented by their host countries. Lubbock maintained an extensive file of these correspondences which he made available to interested students. It was as rich a source of information and contacts of this type as one could hope for.

As Lubbock and I were discussing some of his own recent field work, the telephone rang. He picked it up. "Rosalie, I'm in a meeting—" he started. There was a long pause.

Then, tensely: "Has my, uh, *proposal* gone through?" Another pause, then he placed his hand over the receiver and turned to me. "I think I better take this one," he whispered, a gleeful smile dancing across his face. Then, "Put him through!"

I shifted excitedly in my seat. *A publishing contract for his latest book? Perhaps an invitation from the Russian government to privatize Aeroflot?*

Lubbock was speaking again. "Hello Steven, do you have good news for me?" Another expansive smile. "Wonderful, Wonderful! When do we expect it to happen?"

I strained my ears, eager to catch a snatch of the other party's conversation. *I can feel it. HBS history is being made,* I thought solemnly.

Suddenly, Lubbock scowled. "I hope it won't be any later than that," he said testily. "I have to tell you, I've been getting a lit-tle frus-trated about this . . . Okay Steven, I'll be waiting."

He hung up, then gestured under his desk. "Six months," he said. "Six months I've been waiting for them to get me a filing cabinet to put here. It looks like they'll finally get one to me next week."

A filing cabinet. We swapped administration war stories for a couple of minutes. I told him about the parking debacle on Harvard-Yale day. He told me about special-ordering a garbage can.

Soon it was time to hurry on. Alistair and George's section was having some kind of event that night, so we had scheduled an early study group.

"Well, if it isn't one of Harvard's great malcontents," I greeted Spencer as I arrived at his and Gary's apartment. I was referring to one of the innumerable surveys in *The Harbus*. This week's had been on "student satisfaction." The results were impressive; 83 percent of the 500 students polled were "somewhat satisfied" or "very satisfied" with HBS. Only 8 percent said they "wouldn't recommend" the program to a friend thinking of business school. But of all the happy little sections, Spencer's was the least content, with 31 percent of its members expressing dissatisfaction with the school.

"I hear it's the lousy social life they've got," chided George.

As his section's social chair, Spencer had no choice but to dismiss this charge. "They handed out the surveys on Thursday morning. We had a pub night on Wednesday, and nobody was *asleep* before 2:00. So everyone was just feeling a little grumpy when they filled the stupid things out!" George and I nodded skeptically.

Despite its generally impressive results, the survey had raised some red flags over issues more important than the social stewardship of Spencer's section. People had rated the case study method very highly, but lambasted the grading system (its rating averaged 4.1 on a 5-point scale, with 5 being the lowest). People also complained that the school's international character was underemphasized, that too little attention was given to public sector management, and that recruiting-time options were unnecessarily limited. "Diversity is a farce," wrote one first-year. "Groupthink is induced by the majority formed by former consultants, financial analysts, and bankers."

But by far the most popular target of complaint was the administration and its "invisible, behind-closed-doors policies." Somebody from Spencer's section wrote that the administration had "no respect for the students. This lack of respect manifests itself in [a] myriad of ways: no take-home exams, mindless, trivial work, forced seating, forced curves, forced attendance, and on and on." Another student simply complained of "The abject disregard and disrespect the administration has for its customers . . . I mean products . . . whatever."

We talked about the survey for a while, and agreed that its generally positive results reflected our own attitudes about the school, as did some of the negative sentiments quoted about the administration. But even in this, its Achilles heel, the business school had its bright spots. Spencer pointed out that certain administration figures, such as his own section chair, were quite reasonable people.

I had to agree. Spencer's section chair was the "dean of the MBA Program," and was a deservedly popular figure. To equate him with the monolithic *administration* would amount to an unfair cut (although his title did have an admittedly administrative ring to it). The *administration* was the officious guard who tried to deny me my parking spot. The *administration* was the faceless Politburo that dithered for months over printers and overcharged for petty services. The *administration* was the computer that consigned me to Garden Deck and Spencer to Worm Deck. But people like Spencer's section chair were, well, people like Spencer's section chair.

At that point, FRMA was finally winding down. That week saw the last session of the course. This was a sad occasion, as Toddson had certainly become one of the section's favorite professors. After she finished a course summary and prefinal pep talk, we presented her with a farewell gift. It was a leather-bound, monogrammed dictionary which we had all signed, the perfect offering for a misspelling bee champ of her stature.

An inevitable unpleasantry accompanying FRMA's conclusion was its final exam. This test, like the TOM and Marketing finals before it, would be complicated by the administration's on-going refusal to resolve the printer dilemma. We would *not* be allowed to submit our essays on disk. We would *not* be trusted to leave the exam room at the end of the test period to print in our dorm rooms. There would *not* be any printing facilities made available to us. No, if we were going to continue in our petulant refusal to invest in shoddy portable printers that we would never use again, we were officially on our own.

FRMA's final exam was uneventful; by now these little trials were old hat. Entitled Adventurous Computer Games, it concerned a company that (surprise, surprise) authored video games. Adventurous needed a cost allocation system, as well as the usual assortment of interpretations and manipulations in its financial statements. I walked out feeling guardedly optimistic about my performance.

Much as we would all miss Toddson, it was nice to get FRMA behind us and move on to something new. The class hadn't gotten quite as stale as TOM or Marketing did in their closing weeks, but it was still time for a change. Monday would be our first session of Finance, and Wednesday would see the start of BGIE with the inimitable Nick Patterson.

The second-year grapevine had it that the man scheduled to teach us Finance was outstanding. He would also be one of the few fully tenured professors to stand before Section I. At that point, the only such professor we'd had was Frank Cotton in Marketing. Every section had its allocation of junior faculty, but so far ours seemed unusually large. Although our younger professors had generally been quite good, all of them showed their inexperience in one way or another. The section, then, was excited to finally get some "varsity faculty."

Unfortunately, Trumble kicked off Monday morning's HRM case with a disappointing announcement. Section A's professor for Competition & Strategy (or C&S, a course that would start in March) had recently decided not to teach this year for personal reasons. Our highly regarded Finance professor, who had experience in C&S as well, would now leave Section I to fill this man's spot. The vacancy he left could have most logically been filled by one of the Finance Department's most prominent scholars, who wasn't teaching a course at the time. Our section certainly had a dearth of professors of his stature.

Regrettably, this man happened to be the section chair for Section C. He therefore elected to teach that section, bumping the woman who had been scheduled to teach them over to us.

Not surprisingly, she was yet another junior professor with exactly one year of teaching experience. Section A, which inherited our seasoned Finance professor, had a stellar faculty to begin with. Section C did well by the trade too; they would now have two classes taught by "course heads" (i.e., the professors responsible for the courses' development) and four by tenured professors. By contrast, four of our professors had precisely two years of teaching experience between them.

This drove the section into a fury. We had been expecting our old Finance professor since September, and now, four hours before the start of our first Finance class, we were told to expect otherwise. Trumble's attitude, somewhere between "it's not my fault" and "life's like that sometimes," did little to soothe our ire. To be fair, it wasn't her fault; she had only been informed of the change by voice mail a few hours before. Still, many felt that she should have fought the change on our behalf, something she evidently hadn't done.

One woman asked why Section C's section chair couldn't have been prevailed upon to teach us. Given their overabundance of experienced professors, this would have been more equitable. "Oh come on," countered Trumble. "He already *knows* that section. It's not *easy* to learn ninety-one names, faces, and backgrounds." She was right; this would not have been an easy undertaking for him. But was it really so radical to suggest that such inconveniences were perhaps a part of . . . his job? It wasn't long before a subversive note came my way. WHO THE HELL PAYS THE BILLS AROUND HERE ANYWAY? it read. I replied: ONCE AGAIN, 'I GOT SCREWED,' recalling our all-but-forgotten rallying cry from orientation's section Olympics. For the remainder of the session, Trumble did her best to lead a surly and disgruntled Section I. She was in a tough position; it wasn't her fault, and nobody truly blamed her for what happened. But as section chair and proxy for the administration, she had to deal with our wrath.

The midmorning break saw many bitter little discussions about the development. People agreed that this was yet another example of the school's high-handed and dismissive attitude toward students. True, Section A's C&S professor had very good personal reasons for not wanting to teach in the spring. And true, some kind of faculty shuffling had to happen as a result. But it was disappointing that saving senior professors from mundane chores was viewed as a higher priority than providing students with a balanced faculty. And the fact that the administration thought a last-minute voice mail to our section chair was an appropriate way to communicate the change was viewed as being pretty pathetic. However unconcerned they were about our opinions, they could have at least sent down their own representative to explain the decision, rather than just designate Trumble to get pilloried.

Susan Callahan, our permanent substitute in Finance (who, incidentally, had *also* already memorized all the names and faces from Section C), was in an even worse position than Trumble. She had to walk into a section she could only imagine was bitterly disappointed to see her. We all agreed over lunch not to lodge a formal complaint, start a petition, or do anything else that would make her even more uncomfortable than she perhaps already was. Still, there was an unmistakable grumpiness in the air when she taught us that afternoon. Despite this, she capably led us through a discussion of *Butler Lumber*, a case intended to introduce the capricious art of financial forecasting.

In some ways, Callahan reminded me of Cindy Toddson. She was similar in age, height, and teaching experience. And like Toddson, she had short blond hair, wore glasses, and taught a numerically intense course. But there the similarities ceased. Whereas Toddson's teaching style was bantering and loosely structured, Callahan's was distinctly cool and directive. When class was over, Rick, Jerry, Sandra, and I swapped views on Finance as we drifted out of our classroom.

Sandra, for one, was pleased with our newest professor. Far more than accounting, finance was her strong suit, and she had feared this would be another "high-priced introductory course" that she didn't need. At least for now, these concerns were ameliorated. "We'll probably cover a lot of stuff that I learned at work," she said. "But I'm sure this woman's going to keep all of us hopping."

As for all the scandalized chatter about our change of professors, she found it overblown. "But I'll admit," she joked, "it's nice that people are talking about something other than my love life for a change." Indeed, this must have amounted to a pleasant hiatus for her. A few days before, a group of people from the section had spotted her and Carter walking down Newbury Street in Boston *holding hands*. By nightfall, the rumor had reached almost every Section I ear. "I haven't been such a hot topic of discussion since someone caught me kissing a ninth grader when I was thirteen," Sandra noted.

Sandra bade us farewell and headed off to the Cole Room. Its alumni files had long been her principal resource in searching for a small, entrepreneurial, marketing-oriented company to spend the summer with. By now she had elicited strong interest from at least three firms that closely fit her ideal model of an employer. One was a fast-growing manufacturer and merchandiser of women's apparel in Georgia. Another was an educational software company in California, and the third was a publisher of special-interest periodicals. None had considered offering a summer job to an HBS student before, but all were now on the verge of doing just that.

Sandra's only real hurdle had been in arranging interviews and on-site visits. This was not simple, given her *moral obligation* to be on campus for much of every business day, but in the end fortune smiled upon her. The software company's marketing director had a meeting in Boston one afternoon, and she met with him that evening. The publisher's CEO attended a conference in New York, and she flew the shuttle down to see him after class. As for the clothing company, she just bit the bullet and missed a day of class to fly to Augusta.

As Sandra headed off to resume her proactive job search, Jerry, Rick, and I walked over to Burden Auditorium. The normally tight-lipped administration was scheduled to address its citizenry, a rather unusual occurrence. The meeting's subject was an initiative called Leadership and Learning. I first heard mention of this undertaking in the fall, when occasional communiqués were circulated to trumpet its progress. It was essentially a broad self-diagnosis which the business school had started some time before. Its standing committees had examined such areas as Market Research, Historical Perspective, External Comparisons, and the Learning Environment. These committees had recently completed their Data Collection Phase, and were now presenting their findings. At some indeterminate time in the future, the faculty and administration would Implement Changes based upon the Data.

Leadership and Learning's research agenda had indeed been ambitious. The Market Research committee had polled almost 500 alumni and recruiters for their opinions about the school. Although an overwhelming majority of those surveyed supported the case method, more than half felt that HBS would benefit from a limited adoption of lecturing in some classes. Only 18 percent of alumni felt that having a forced curve undermined the school's teaching objectives. This contrasted sharply, of course, with the overwhelmingly negative student view of our grading policy demonstrated in the recent *Harbus* poll.

More interesting to me was the survey of the student body and its attitudes, which was overseen by Sam Lubbock, our Ethics professor. Lubbock's group had polled the classes of '92 and '93 extensively, and had also conducted several student and faculty focus groups. When asked to rank order their reasons for coming to HBS, no fewer than 55 percent of students placed "reputation" at the very top of the list. Roughly 80 percent listed it among their top three criteria. "Quality of faculty" was among the top three factors for only 10 percent of students, while the venerable "case method" was up there for a mere 27 percent.

I found Lubbock's discussion of the student body's ongoing evolution to be particularly compelling. It included a comparison of the classes of '92 and '65. Whereas the earlier class pulled roughly two thirds of its students directly from college (32 percent) or the military (30 percent), by the time the '92s arrived, those avenues accounted for 0 percent and 4 percent of incoming students respectively. Meanwhile, the proportion of women had grown from 2 percent to 28 percent, and of minorities from 1 percent to 15 percent.

The representative from the Learning Environment committee spoke with unusual frankness. He acknowledged that there was a "universal view" among students and faculty that communications skills, while critically important, were inadequately taught at HBS. Also, a "vast majority" of faculty found the section size too large. A subject on which he contended there was no clear consensus was the grading system, although he conceded that students were "clearly dissatisfied" with the quality and quantity of feedback they got. The speaker concluded by saying that HBS had developed an "undesirable resistance to change." To the extent that the first-year curriculum would be revised, it should happen in a "clean slate" manner, rather than through rounds of incremental adjustments.

The student body's appraisal of the committees' findings was a pleasant and unexpected display of comradeliness from our normally aloof administration. However, it soon became clear that this uncharacteristic bout of *glasnost* had its limits. When a woman from *The Harbus* requested paper copies of the presentation's data-rich overhead slides, she was flatly denied. The findings, it was implied, were of no concern to the 1500-odd students who didn't happen to attend the meeting. After considerable prodding, an administration representative reluctantly agreed to review the statistics that the *Harbus* reporter had managed to write down during the presentations. Errors in these frantic scribblings would be pointed out, but *not* corrected.

As soon as the Leadership and Learning presentation ended, Rick hustled me out of Burden. A lecture on capital markets in the developing world was about to start in Aldrich, and he was eager to get to it on time. Rick's enthusiasm for punctuality stemmed from his summer job interests, which by now lay largely on Wall Street. This new obsession was a product, oddly enough, of Harvard's assigned seating policy. He sat between two investment bankers in class, and they had long since turned him into an aficionado of *The Wall Street Journal*'s C (or Money and Investing) section. "I especially like the credit markets report," he said to me once. "I'm getting pretty good at predicting how different economic indicators will impact the bond markets. It's fun; it appeals to my quantitative side."

Intriguing as he also found "tombstones" announcing deals, articles on M&A transactions, and other murmurs of high finance in those pages, Rick wasn't much attracted by the investment banking side of Wall Street. He didn't want to make the lifestyle sacrifices I-banking required, and didn't think he'd enjoy managing client relationships in a service industry. This had led him to think very seriously about Sales & Trading. Particularly trading.

We got to the lecture right on time, and found two empty seats right next to Carter. The presenter, a senior banker from J. P. Morgan, discussed the process of underwriting debt and equity in Latin America and Eastern Europe. While not explicitly a recruiting pitch, it definitely made me wish I'd sent a résumé to J. P. Morgan. The bank, it seemed, could provide a rare opportunity to work in a top-flight, Western professional setting in a variety of emerging economies.

J. P. Morgan was an interesting institution for other reasons as well. It was the first commercial bank to gain equity underwriting powers since the Glass-Steagall Act of 1933 severed the realms of commercial and investment banking. Other institutions, notably Banker's Trust, were expected to follow this lead, but for now, Morgan was the only game in town. The bank was also said to take a long-term, almost nurturing approach toward its human resources. While some Wall Street firms were said to burn out their employees and then show them the door, Morgan was said to place a sincere emphasis on personal and professional development.

After the lecture, Rick and I chatted briefly with Carter, who was by now fully focused on investment banking in his summer job search. He was particularly drawn by J. P. Morgan, as they had a strong presence in Latin America. Carter had focused upon Spanish and Latin American studies as an undergraduate, and liked the idea of merging his professional and academic interests.

I went by my mailbox after the lecture, where I was astonished to find an invitation to dine with J. P. Morgan on Wednesday night. Could this mean it wasn't too late to apply for a summer position with them? I called their recruiting office, accepted the dinner invitation, and was told to go ahead and send in a résumé for consideration. The Gold List only mentioned positions in Corporate Finance, but the woman I spoke to said they had a Sales & Trading summer program as well. Without thinking much about it, I addressed my cover letter to the Sales & Trading group. This later proved to be an unfortunate mistake.

Another piece of recruiting excitement came later that night when I was flipping through the *10-K*. This newsletter was our weekly update from the career center. That week, twenty-one new companies and divisions had signed up to recruit summer interns at HBS. Among them was Fireworks Partners. I had read about Fireworks in *The Wall Street Journal* only a few days before. It was a venture-capital-like group recently set up by IBM to oversee its multimedia-related operations. Fireworks was also mandated to acquire independent multimedia companies, nurture them, and eventually take them public. It was hard to imagine a more interesting setting for someone interested in emerging technologies, and I was astounded that the group was coming to campus. Please, just give me an interview, I thought as I typed up a cover letter.

The recruiting rush continued throughout the next day and into the evening. William Simmons, who was the section's official Finance Club representative, arranged a small lunch at Kresge for people planning to interview for Corporate Finance jobs. Perhaps a half dozen of the section's former bankers spoke informally about the industry and their personal work experiences. Several of us came to ask the questions we felt too foolish to pose directly to recruiters.

I spent much of the afternoon plowing through a week's worth of *The Wall Street Journal*, flagging articles about the companies I hoped to interview with and their industries. I was attuned as ever to pieces about multimedia and Silicon Valley. But I also started to focus on finance, as Wall Street interviewers were known to probe candidates' knowledge about conditions in the markets. A former banker once explained the logic behind this practice to me. "If a banker's interviewing someone who can give a knowledgeable summary of what the Long Bond is up to, he'll figure that person has a certain passion for the market, and knows how demanding Wall Street life can be. But if he comes across someone who doesn't even know what the Long Bond is, he'll figure the person's just dallying, and would be better off working for McKinsey."

I clipped some good articles on the rallying bond market and the potentially overvalued equity market. And of course, I focused a good deal of attention on the notorious Long Bond (shorthand for the thirty-year U.S. government treasury bond). All of this helped me feel prepared and confident when I headed out to the J. P. Morgan dinner that night.

As it turned out, my afternoon's research had little relevance to the evening's chatter. True to their balanced, "renaissance" image, none of the Morgan people were inclined to spend a whole evening discussing government securities. Conversation at our dinner table ranged from Japanese literature to Kenyan politics, and the people I met from the bank struck me as affable, outgoing and fun. I managed to talk to two people from the bank's Emerging Markets group that night. These conversations left me convinced that their department would be a terrific place to work. Halfway through the dinner, I began to worry that I'd sent my résumé to the wrong group, as it seemed the Emerging Markets people drew more on the Corporate Finance summer interns than their counterparts in

Sales & Trading. I expressed my concern about this to a few
Morganites, but was assured that my résumé would get into the
proper hands.

The next afternoon I continued with my interview preparation at a Finance Club-sponsored seminar on "How to Interview
for a Job in Investment Banking." Presenting were the recruiting coordinators from Merrill Lynch and J. P. Morgan. Both
of them held MBAs, had entered their respective companies
through the Corporate Finance path, and had later shifted over
to recruiting. This made them very familiar with both sides of
the MBA recruiting coin, which gave their presentation a well-
balanced perspective.

Their bottom line was that we had better know plenty about
Wall Street before interviews started. Know the markets, they
urged us. Know the trends. *Be sure* to know the firm you're
talking to. Know its reputation. Know where it makes its money.
Know its strong coverage and functional groups. Understand
its culture. Be well-versed in its recent triumphs and tragedies.
But most importantly, demonstrate a clear job interest by having
an internally consistent job search. "If you're interviewing with
Salomon," the Merrill guy said, "you can bet they're gonna ask
you who else you're talking to." He smiled, warming to a joke.
"And if you tell them Dillon Read, Lehman Brothers, and
Brown Brothers Harriman, you're gonna look awfully unfo-
cused!" Everybody laughed warmly at the absurdity of doing
this. Meanwhile, I panicked. *I'm the only one here who didn't get
the punch line!* I thought. Hell Weekend was closing in fast, and
I had a lot of homework yet to do.

All this pre-Hell hoopla made it easy to lose sight of academics. But the start of our new classes luckily had shifted at
least some attention back to this important area. Finance moved
along steadily, if unspectacularly. The first couple of weeks
focused on various aspects of financial forecasting, and for now
it was hard to tell what Callahan was going to be like. Meanwhile,
BGIE got off to an exuberant start. Patterson was energetic and
had a good deal of experience with the course. The classes he
put together were refreshingly entertaining, but still drove
home the important points.

His course sought to examine political economies by using
some of the analytic tools we usually applied to companies.

What were a country's strategic objectives, and how did it pursue them? How did it mobilize and deploy resources? What were the underlying fundamentals of its financial state? The first case of the course discussed Japan at the time of the nineteenth-century Meiji Restoration. Later we shifted focus to the United States at the time of the Great Depression and the New Deal.

All told, the new classes amounted to a slightly more moderate workload than what we'd become accustomed to in the fall. Only Finance was on a par with Marketing and TOM in terms of the time it demanded. The textual portions of its cases were quite lengthy, and were invariably followed by pages and pages of numerical exhibits. HRM cases, by contrast, were "soft," interesting, and quick. BGIE and ME lay somewhere in the middle in terms of the time they required. I was grateful for the lightened load, as summer job research had become a hectic ongoing commitment. For the first time all year, my life seemed to maintain its frenetic pace straight through the weekend.

One night, Gary showed up at study group with a pronounced limp. He had blown out his knee playing basketball that afternoon, and spent much of the day seeking treatment from Harvard's Soviet-style health care system. Afflictions like his were increasingly common. Intramural basketball had started, and competition was fierce. Most sections (both first- and second-year) fielded teams in all three skill-graded leagues.

"So how's the Ministry of Health?" Spencer greeted him.

"Mobbed. Like a little HBS outpost in Cambridge." Clearly, Gary wasn't the day's only casualty. "The nurse I talked to said something like half the cases they treat over there are B-school sports injuries."

I had heard this grim statistic before. If accurate, it was awfully impressive, as we only accounted for perhaps 15 percent of Harvard's total student population. And the indications were that it was all too accurate. By now, Spencer and I were the only people in our study group who had emerged from five months of Shad completely unscathed. A guy in my suite had been walking around in a monstrous leg cast for months. And our classroom's Sky Deck had started to look like an infirmary. Two guys up there had recently careened into each other on the basketball court. One could no longer open his right eye, the other was missing his front teeth. Another Sky Decker had been in a neck brace for days.

"We've gotta realize, we're not a bunch of college kids any-more," Spencer, 26, observed wearily.

"Yeah, I know, we're gettin' to be old men," agreed Gary, 27. "But we have to release stress somehow. This Hell Weekend stuff's been getting to people."

Release stress? I hoped this wasn't really behind all the physical damage on the court. If it was, we were in for a blood bath in about a month.

14

THE GATHERING STORM

THE FORMAL PROCESS of signing up for on-campus interviews was to commence on February 8. A number of recruiters, notably the larger consulting firms and some of the Corporate Finance programs, would conduct their first-round interviews off campus. This technically left them free to ignore the on-campus schedule, but to do so would have been unwise. Because once interview sign-ups started, students' calendars would fill rapidly. Many would be hard-pressed to find time in their schedules for off-campus recruiters that failed to offer sign-ups before the eighth.

For this reason, it was widely assumed that most recruiters would mail out their interview invitations at the same approximate time. The school had designated Friday, January 29, as the last date by which this should be done. This made Monday, February 1, an anxious day indeed. That afternoon, I joined a solemn throng heading toward the dormitory mailboxes after classes ended. Much of the idle chatter that usually flowed in these corridors was absent. As we approached the end of the last hallway, faces froze and steps quickened. This is what it was like when we went to pick up the TOM midterm, I realized.

When I got to the mailroom, it was full of disgruntled people. "Not a bloody thing!" complained one man to nobody in particular.

"I'm still waiting for nine letters!" mourned a woman to her companion. Several other people were slowly shaking their heads as they sifted through their mail. I opened my box. There was a bank statement and a phone bill, but not a whisper from any of the recruiters I was still waiting to hear from. Invitations from Deloitte & Touche and Morgan Stanley had trickled in during the previous week, but responses from Apple, American Express, the Boston Consulting group, Fireworks Partners, J. P. Morgan, Salomon Brothers, Merck, Microsoft, and Sony were all AWOL. I imagined the stern directives the administration must have served these firms about getting invitations out on time. Perhaps our school was more tolerant of disobedience from recruiters than it was from its students.

The following morning, the HRM department treated the first-year class to some much-needed comic relief from the specter of empty mailboxes. At eight-forty, hundreds of us rallied in Shad's massive main gym for a long-touted "section effectiveness exercise." The sections had all been divided into teams of ten. We now had thirty-five minutes to build "towers" out of materials provided by our academic overseers. All of this was meant to "deepen [our] understanding of coordination and teamwork through direct experience."

Our team convened in Au Bon Pain before the Exercise began, and Samuel, our appointed chieftain, put forth an Action Plan. Some of us would separate materials. Others would strategize construction. Still others would specialize in Sub-Assembly. And as for Samuel, he would Lead. Jerry, who was also in our group, was not in the best of moods. "I'm not sure what I think about all this Northwestern crap," he muttered darkly. He was referring to the predilection of Kellogg, Northwestern's business school, toward team-focused high jinks like these.

In the middle of our squad's designated sector of the gymnasium was a grocery bag stuffed with paper cups, cardboard tubes, construction paper, and other miscellaneous clutter. A tower? The signal was given to start and we frantically set to work. Things immediately bogged down as ten fiercely independent people propounded conflicting visions of What To Do Next, but we eventually settled into Samuel's division of labor. The engineers puzzled over how to best make a tripod out of three cardboard tubes. A TOM star prototyped a few Sub-Assemblies and got the Sub Assemblers working. Meanwhile,

Jerry and I set to crafting tinsel chains out of paper clips. Our tower would be evaluated partly on its aesthetic merits, we reasoned, so somebody had to make decorations.

Many teams around us meshed miraculously, producing strange and wonderful monuments from their little bags of miscellany. One group crafted a colorful, flowing structure that looked to be straight from the imagination of Dr. Seuss. Another produced an elegant but sturdy latticework that thrusted defiantly toward the ceiling. Still another built a dainty Maypolelike construct that rocked gently but never fell. All we could manage was a sorry little runt of a tripod with a few styrofoam cups dangling precariously from its sides.

The panic finally set in when we had about five minutes to go. Where others had engineering marvels, we had a collection of cups, tubes, and paper, which had looked far more impressive when it was still in its grocery bag. Samuel tried valiantly to forge some consensus on how to make the damn thing *tall* before time ran out. Eventually we adopted the improbable strategy of slapping everything on top of each other and hoping it would stick. Tripod, Sub-Assemblies, and random bits of raw material were stapled, taped, and mangled into position. With about a minute to go, an unsightly multihued minaret suddenly took form in our midst.

With thirty seconds to go, it lurched sickeningly to the right. Three Sub Assemblers leapt to its aid. For a mad moment they struggled, hands thrusted upward, in an effort to save our crumbling magnum opus. But the strain was too much, and the slapdash framework rained down in fragments upon their heads. Jerry and I sullenly applied our handspun tinsel to the wreckage as the final seconds ticked away.

The unenviable chore of "selling" our handiwork now fell upon me and Martyna, an articulate veteran of the publishing industry. As "communications whizzes" (this unlikely handle falling on me, presumably, because of some occasional rambling contributions to *The Harbus*) we were chosen to argue our tower's merits to the section's evaluators. Much of the team faded sheepishly into the background as the judges approached. Martyna and I meanwhile tried hard to effect an air of smug satisfaction and accomplishment.

The evaluators arrived. Martyna began our pitch. "As you can see, our tower represents the decline of cities." The evaluators smiled and nodded, willing to maintain the polite fiction that the wreckage surrounding us was deliberately planned.

"Yeah," I added. "It's also symbolic of our opposition to . . . imperialism."

"Imperialism?"

"Sure," I continued unconvincingly. "Towers are triumphal structures, erected to commemorate imperial conquests. And they also symbolize, uh . . ."

"Male domination," Martyna finished.

"I see," said an evaluator. "Now, if you had to pick a single word to sum up this . . . *tower* and your experiences with it, what would it be?"

"Buffalo," Martyna deadpanned, referring to the team that two days before had suffered the most humiliating defeat in Super Bowl history. The evaluators nodded compassionately and moved on.

They must have appreciated our sense of humor, because the next day our tower was rated as the second-most "successful" in the section. This infuriated our rivals as much as it tickled us. But whimsical as our ranking may have been, there was a valid business lesson imbedded in it. Important as Engineering, Design, and even Sub-Assembly are, Marketing is sometimes king.

After the tower debacle, Carter and I hastened down to our mailboxes, where we were both greeted by a miserly pinch of junk mail. "This is absurd," Carter complained. Although most of the consulting and Sales & Trading recruiters had by now sent out invitations, few others had followed suit. Carter had submitted all of his résumés to the still-silent Corporate Finance community, and was by now sick of waiting on their responses. I was a bit calmer, having already gotten the nod from a few firms. But the sluggishness of the companies I hadn't heard from was getting to me as well.

As we were walking by the class pigeonhole rack a moment later, I was surprised to see a Federal Express envelope in mine. It was from S. G. Warburg, a London-based investment bank, and contained an invitation to interview with their Corporate Finance group. "What do you make of this?" I asked Carter, handing him the letter. "I didn't even send them a résumé!"

He looked it over and shrugged. "Maybe they like the fact you speak Arabic," he guessed. I later learned that several firms had unilaterally offered interviews to people who hadn't requested them. As with the previous months' dinner invitations, they apparently used the résumé books as a screen.

The next morning the cycle started afresh. Class. Lunch. Junk mail. Class. The ongoing lack of letters from recruiters frustrated and distracted me, enough so that I found it difficult to focus on BGIE in the afternoon. The day's subject was Herbert Hoover and the Great Depression. I would have normally found this interesting, and Patterson was doing a bangup job as usual. But I kept coming back to the same question: When am I going to hear from everybody? Interview sign-ups were less than a week away! As penance for my lack of focus, I idly penned a Hoover-related note.

Section I Hoover Challenge:

GET THAT HAND IN THE AIR!!!

1) *$2.50 to the first person to ask when this guy found the time to invent the vacuum cleaner.*
2) *$5.00 to the first person to ask how this guy had the energy to run the FBI for 30 years after being president.*
3) *$7.50 to all persons to discourse at length on any subject, provided that they say "Hubert Humphrey" at least three times instead of "Herbert Hoover."*

I sent my handiwork up to the Power Deck, where it elicited some stifled chuckles. I had lofted countless Challenges like this over the months, and had yet to be taken up on one. Today was no exception.

After the class ended, Carter and I resumed our griping about the silent recruiters. We were both particularly disappointed with J. P. Morgan, a company we had expected kinder treatment from. "How can they keep stringing us along like this?" Carter pondered rhetorically.

Fortunately, Jerry heard our complaining and came over. "Quit moping, boys," he greeted us. "If you want to know which interviews you got, just head over to the Career Development Office. A lot of companies have sent the school their lists of interviewees, and they're on file there." Somehow it wasn't surprising that Harvard found out where we had interviews before we did.

Carter and I trotted across campus. Sure enough, the office Jerry directed us to was buzzing with first-years who had learned of this new information source. We grabbed a bulky black binder containing interview lists. "Incredible," Carter fumed after we opened it. None of the leading Corporate Finance programs had sent their interviewing rosters. The news for me was regrettably more definitive. Lists from Apple, Microsoft, and Merck were in the binder, and my name appeared on none of them.

"Dude, you got dinged," Carter observed sympathetically. Dinged. This popular euphemism sounded less categorical than *rejected*, but it meant the same thing.

A few days later, the ding letter from Merck's Human Health Division arrived. It was an unintentionally humorous piece. "Unfortunately," lamented their manager of Economic Affairs, "we must inform you that we will not be able to pursue employment opportunities with you . . ." Pursue employment opportunities with *me*? I wondered if I should write to tell her that I wasn't hiring anybody. How humiliating, I sniffed haughtily. I've been dinged by an illiterate.

Difficult as I found it to get some of the interviews I wanted, and frustrated as Carter was with the investment banks' sluggishness, those who were set upon summer jobs in marketing faced far tougher roads than either of us. Because whereas McKinsey hired by the dozen, few consumer products' companies made more than one or two summer offers at HBS. This made the competition for those slots brutal.

Sandra was one person who knew this firsthand. Although her independent job search had already netted her one firm offer, she thought interviewing with some of the big consumer products' firms would be a valuable experience. "That idea proved to be very damaging to my ego," she confided to me over dinner one night, in tones of mock woe.

"I find it hard to believe that a mere industry could do much to rattle you, but let's hear the sob story," I replied.

"Well, these companies get swamped with letters and résumés from HBS students. I think they just burn them all, and choose their interviewees from the résumé book, because there is *no* correlation between the people who request marketing interviews and the ones who get them." I nodded, thinking of my own mysterious invitation from Warburg.

"So I guess when you're screening a book of 800 résumés for people to recruit into marketing, another Yalie from Wall Street doesn't tend to catch your eye."

Luckily, Sandra did have a few things to recommend her to the marketing firms. Her résumé emphasized the work she did in the consumer products' industry while at Morgan Stanley, and this got her interviews with two good companies. But although she had now cleared a daunting hurdle, a far higher one still separated her from a job offer. One of her two companies was said to be interviewing twenty-four students for one summer position. This was a grim statistic. Few consulting or investment banking firms boasted interviewee-to-offeree ratios even approaching 24–1.

Sandra was now doing what she could to improve these odds; she was watching lots of television. "They say these people always ask you about ads. And I've hardly seen anything but a couple of *Simpsons* episodes since August." Luckily for Sandra, the Marketing Club sponsored a sort of remedial ad clinic, in which a second-year discussed dozens of recent spots by major marketing companies.

By the day interview sign-ups began, I still had yet to hear from an upsettingly large group of companies. The Boston Consulting Group had responded favorably a few days earlier, but there hadn't been a peep from the others. It amazed me that some on-campus interviewers had yet to even fax the school a list of their interviewees. After all, a third of the first-year class would finish their sign-ups that afternoon. By then, many people would have no time left in their calendars on the heavy interview days.

Improbable as such scheduling gridlock may sound, it was an inevitable result of Hell Weekend's unique logistics. Although the winter recruiting season technically stretched into late March, virtually every major investment bank and consulting firm began interviewing on that first Friday or Saturday. My more energetic (and less focused) classmates had by now garnered more than a dozen invitations for those days. And since some recruiters (particularly consultants) had first-round interviews lasting upwards of two hours, the schedules of such people filled up quickly.

I personally thought that anyone who would begin Hell Weekend with sixteen back-to-back interviews was in need of counseling. And daunting as such a hectic first round could be, the prospects of actually doing well in it were potentially more frightening. Second-round interviews typically came in the latter half of Hell Weekend, and often lasted two hours or more. Time constraints could therefore force an overly committed interviewee to cut some firms from consideration after the first round.

Empowering as this may sound, it would be an uncomfortable process. You could go for glory, meet with all the prestigious firms that invited you to a second round, and potentially get rejected by all of them. Or you could conservatively go for less competitive jobs, and thereby forego interviews with some companies you're more interested in. Which was the wiser path? Gary from my study group seemed likely to face this dilemma. He had a résumé that wowed almost everyone who read it, and he now had over a dozen first-round interviews scheduled for Hell Weekend. All would be with consulting firms or financial institutions.

Thanks to a relatively restrained résumé-sending campaign (and several unwelcomed ding letters), my own schedule was less overwhelming than this. For now, I only had four companies scheduled for Friday and one each for Saturday, Sunday, and Monday. This would leave me plenty of time to slip off to Shad, even if things went well. While Jerry also had seven interviews coming up, he was nonetheless more focused than I was. Whereas my interviews were for jobs in four distinctly different fields, all of his were in one: management consulting.

Perhaps Rick was more focused than any of us. Now committed to the idea of getting a Sales & Trading job, he planned to skip the rest of Hell Weekend entirely. This approach, he realized, was almost dangerously narrow. Sales & Trading jobs were notoriously hard to come by, and most companies were said to prefer people with some sort of financial background. Still, Rick was confident. "Everybody tells me that the key thing they look for is focus. They want people who show enthusiasm for the capital markets, and who have been keeping abreast of them in their spare time. They'll definitely have that in me. And I don't think an engineering background can hurt when you're interviewing for a job with as big a quantitative side to it as trading." Rick also took heart in the fact that all six of the Sales & Trading programs he wrote to had offered him interviews.

Regrettably, Carter didn't generate such enthusiasm on Wall Street. A few days before, his mailbox was stuffed with ding letters from Goldman Sachs, Morgan Stanley, and J. P. Morgan. Although he secured interviews with Bankers Trust, Merrill Lynch, and other top firms, the unanimous rejection from his personal Big Three was bruising. I found it astonishing that somebody with so solid a background in commercial banking had fared this way.

"I think it might be the pedigree game," was Carter's best guess as to why this had happened. "Emory's a respectable school. Commercial banking's a respectable field. But face it, it's not like I came out of Princeton and McKinsey. I think the Goldmans and the Morgans of the world value those brand names a lot. And face it, they have to come up with *some* methodology for sorting through the résumés quickly; there's no way they can sit down with everyone who asks to interview with them."

As the Gold List/Hell Weekend job search rolled along, I was still struggling to keep my high tech search in gear. In the wake of the Microsoft and Apple dings, my only hope for an on-campus interview in this area was now IBM/Fireworks. I continued to ferret about in the Cole Room doing research, and began scheduling meals with friends and friends-of-friends who had worked in Silicon Valley.

Everybody I talked to was supportive and informative, and I soon had a long list of people to telephone out in California. Making these calls was a frustrating process. Many people didn't even return my calls, and those who did had the same story; we're not coming to Harvard this year, but you're welcome to come in and talk when you're next in the area. It seemed that while there were some possibilities out there, they weren't about to hop on a plane and come to Boston for my convenience.

Clearly it would be wise to visit California, but when? We had no days off until Hell Weekend. And while Hell Weekend itself was a four-day hiatus from classes, I would obviously be busy then. And if I got any offers during this period, I wouldn't have much time to make up my mind about them afterward. Harvard policy stipulated that recruiters could not require responses to their offers before March 22. So if I did well during Hell Weekend, I'd only have a couple of weeks to find my way out to Silicon Valley. This would be no easy feat, as we only had one business day free of classes during that interval. Even if I did fly to California for that sole day off, I would at best manage first-round interviews with two or perhaps three firms. And this would be a mere ten days before the Gold List response deadline. So basically, I had to:

a) Schedule interviews with appropriate managers at companies 3,000 miles away via friend-of-friend phone networking
b) Impress these managers enough in an hour or two to get a summer job offer, and
c) Persuade them to make a firm commitment to me in less than ten days

It didn't take the proverbial rocket scientist to figure out that this just wasn't going to happen.

The whole recruiting schedule was beginning to feel crazily claustrophobic. It's December. You figure, Hey, all these companies are coming to campus so I may as well talk to a couple of them. You casually submit some résumés. You're granted a few interviews. You do well over Hell Weekend. You get an offer from a respected consulting firm or I-Bank. And then you have three weeks to tell them yes or no. So what do you do? Throw away a $20,000 summer job for a *chance* at something in Silicon Valley (or the movie industry, or the World Bank, or wherever)? Right in the middle of an $80,000 run of living and tuition expenses? Unlikely.

This is called getting sucked in. But of course, it doesn't have to be the end of the story. Because you could always take the lucrative summer job, squirrel away some cash, and start your "real" hunt the following September. But then where are you? Say you took a summer job with a consulting firm which has now offered to pay your second-year tuition if you'll *just say yes* to coming back. They're also offering a healthy six-figure package, including bonuses. So what do you do? Toss it for a crack at Silicon Valley? Hollywood? Unlikely.

To be sure, there was nothing inherently bad about all this. On the contrary, it was an awesome, almost miraculous process that Harvard put together on our behalf every year. But still, this was one significant weekend coming up. And it wasn't just about summer job interviews. Certain companies almost never gave full-time (i.e., post-graduation) offers to people who didn't work for them either before business school or during the summer. Miss the boat with these folks over Hell Weekend, and you've probably missed it forever. And historical data indicated that almost a quarter of us would return to our summer employers after graduation. When you thought of how casually, almost randomly, many people landed in their summer jobs at business school, this was a frightening statistic. For hundreds of us, it seemed, a few short hours of poise and polish in February would set the stage for the next several years of our lives.

In light of all this, it would have been nice to have a chance to snoop about the non–Gold List world before the crazy rush of Hell Weekend. True, I could have theoretically done this over Christmas. But virtually nobody drafts high-priced summer employees six months in advance. And as for after Christmas, Harvard's schedule offered blessed little leeway for extracurricular snooping. Unless, of course, one was willing to *miss some classes*.

This very issue came up that week in HRM. We were discussing Pennsylvania Pharmaceuticals, a company that wasn't sure about how to deal with its first batch of newly hired Harvard MBAs. Somehow the issue of missing class for recruiting and job-hunting came up in the case discussion. Trumble immediately reminded us of our *moral obligation* to make it to every session of every class. And in case this wasn't convincing enough, she reintroduced the specter of docked grades for "unexcused" absences.

This abruptly reminded me of my conversation with the second-year on that train back to Boston after Columbus Day. Harvard, she had argued, tended to "funnel" people toward Gold List companies. Her words didn't really sway me at the time. After all, with our school's alumni network, name recognition, and well-stocked research rooms, it was difficult to imagine a more empowering place for the broad-minded job hunter. But as Trumble enunciated the Harvard party line for the umpteenth time, the second-year's arguments suddenly seemed very persuasive. Those people who were certain that they *didn't* want Gold List jobs were fine. They could use Hell Weekend and other recruiting-related days off to pursue off-campus job searches. And those who knew that they *did* want a Gold List job were even luckier. They could take their fourteen Hell

Weekend interviews and check out consulting, finance, marketing, or perhaps a dozen other industries.

But for those of us who weren't sure, who wished to explore both sides of the fence, the default value was almost sure to be the Gold List. Because if you came away from Hell Weekend with any appealing offer, you could only investigate alternatives to it at significant academic peril. After all, you had a *moral obligation* to come to class despite your professional aspirations. And HBS dealt sternly with the ethically bankrupt. "Funneled" again.

After class, I hit the Career Development Office to see if any new lists had arrived. It was tough to maneuver through the chaos of interview sign-ups to the shelf where the invitation rosters were filed. The only significant change was that the Salomon list was finally in, and my name was on it.

On my way out, I came across Hans, who was heading in. "Howdy Hansel," I greeted him. "Any interviews coming up?" I remembered that he wanted to work for a European industrial company, and was uninterested in most of the on-campus traffic.

"Why yes," was the unexpected response. "Bain, McKinsey, and BCG. All for Frankfurt or Munich offices."

"Whatever happened to Airbus and Volkswagen?" I asked.

Hans shifted uncomfortably on his feet. "Oh, they are most slow in responding to my queries. All the European industrial companies either don't write back, or insist that I fly out there at my own expense to interview. You know how difficult it is to miss classes for this." I nodded. I knew all too well. "But still, I am trying. And meanwhile it doesn't hurt just to interview with the consultants, does it?"

I nodded again, rather absently. *Meanwhile, it doesn't hurt just to interview with the consultants.* I knew a man on the verge of getting sucked in when I saw one.

Despite the pre-Hell panic, the section was still finding time for nonacademic pursuits. Perhaps the most significant of these was the mighty Sadhu Fund, the one which Sam Lubbock had inadvertently initiated by leaving his hundred dollars on the table at the end of our last Ethics class. As one of the section's prominent Save the World figures, Carter was helping to lead this charge. He launched two Sadhu committees, which he charged with defining the fund's mission and structure.

The core concept remained unaltered. The fund would be a permanent vehicle for keeping the section united and giving something back to the world after graduation. Our committees defined this concept more closely. Over the years, we would all strive to provide the fund with the material resources it needed to fulfill its mission. Meanwhile, any fund member who encountered a Sadhu in their lives could petition the fund on that Sadhu's behalf for financial help. A Sadhu could be any individual or organization needing skills or resources it was unable to obtain on its own.

The fund would also have an important nonfinancial side. Every several months, its directors would organize a newsletter in which people could write and update the section on their whereabouts and doings. This would serve to keep us connected as a group, a worthy cause in itself. It would also be a medium for alerting the section about Sadhus needing help. Jerry, for example, might become aware of a school in need of computers. If he put a message in the Sadhu newsletter, it might then catch the eye of somebody whose office was replacing its MIS system. The office's old computers could then be donated to the school, and there would be one less hungry Sadhu out there. The power of this network would theoretically increase with time as we spread out and rose in our careers and communities.

In the midst of these uplifting Sadhu-related developments, the gray reality of pre-Hell persisted. Sunday was Valentine's Day, a fine day for Carter and Sandra, but hardly a blip in the lives of the unpartnered. In honor of the occasion, *The Harbus* polled the student body on its "mating habits." Of the 66 percent of us who were neither married nor engaged, roughly 40 percent had dated another HBS student. The editors noted that twenty surveys were disregarded because of "exaggeration of information" (special apologies for this censorship were extended to "the prolific woman in Section H who reported having dated 90 people in her section and slept with 800 students at HBS"). Ours was among the least incestuous sections, as only 8 percent of us had dated a sectionmate (Carter and Sandra alone accounted for one quarter of this tally). Section F was the most self-sufficient, with 28 percent of its unmarried members reporting to have done this.

The survey also asked people about their "most romantic experience at HBS." Most responded with ironic angst. "I think somebody helped me on with my coat," wrote one unhappy person from Section H. "Building spread sheets, scraping the snow off the top of my car," reported another lonely soul. "Discussing a case in the moonlight on the way to Kresge for study group," wrote yet another. "Screwed by cases every night" wrote a fourth, perhaps on behalf of all of us.

Hell Weekend took further shape when classes resumed on Monday. I finally got my interviewing status from American Express (yes) and Sony (forget it, kid). This meant that only IBM's Fireworks Partners and J. P. Morgan remained silent. Fireworks didn't surprise me; their job description first appeared only a couple of weeks before, and they were probably still sifting through résumés. Besides, the unit had only been formed a few weeks ago, and surely still lacked formal mechanisms for dealing with recruiting.

As I was leaving Shad late that afternoon, I ran into Carter. "Dude," he greeted me, "did you get the Fireworks interview or what?"

I shook my head. "Still no word. I'll call 'em if it gets much later."

"Better check again," he advised me. "I just saw a guy from another section. He said they faxed their list in a couple of hours ago. The Career Development Office closes in five minutes, so you better hop."

I bolted off and got there moments before they locked the door. Sure enough, the Fireworks listing had just been filed. They were scheduled to come to campus on the Monday of Hell Weekend, and would speak with eight people. Robert Reid would not be one of them. *Come on!* I read the list twice; I definitely wasn't on it. Now what? My one chance at a high tech interview (and an awfully attractive one at that) was now gone, outathere, seeyabye. "I'm sorry, sir," came a voice over my shoulder as I flipped through some other job listings. "It's four-thirty and time for us to close." Four-thirty. There was something oddly familiar about that phrase. *Oh no—William!*

My buddy William Simmons had asked me and a few other people to help him work on a speech that afternoon, and I was now running late. The guy's energy level was an ongoing marvel to me. Like the rest of us, he was dealing with cases, classes, and the logistics of Hell Weekend. On top of all this, he was now running for president. In the past, the nominal leader of the student body had been selected by the General Affairs Council, a body of eighteen representatives from each of the first- and second-year sections. But this year, the Student Association President would be chosen by popular election for the first time, and William was one of four people who had thrown their hats in the ring. Tomorrow the candidates were scheduled to address the student body. William was now anxious for some coaching.

As I headed to our meeting place, I considered William's candidacy and its chances of success. One of his rivals was an editor at *The Harbus*. He had graduated Harvard College with William, and was, in fact, one of his better friends. Both of them were well-known and highly regarded around campus. The other two candidates both came from the same section, which probably meant trouble for them. With the vote cutting four ways, any candidate who couldn't count on the undivided support of at least his own section would be at an immediate disadvantage.

But how would people from the six sections that didn't produce candidates (or the second-years, who were also allowed to vote) differentiate the field? Unless you knew one of the guys well, you'd probably base your decision on one of the "candidate surveys" that ran in *The Harbus*, or on the campaign fliers that by now cluttered our pigeonholes. Most of this stuff was written in the generic Concerned Student Leader style we had seen since junior high school. One candidate, whom I had come to think of as Mr. Student Council, typified this approach. His writings in *The Harbus* included a presumptuous reference to his "future presidency," and his fliers consisted largely of his own name in massive type.

My editor friend from *The Harbus* would probably make an outstanding president, but suffered from campaign material that read too much like a management consulting job description:

As your President, my agenda will be to:
• Determine the CONTENT of what we want to voice
• Build a STRUCTURE as a conduit for our voice
• Turn content into ACTION

Or,

> I will create task forces comprised of students from all
> sections that will focus on issues and implementation
> each with a mandate to formulate an action plan within
> a short time frame.

The fourth guy, who was also from Mr. Student Council's section, was the election's logistics whiz. His pigeonhole propa-
ganda came in envelopes personalized with our names on the
front. More impressively, most people received letters written
in their native language. At least with the international crowd,
this guy would be a force to be reckoned with.

Of course I was biased, but I thought William's pre-election
publicity was nicely differentiated. He showed a refreshing willingness to confess to a less-than-omniscient understanding of
our complex world ("I do not have all the answers to all of the
problems that we have here at HBS. What I do have is an ear
to listen, a mind to understand, a voice to communicate, and a
will to act"). And in a *Harbus* piece, while others trumpeted that
they were "the founder and president of three small organizations," William listed a cascade of 22 things starting with the
letter L that he *liked*. Rather than coming off as a student government drone (perhaps an uncomfortable reminder of what
many of us had been in high school) William came off as, well,
William.

I arrived at the lounge in Morris Hall, William's dormitory.
The other members of the informal Committee to Elect William
Simmons SA president were already there. After we settled
down, William pulled out the notes to his speech and spoke.
His sonorous voice filled the room as he sermonized on what
was wrong with Harvard Business School. "So . . . how was it?"
he concluded sheepishly.

And so the workshop began. William took our constructive
criticism in stride, and vowed to have a truly stupendous speech
ready tomorrow. Throughout all this, I sensed that, for the first
time in perhaps decades, William was *slightly nervous*. After all,
tomorrow he would address a large and erudite crowd. Of
course, attendance at the speeches wasn't mandatory and there
was a small chance that some people wouldn't show up. Perhaps

there was even a large one. "Exactly how many people are you expecting?" I asked William.

"Oh, maybe five or six hundred," he replied, blanching somewhat at the thought.

The next afternoon, I showed up twenty minutes early to get a good seat in the auditorium. The place was still empty, so I had my pick. I sat on the aisle about ten rows from the stage; close enough that William could see me and take heart in the presence of a sectionmate, far enough back that his booming tenor wouldn't bowl me over. Five minutes later, a handful of people from Mr. Student Council's section showed up. They sat in the same row as me, perhaps twelve seats away. Ten minutes later, three or four more William supporters trickled in.

William's estimation of the audience's size turned out to be on the aggressive side. Five or six hundred? Not quite. In the end, roughly two dozen people chose to shun the unseasonably warm weather for an hour of SA presidential campaigning. Virtually every member of the sparse audience was fiercely partisan to one of the candidates, and on hand mainly to cheer loudly at the mention of his name. Clearly, no critical bloc of swing votes would be charmed by oratorical fire today. William spoke well, as did his rivals. Mr. Student Council one-upped the competition by bringing overhead slides and a sidekick to change them during his speech. But somehow, the whole event was a rather empty exercise.

After the speeches, I passed by my mailbox for the daily ritual and was treated to an unexpected surprise. Among the usual array of bills and junk mail was a slim envelope from IBM. I almost pitched it, not wishing to subject myself to yet another ding letter. But then I ripped it open (perhaps in search of a consolatory sense of grammatical superiority). I must have read it over three times. This was not a ding letter, but an invitation to interview! So what was the meaning of the list at the Career Development Office? The last time I read the letter, it struck me; this was an invitation to interview for a *full-time* position. My résumé evidently ended up in the second-year batch by mistake. The important thing was that the folks at Fireworks were willing to talk to me after all. I raced over to the Career Development Office. Sure enough, my name was there on the second-year list. A quick call to IBM straightened things out, and I was on the summer list.

The next day it was announced that William had narrowly beaten the *Harbus* editor in the election. The logistics whiz and Mr. Student Council finished further behind, having split their section. William carried most of the nonpartisan sections, as well as the second-year vote (although this latter achievement was perhaps less impressive than it sounds, as only twenty-eight second-years had bothered to vote at all). William was now the school's first popularly elected Student Association President.

While most of the section was thrilled about this, few of us had time to reflect on William's victory, let alone celebrate it. By now, most people's hands were plenty full with their own affairs. The real business of Harvard Business School was now upon us.

15

HELL

NOT SINCE THE night before the first TOM midterm had the campus seemed so withdrawn, hushed, and wound-up. It was the last Thursday in February, and in a few short hours, Hell Weekend would commence. The fortunate, focused, or care-free few who were blowing off the whole circus were by now gone for an extended weekend. This group consisted mainly of those who had already accepted offers to return to their pre-HBS employers or who were strictly pursuing off-campus opportunities.

Sandra was one of these fortunate people. Her only on-campus interviews would be with marketing firms, and none of them would take place for another week. So as the rest of us waited tensely by our phones for decisions from recruiters, she would be carefree and skiing in Vermont with some old college friends. Why didn't I decide to focus on marketing? I thought when she told me of this. Why?

Carter was less than pleased about Sandra's disappearance. "This isn't exactly the easiest weekend to deal with by yourself," he pouted. "It's not like Melissa's taking off for Vail and leaving Jerry behind."

"Come on," I admonished. "Melissa and Jerry are *married*. And remember, for better or worse, most of us are dealing with this one by ourselves too."

Carter was unswayed. "Well if I were Sandra, I wouldn't be off in another state having fun right now." But Carter was not Sandra. And Sandra was, indeed, in Vermont.

Back on campus, it was an evening of apprehension before the world's most concentrated corporate rush week. Classes had continued in a business-as-usual manner throughout the preceding days, although preparation levels had slipped noticeably. I personally logged my share of hours in the Cole Room in decidedly unacademic inquiry, which allowed for only the most cursory case preparation. Most of my research was focused on getting smart about the companies I would interview with.

Many people were far more assiduous in their interview preparations than this. Some of my classmates had by now gone through several "mock interviews." Certain preprofessional clubs, notably the Management Consulting and Marketing Clubs, offered these to their members. In them, a second-year veteran of the appropriate industry would play the role of inquisitor, and put first-years through rigorous simulations of Hell Weekend interviews.

By now all the companies I had requested interviews from had responded to me. The last to do this was J. P. Morgan's Global Markets group (the Sales & Trading unit to which I had submitted my résumé). The group's recruiting coordinator finally called late the night before and said that he wouldn't be able to make it up to Harvard after all. I was granted a first-round interview, but would have to go down to New York to have it.

When I called to set up an appointment, I was told that he would be available only mornings. It seemed that this would inevitably conflict with my classes, so I told the secretary that I'd have to call her back after my schedule had become clearer.

Despite this minor frustration, I felt good about my Hell Weekend schedule. All told, I was slated to meet with ten companies over the next six days. Hell Weekend proper only stretched from Friday to Monday (both of these days were free of classes), but a number of companies (including three that I planned to talk to) would begin interviews during the subsequent week. I had scheduled most companies at the earliest available hour and date. This left my afternoons and much of Saturday free for later-round interviews, if needed. This also meant that Friday would be particularly busy. I planned to meet with four companies on that day, beginning with the Boston Consulting Group at 8:15 A.M.

BCG had one of the longest first-round interviews of any company in the Hell Weekend roster. It would consist of three consecutive forty-five minute meetings with consultants from different offices. A number of people had expressed frustration about this little marathon. "What are they thinking, anyway?" pondered Jerry one morning. "I'm sure they can tell they don't want to hire certain people within five minutes of meeting them. When that happens, the rest of the interview must be a monumental waste of time for everybody. Over two hours! I've got a lot of stuff to schedule, and this doesn't make it any easier."

I understood Jerry's sentiments, but could see the situation from BCG's perspective. They screened tightly in granting interviews; a number of very sharp people had not been invited to meet with them at all. This may have made them confident that everyone who walked through the door was worth at least two hours of their time.

After my BCG interview, I was scheduled to meet with McKinsey, then Morgan Stanley's Sales & Trading group, and finally Salomon Brothers' Corporate Finance team. By the time this last interview wrapped up at 3:30, I'd probably be ready for a long nap, a couple of hours at Shad, and maybe a beer or four.

And now this whole marathon was less than twelve hours away. It seemed that the ideal preparation for it would be an uneventful evening and a full night's sleep. With this in mind, I quietly settled down with a book after dinner, feeling generally smug about my mature and relaxed attitude about Hell Weekend. I managed to maintain it for roughly twenty minutes.

Around eight-thirty, it occurred to me that I'd given next to no thought to what I was going to say tomorrow. I had been so caught up in considering what I wanted to *do* for the summer that this important subject had somehow fallen by the wayside. Astonished that I hadn't done so earlier, I picked up a copy of my résumé and started thinking through the issues it might raise in somebody's mind. Awright kid, what were you doing in Egypt for a year? What did Bain teach you about finance? Why did you run off to Poland? How many privatizations were you involved in there? I should be ready for questions like these; fumbling for answers would impress nobody.

After grilling myself in this manner for perhaps an hour, I considered the firms I was scheduled to talk to. What was McKinsey most likely to ask me? An obvious question came immediately to mind: Why would an ex-Bainie be interested in working at McKinsey? It wasn't hard to come up with an answer to this. Although there was a chance I would return to Bain long-term, it made no sense to spend the summer with a firm I already knew. It was better for both parties that I investigate other companies, and that Bain get to know other first-years. And because I enjoyed consulting and was seriously considering returning to it after graduation, it made sense to learn more about other consulting firms now.

I started conjuring up questions the other firms might ask. I found I was best prepared for the investment banks, as I had already given a good deal of thought to what interested me about their business and why. Besides, much of my research over the previous weeks had been in anticipation of the curve ball questions some of those guys were known to pitch. *Okay, kid. If you're so interested in Wall Street, tell me what the Long Bond's been doing lately?*

I had been warned that this question was almost sure to come up. And the thirty-year treasury bond was indeed up to some interesting antics. Bond markets had been rallying for weeks, driving prices on the thirty-year to record highs. Smug government officials portrayed this as a vote of confidence in their ability to manage the economy, as high bond prices indicated that the market anticipated low interest rates. Others argued this belied only a conviction that the administration would push the economy into a tailspin, as low interest rates often accompany recessions. I reviewed my collection of recent articles on the capital markets, nervously telling myself that no Long Bond question was going to catch me off guard.

The next morning was clear and cold. I donned the suit, shoes, and tie that I had laid out carefully the night before and hustled across the river. BCG recruiting would take place in the Charles Hotel, right off of Harvard Square. I checked my coat and went up to the suite that served as their command center. Outside of it was a long table staffed by administrators who took my name and handed me a small envelope. Inside it were four cards; three were short biographies of the people I would meet with that day, and the fourth was a summary of how BCG's recruiting process would proceed after the first round.

I entered the luxurious suite, which was half-full of first-years anxiously waiting to be paged. It was as if we were all at a plush dentist's office waiting to be called in for root canal work. The company had provided a generous spread of food and drink, but most of us assiduously avoided it, horrified by the thought of sullying new suits and starched shirts with fruit fragments or bagel crumbs. Every so often a BCG person would stroll in and take an interviewee away. Eventually one of their partners walked in looking for me.

As soon as we got squared away in the room he was using for interviews, he glanced through my résumé. "There's something I'm curious about," he said. I braced myself slightly. Bain vs. BCG? Privatization in Poland? Long Bond? I was ready for anything. "Tell me a bit about the virtual reality industry and where it's heading." The *what*? Then I remembered—at the top of my résumé was a half-line reference to my consulting project with the local VR company. The man sure had an eye for the unusual. So I told him about the company, some recent trends in the VR industry, how certain market segments were shaping up, and where it was all likely to lead. In retrospect, the question wasn't surprising. The guy's bio card said he was an engineer by training, with experience in both nuclear physics and software development. It was no wonder he found the subject of VR interesting.

Eventually we got started on the case portion of the interview, which was the part I had been looking forward to. Case interviews were a hallmark of strategic consulting firms, and I had been through my share of them as an undergrad. In one, the interviewer would present a business situation, usually from his or her own consulting experience, and ask the candidate to "solve" it. The interviewee would start by asking a series of probing questions, thereby developing the background needed to assess the problem. Based on the information so gleaned, he would develop an analysis of the situation and a series of recommendations for resolving it. Candidates were not expected to have prior expertise in the industry in question. In fact, it was preferred that they did not. Interviewers were interested in how people thought about things, not in their familiarity with whatever industry the case happened to concern.

The BCG partner drew a graph on a piece of paper. There was an X axis, a Y axis, a downward-sloping line, and four points clustered around it. "Okay," he started. "You're a general manager. These four points represent factories that you're responsible for. In five minutes, you have to allocate bonus money to the directors of each of them. This is all the information you have. Who gets the most money?".

I started asking questions. What did the X and Y axes represent? (fixed overhead cost per unit versus factory volume). Did this mean that the bigger factories had almost the same *total* fixed overhead as the smaller ones? (yes, well, somewhat . . . you tell me). Was the fixed overhead allocated by the corporate office, or was it under the control of the factory director? (under the director's control). Did the bigger factories tend to be older or newer than the smaller ones? (older). After a few minutes of this I realized that I wasn't looking at a "normal" graph, but rather a *logarithmic* graph. Point A wasn't plotted against Factory A's total volume, but rather the logarithm of its volume.

I had last been exposed to log and log-log graphs in Bain's training program, but that was a long time ago. This made the situation frustrating; I *knew* how to solve the thing, but it just wasn't coming to me. I floundered away unhappily until the interview ended, and left badly shaken up. I had expected that case interviews at HBS would be tougher than they were back in college, but this was ugly!

My next interview was with a woman from the company's Boston office. Her case concerned a company that made envelope-stuffing machines. Their sales had recently started to slip, and they called BCG in to help figure out why. One problem they faced was that they had no real idea of how big their market was, or what proportion of it they controlled. How could they get a handle on these important issues, and how could they redress the erosion of their sales? I took a crack at assessing the market size, then made some guesses about why sales were down. There were no log graphs, and I felt the session went much better than the first one.

I went back to the central suite to await my third interviewer. The minutes ticked by steadily. I was scheduled to go

in at 9:45, which would get me out just in time to make it to
McKinsey by 11:00. At 10:00, I was starting to get uncomfortable. I didn't want to cut this last interview short, but I simply
had to leave by 10:30. Soon it was 10:05. Then 10:10. The guy
finally strolled in at 10:15, having gone "slightly overtime" with
his previous candidate. Midmorning and they were already a
half hour behind schedule. This augured ill for their afternoon
appointments; I was silently grateful that I hadn't scheduled
mine for 3:00.

I told my interviewer that I had to leave on time, so we
jumped right in with a truncated case discussion. This one concerned a company that made frozen dinners, and was set in the
late eighties. The company had first entered the market a few
years earlier, intending to sell higher-quality meals at low-end
prices. Their strategy succeeded, and eventually forced the
other high-quality producers to cut prices. Competition was
now getting fierce, and it was increasingly difficult to win shelf
space in grocery stores. Meanwhile, a large health-oriented
niche market had emerged. The company asked BCG to assess
the new market's attractiveness.

I made a quick stab at analyzing the new segment's profit
margins, its growth prospects, and the synergies between it and
the areas in which the client already did business. It seemed
that the new segment's circumstances were remarkably similar
to those of the wider industry back when the client first started
making frozen meals. I suggested that a modified version of
their original entry strategy might therefore be effective. Because the new segment was also the only growth area in the
client's market, it seemed that they should proceed without
delay. The consultant told me that I'd done a good job, then let
me scramble out the door.

McKinsey was holding court in the Guest Quarters Hotel,
which was some distance away. I got there just in time.
McKinsey's operation was a marvel. Something in excess of 400
students were said to be interviewing for domestic postings with
them, as well as another 250 for international work. There was
some crossover, as a few people were in both tracks, but it was
clear that a substantial majority of our class was interviewing
here. To accommodate this demand, the firm had booked out
several of the hotel's expensive floors.

The first round consisted of two interviews, both a half

hour long. Like BCG, McKinsey had a Grand Central Suite serving as its waiting room and logistics center. It was positively humming with first-years and McKinseyites who came and went at a steady clip. The place reminded me more of an airport terminal than a dentist's office. At precisely eleven my interviewer, a consultant from the Los Angeles office, walked in. He explained that he would only talk through my résumé, and that my next interviewer would give me a case.

The first things he asked for were my GMAT scores and my undergraduate grade point average. "I know it's obnoxious to ask for this stuff," he apologized, "but we need a semi-objective standard from which to compare everybody." I gave him the numbers he needed, and we began on my résumé.

"So," he started, "tell me a bit about the virtual reality industry."

I talked through what was becoming a well-practiced VR rap. We then went on to discuss Poland, Bain, and Egypt. It was a fun and amiable chat, and I felt things were off to a good start. My interviewer had worked at BCG for a while, so he didn't see anything bizarre about an ex-Bainie talking to McKinsey. I asked him what he felt distinguished McKinsey from BCG and other consulting firms. "Probably the fact that it's really *one* firm worldwide," he answered. "BCG offices, and I think Bain offices as well, are fairly autonomous, and their cultures vary somewhat from location to location. But at McKinsey, you feel that anyone you talk to in the firm, whether they're from Saõ Paulo, Bombay, or San José, is coming from the same basic perspective."

The next guy I met with was from the San Francisco office. We spent most of our time working through a case, but like his colleague he couldn't resist asking a few questions about virtual reality. The case he presented concerned a certain newspaper agency, which was structured as an alliance between a small city's morning and evening papers. The agency was losing money. Why?

By the time the interview was over, I was reasonably sure that I had done alright on the case. I also really liked my interviewer, and he was from the office that interested me the most. San Francisco! I thought happily as I walked out. Great town. Great firm. Great office!

Down in the hotel lobby, I ran into a friend of mine who

was just arriving. He looked a little ashen-faced. "Hey," I said
cheerfully. "There's nothing to be worried about here. These
guys don't bite!"

"Oh, I'm not scared of McKinsey," he answered. "I'm just
a little shaken up from my Salomon interview. Those guys do."

Trouble. "What happened? Did they ask you about the
Long Bond?"

"The what? No no, not that. They wanted me to estimate
a reasonable hurdle rate for a new piece of equipment in a
Procter and Gamble factory. I don't even know what a hurdle
rate is!" With that, he made his way to the elevator.

Salomon, it seemed, was playing hard ball. But so far, it
sounded manageable. Long Bonds may have been stretching
my experience, but one of my projects at Bain had left me
familiar with hurdle rates. Bring 'em on, I thought.

My next interview was with Morgan Stanley's Sales & Trading group. It was held on campus, and was a decidedly understated affair. They were set up in a building next to one of
the first-year dorms. In contrast to the consultants' bustling
hospitality suites, they only had a modest reception area where
an administrator checked off names and dispatched interviewees to one of two rooms.

The guy I met with was low key and easy to talk with. We
chatted casually for about a half hour, mainly about the roots
of my interest in Sales & Trading. At the end of the interview
he threw out an unexpected question. "So, who do you think's
gonna win Best Picture at the Academy Awards?"

"Well . . . maybe *The Crying Game*," I answered, not sure of
where this was leading.

The guy nodded for a moment. "Yeah. Anyhow, I hope
we'll be in touch with you by Monday. Thanks for coming by."

I walked out a little perplexed. What was that all about?
Then I remembered; in the "personal" section of my résumé,
I indicated that I liked film. Maybe I struck this guy as a unidi-
mensional dork with imaginary outside interests, and he felt
compelled to check my credentials. I felt like the half hour went
well, but had no idea if I'd get called back. I had heard that the
Sales & Trading folks looked more for a personality fit than
anything else. I hope he liked *The Crying Game*, I thought.

I had about ten minutes to stroll over to the Salomon interview. When I got there, I found that the two people I was slated

to meet with were running late. Luckily Minouli, the associate I had now seen at a few Salomon functions, was on hand. We talked for a bit. Soon we were joined by Jack, the guy who had spent a summer at the company I later worked for in Warsaw. By now I was really getting to know these two, and I liked them quite a bit.

Eventually the door of my interviewing room flew open. A student dressed in a track suit and carrying a squash racquet skipped out, presumably late for an appointment at Shad. I looked down at my conservative suit and tie. Was I overdressed? I entered the room. This would be a "two-on-one" interview. Across from me were a man and a woman who were perhaps two years out of business school. "So Rob," started the woman. "We're going to begin with what's probably an odd question, but we're both curious about it. What's the deal with this virtual reality company?"

Once we had that formality straightened out, the man looked at his watch. "I guess we have about twenty minutes left," he said. "Why don't you tell us why you're interested in investment banking?"

Twenty minutes! This approach was unexpected but smart. The banks and consulting firms were always swamped with people interviewing just because it was the thing to do. By asking candidates for extended monologues on the appeal of investment banking, these two could figure out quickly who was genuinely interested in the field. The what-the-hell interviewee would lapse into an uncomfortable silence after a minute or two, while the true Wall Street aspirant would have to be cut off at the end of the time slot. Luckily, I had given this subject enough thought that I was able to babble about it at length.

I walked out sensing that I had done well. This was confirmed a few hours later when the woman I'd met with called to invite me to a second-round interview. It would last two and a half hours, and would be held in an off-campus hotel tomorrow. So far, so good, I thought. McKinsey and BCG weren't scheduled to call until Sunday, Morgan Stanley on Monday. So this would be the day's only feedback, and it was positive.

My next morning started early with Deloitte and Touche, which was off campus at yet another area hotel. As with McKinsey, I would have two half-hour interviews. But because the firm was "operational" rather than strategic in orientation, their interviews wouldn't be case-style. Instead, they would be in-depth discussions of my résumé and interests. My first interview was with a vice president who ranked highly in the firm's telecommunications practice. We talked at length about the convergence going on between this area and the media industry, a subject he had some interesting insights on. Our conversation confirmed my initial take on the firm. This was a group of bright, down-to-earth individuals who happened to consult for a living, but didn't let work devour their lives. I liked what I was seeing.

My next interview was with a particularly tough-minded vice president. She put me through a gauntlet that made my logarithmic debacle with BCG look like a walk in the park. She began by asking me where I'd like to be in ten years. I said I hoped to be involved in the converging media/high-tech/telecom industry. Ideally, I'd like to be working for a growing, medium-sized company at a fairly senior level.

Before I could finish painting this rosy little picture, she cut me off. "Deloitte and Touche is different from Bain in a lot of ways. One thing we really want from our people is long-term commitment. If you come to work with us now, in ten years you'll be on the verge of making partner and really adding some value to the firm. The last thing we need is someone who's just going to walk off at that point. So why should we hire you over somebody who knows they'll want to build a career with us?"

I pointed out, as tactfully as I could, that anybody who told her at my age that they were ready to commit to two decades with a firm they had yet to work a day for was full of it. She smiled at this. "Point well taken," she said, then moved on to the next startling subject. "So tell me, Rob, what's the worst thing about you?"

The *what*? Now this struck me as an obnoxious question, one that was hard to view as a sincere attempt to gauge my potential as a consultant. I stammered some lame story about how I could get overly focused on certain ideas or projects at the expense of living a balanced life. What did she want?

Not this, evidently. "Oh come on, Rob. If *that's* the worst thing about you, you must be some kind of a saint."

Saint Rob, I thought. Kinda funny ring to it, but the world'll get used to it.

She eventually let the issue rest, and we moved on to chat

about my work in Poland. At the end of the interview, she thanked me for my time and asked if I had any questions. Part of me harbored a shriveling hope that I still had a shot at a second-round interview. Be cool, it counseled; ask something innocuous and then leave. But the mischievous fourteen-year-old boy inside of me that I usually kept in check was lobbying fiercely for attention. "Say it!" it was all but hollering. "*C'mon, say it!*" Ah, what the hell!

"Tell me," I said, shifting slightly forward in my chair. "What's the worst thing about *you?*"

She smiled again. "Occasionally I'm a little too frank with people." We both laughed at this, and I headed out.

Deloitte and Touche had chartered a minivan to shuttle interviewees back and forth between campus. The other passengers on the ride home got a real kick out of my worst-thing-about-you story. Soon everyone was swapping tales about interviewing fiascoes.

For some reason, most of these involved investment banks. One woman told of a guy from her section who interviewed with a loutish trader from New York. "So tell me," the interviewer began, once he settled into his seat, "what separates you from the next asshole?"

The student, not missing a beat, gestured at the desk between them. "At this point, nothing but a table," he answered.

Another student told of a Latin American fellow who was particularly keen to land a job at a top investment bank. On Friday, he found this guy hanging his head in shock after an interview. The unhappy Latino looked up. "I told the man I like to play squash, so he asked me if I was an *aggressive* player or a *strategic* player. . . . I didn't know what to say, so I told him I was a strategic player!" Again he lowered his head in sorrow and confusion. "And I just can't figure it out. . . . Did I say the right thing?"

The day's funniest story concerned a guy who was, according to the woman who told us about him, one of the brightest people in her section. On Friday he walked into an interview he'd been looking forward to for weeks. The interviewer started by asking him why he was interested in the firm. The guy started in with a well-prepared answer. "Dillon Read is certainly *the* premier boutique firm, and I really want to work for a smaller bank. I like the fact that you guys still have a true partnership, as I intend to be a long-term employee of whatever firm I join. Also, your expertise in the energy industry is well-known, and this area interests me considerably." He spouted on for about five minutes more, detailing his enamoredness with Dillon Read.

Eventually the interviewer took pity on him. "I should probably tell you that you're interviewing with Kidder Peabody right now. I think Dillon Read's coming to campus tomorrow."

Hearing all of this before my Salomon interview was like listening to ghost stories before sleeping alone in a big creepy house. Imagine referring to an investment bank by the wrong name in an interview! You could bet that story would flit around the office for years. After lunch I headed across the river. *Salomon Brothers*, I reminded myself. *Salomon Brothers. Salomon Brothers. Salomon Brothers.*

Minouli and Jack were manning the hospitality suite when I arrived. This was no O'Hare-like hub for aspiring consultants; Salomon had already narrowed their field down to a little more than a dozen candidates. Minouli immediately escorted me to my first interview. It was with Stanton, the managing director I had dinner with so many months before. This was good; I enjoyed his company on that night, which made me comfortable talking to him now. His interviewing strategy was similar to that used by his colleagues on Friday. He asked me broad questions about my interest in Salomon and in banking, leaving me a long leash to demonstrate what I knew (and didn't know) about the industry. By the end of our meeting we were laughing and joking as we had at dinner, and I walked out feeling fine about the interview, Stanton, and Salomon Brothers in general.

The next interview was with two guys who asked me some résumé-oriented questions. It went pretty smoothly. The last was with a senior banker who headed up one of their Capital Markets groups. After studying my résumé for a moment, he looked up. "I'm sure you've heard that investment bankers are known for asking unusual questions in interviews," he began.

Here it comes, I thought excitedly.

"I'm hardly one to break tradition, so forgive me if I catch you off guard with this one."

The Long Bond, I thought. I'm ready for it!

"Tell me, in your opinion," he said as he set my résumé down, "what makes a successful company in the virtual reality business?"

So we discussed this and its (apparently quite fascinating) industry. Then we moved on to Salomon, Capital Markets, and my own interest in Finance. At the end of the interview he asked me if I had any questions for him.

By then there was only one thing left on my mind. "Tell me what you think of what the Long Bond's been up to lately," I said.

"The yields are going down, kid. Way down. You heard it here first. We'll call you by Monday."

That night I had dinner with some guys from the section in a dumpy restaurant off Harvard Square. Carter was flying a little low, as he'd already taken a few dings. And hell, he was lonely for Sandra. Jerry was in a great mood, as he'd already gotten more than one callback. The rest of us fell somewhere in the middle. It wasn't long before the Hell Weekend war stories began. Jerry started us off with a tale about a Boston-based consulting firm known for its internal scientific and technical expertise.

"You wouldn't believe it," he said. "I had a *four-hour* interview with those guys today." We all looked at him aghast. BCG was pushing it with two hours. Four was an outrage. But Jerry explained that the interview was this long because it was folded in with the company's national recruiting effort. Each year they picked one weekend in which they flew candidates from around the country to their Boston headquarters for a full set of interviews, and this weekend happened to be it. "They usually schedule the thing so it won't land on Hell Weekend, but they claim Harvard switched the dates on them this year," Jerry added.

This made better sense, but the format the firm used still sounded awfully silly. "It started out with a group interview," Jerry reported. "There was one partner sitting there interviewing five of us at once. It was the most moronic thing you ever saw. Everyone was trying to outposture everybody else."

"And what kind of questions were there?"

"Oh, real winners. He started by asking everyone to tell him something about themselves that wasn't on their résumé. People talked about all the likely stuff; backpacking around Asia, starting little companies in high school, that kind of thing."

We all chuckled. "So what did you tell him?" somebody asked.

"Well, by the time he got to me I'd already decided that

the whole thing was a farce. So I just stood up, said 'my favorite color is blue,' and sat down." This earned Jerry a hearty applause from us, but no job offer from his interviewers. This fortunately didn't worry him, as he was doing quite well in his interviews otherwise. No other firm had failed to call him back for a second round, and two already seemed on the verge of making him offers.

At that point, Rick chimed in with a story that explained something I'd seen the day before. "I heard of this one dude from another section who'd give anything for a job with Salomon," he started. "Their Corporate Finance side agreed to talk to him, and he was real excited. But for some reason, he thought his interview was on Saturday rather than Friday. So yesterday he was heading over to Shad for some squash, and happened to walk by the bulletin board with the master interviewing schedule on it. As he was passing by he glanced up, and realized that he was supposed to have met with Salomon that morning. He'd already missed his damn interview by four hours! So he ran over to where they were interviewing, told them he'd made a mistake, and begged for a second chance. They figured, what the hell, and talked to him. So the guy ended up with a second-round interview!" Everyone laughed at the guy's forgetfulness, cheered his gutsiness, and marveled at how it had paid off. The story, of course, had extra meaning for me, because this was the person who had interviewed immediately before I did.

Around that time, Hans walked in with a German fellow and an American that I vaguely knew. All three had already received their first job offers. Hans and the German guy both got positions with McKinsey in Europe. By now, I knew of several other European students with consulting offers on their home continent. European recruiting tended to be quick and concentrated, as the partners who conducted it had a long way to travel and couldn't afford much time away from work.

Hans sat down and explained the peculiarities of this fast and furious process to us. "With McKinsey, there were many non-HBS people interviewing," he told us. "In fact, I heard that every interested German from every major U.S. business school was brought to the Guest Quarters for interviews this weekend. There were also a few of us Austrians. Anyway, when you arrived there, you were given two interviews. After that, your two interviewers met to decide whether to give you a third one.

After the third interview, the three interviewers met to decide whether to give you a fourth one, and so on. If you made it through the fifth interview, they'd give you a job on the spot. BCG was similar; after three interviews they told you immediately whether you had a job."

The American guy with Hans told us that his offer came from Kidder Peabody, an investment bank. I idly wondered if my answering machine at home held similarly big news from Salomon. Although we happily congratulated our classmates, a certain tension settled on our dinner group. These guys already had offers. Where did that leave us?

When I got home, my message light was blinking frantically. I nervously hit the play button. No big news from Salomon, but there was surprising news from Deloitte & Touche. They wanted me in for a second-round interview tomorrow. It seemed my petulance with the New York partner was forgivable after all. Around eleven the phone rang and I pounced on it. It was McKinsey, calling a day ahead of schedule. Could I come in for a final round interview on Tuesday? "You bet," I said.

Sunday morning was yet another whirlwind, starting with Goldman Sachs's Sales & Trading group. Their setup was substantially more elaborate than Morgan Stanley's. There were perhaps seven or eight Goldmanites up from New York, and they even had one of the refreshment spreads I had come to associate with consulting firms. I was sent in to talk with two people from the Sales group. The guys were, well, salesmen. Smooth, polite, and gregarious, they gushed over my résumé and seemed fascinated by everything on it.

They did their best to show that they cared about *me*, not only as an *interviewee* but as a *person*, and not only as a *person*, but as *an HBS student with a newfound interest in finance*. They gave me a reading list. They invited me to a special dinner they would hold in Boston in April. Afterward, one of my interviewers introduced me to a senior banker from the London office ("with your background in Arabic, we may just want to point you in that direction"). He later sat me down with a guy who grew up in my hometown ("this fellow was Darien High School class of something-or-other. I'm sure you have some mutual friends.") I left my half-hour interview almost two hours later, rushing to make the microbus to Deloitte and Touche's site.

Of course, I had heard about the Goldman Sell before. The firm was said to take a canny, long-term view of every HBS student it came into contact with. Whoever wasn't chosen to become a Goldman employee, it was said, was deferentially viewed as a potential Goldman *client*. Recruiters therefore handled even the lowliest dingee with the utmost respect and care. Because years later, that person might have wealth to invest, bonds to issue, or a company to take public. And at that point they'd want him to remember Goldman fondly. Thus the reading lists, the special dinners in April, and the London handshakes that made us all feel so good.

Although one could argue that Goldman's approach had a certain tinge of insincerity to it, I appreciated the extra effort they went through. It was certainly preferable to the offhand treatment meted out by some firms. Job offer or no, I would surely come away from it all thinking of Goldman Sachs as a class act. And besides, the morning went so well! Still, I reminded myself, many people left Goldman interviews feeling as I did only to be dinged in the first round.

The Deloitte and Touche interview, a single hour-long session with two partners, went better still. We had a free-ranging conversation about consulting, my background, and Deloitte and Touche's strengths. Nobody asked me about the worst thing about me, and I walked out feeling terrific about the company. Early in the evening, one of the partners called back to extend me a summer offer. The shocker was the location; my offer wasn't from the San Francisco office as I had hoped, but rather from Detroit.

"Detroit?"

The partner chuckled. "There's always a bit of a pregnant pause when we mention that location to somebody. Let me tell you why we think you'd like it there." Detroit, he said, was one of the most highly regarded offices in the system. "The caliber of personnel there is second to none," the partner concluded. "We're sure you'll like the office, and urge you to give it your most serious consideration." He then told me that the firm would host a dinner on Monday night for its Harvard offerees. I told him I'd be there and thanked him for calling. After we hung up, I mulled this all over. *Deloitte in Detroit.* It had a certain ring to it.

As I was getting ready for bed, it struck me that I must

have gotten dinged by BCG. They had promised to call between one and three in the afternoon, and by now it was almost midnight. This wasn't much of a shock; the Log graph fiasco hardly constituted a formidable showing. But given that I had invested two solid hours in my interviews with them, I was surprised that they hadn't bothered to call with the bad news. After all, virtually every other consulting firm had done this for people they had dinged after half-hour interviews.

A number of people were grumbling about this very subject at breakfast the next morning. BCG had in fact, called finalists during the designated hours on Sunday, shunning the rest of us entirely. "Monitor, Booz-Allen, Bain, I've been dinged by the best of them," muttered one jilted student. "But BCG was the only one that couldn't be bothered to call and say no thanks." Jerry held his peace throughout this grousing. BCG had invited him to a second-round interview, and he was in no mood to bad-mouth the firm over a minor administrative policy.

Conversation at our table soon turned to more war stories about recruiting. But unfortunately, I didn't have time for them, as in a few hours, I would walk into what I fully expected to be the most interesting interview of the year. IBM's Fireworks group was in town, and I had homework to do. I went to my room and pored through my clipped articles on IBM, Fireworks, multimedia, and several other subjects. I wanted to be ready for any question they might throw at me.

As it turned out, I wasn't thrown many questions at all. Instead, my interviewer was happy just to let me prattle on about the multimedia world and IBM's place in it. At the end of our meeting, I asked how the recruiting process would unfold. "Well, we plan to move quite quickly," he answered. "You should hear from us in about three weeks."

"So will there be a second-round interview in Atlanta?"

My interviewer smiled briefly, as if amused by the thought. "I considered that, but who needs it? It's just for a summer job." Just a summer job. So this was it; after a half-hour interview, Big Blue was ready to pull up and shoot. Given a few weeks to mull things over, of course. The contrast between this approach and that of the hyperformal consultants and bankers couldn't have been starker, but what did I know? Maybe this was how technology companies worked.

When I got home, my message light was flashing again. Stanton, the managing director at Salomon, had called. My stomach fluttered a bit as I picked up the receiver to call back. *I really want to get this job*, I realized.

Stanton's secretary put me right through. "Rob! Glad you called back! Listen, I have some exciting news for you . . ."

The news was exciting indeed. I had an offer, and they wanted me to visit the office and meet some more people soon. I looked at my cluttered calendar. "How's Thursday afternoon? I can get down there after class. Maybe 3:00?"

"Perfect. I'll look forward to it."

After we hung up I looked at my calendar again. Maybe I could squeeze in that appointment with J. P. Morgan while I was down there. I called them up, but the secretary who set recruiting appointments for Global Markets was out to lunch. I left a message asking her to call back that afternoon. She didn't get around to it. I also didn't hear from Morgan Stanley or Goldman, which basically meant they had dropped me. This was disappointing. But with a Salomon offer in hand, I wasn't too worried.

Around eight o'clock, Jerry and I joined a carload of people heading over to the Deloitte and Touche dinner. There were perhaps twenty HBS offerees, down from the two hundred or so who had interviewed first round. The offers had come from cities across the country. At dinner they sat me next to a recent HBS grad who was now in his first year in Detroit. He was enthusiastic about the office, and said the city was a surprisingly nice place to live. I decided I should fly out and see for myself.

That night, Rick called to see how things were going. He congratulated me on my progress, and told me things were going well on his end too. Unlike me, he had heard back from the Sales & Trading groups at Goldman and Morgan. He would have second-round interviews with both of them during the coming week.

Hell Weekend was now officially over, but interviews continued to rage on after classes began on Tuesday. In fact, Tuesday was my busiest interviewing day so far. Immediately after Finance class I sat down with S. G. Warburg. Though prominent in Europe, the firm was a minor player in the United States, and I didn't imagine they had much of a training infrastructure for summer associates. For this reason, I doubted if I would find them as interesting as Salomon. Still, I was curious to find out why they had asked me to meet with them.

My interviewer glanced through my résumé. "So tell me," he began, "why are you here?"

"Actually, I was hoping you might answer that question for me," I said frankly. I explained how Warburg's interview invitation had come to me unsolicited.

The guy took a halfhearted stab at why his own Human Resources department might have singled me out, then proceeded with the usual questions about my background. Among them were a couple of oddballs. "Tell me something about yourself that you'd never want an interviewer to know," he asked me.

"I'm adopted," I said. Though I had never been shy about this fact, I figured it would seem personal enough to satisfy his nosiness.

He continued. "What's your biggest interest that falls completely beyond the realm of Wall Street?"

"Writing," I confessed recklessly, suspecting that the recent success of *Liar's Poker* would make a banker think twice about recruiting from the literati.

The only truly objectionable thing he asked about was my grades. Harvard had a clear rule on this; under no circumstances were recruiters to request grades from first-years, and under no circumstances were we to provide them. I politely reminded him of this, upon which he asked for some "alternative proof" of my sentience. I referred him to my GMAT scores and college grade-point average.

At the end of the interview he smiled and said I'd done well. For those who made the cut, the second round would start later that night, so I should try to keep my schedule flexible.

After a few minutes' rest, I headed back to the Guest Quarters for my final-round interview with McKinsey, a two-hour session. I got to the hotel and rode up to the familiar top-floor suite. The once-bustling room now verged on tranquillity, giving credence to the rumor that McKinsey had already culled its candidate pool by 80 percent.

My first two interviews were with partners from the West Coast, and seemed to go well. Both were dominated by case discussions. The first was about an aluminum smelting plant (thank God for TOM). The second concerned a real estate partnership. I liked both of my interviewers, and was impressed with what they told me about the firm's technology practice.

My third interviewer was another partner and followed a different format. "I'd like to tell you something about our summer hiring regime," he said after we exchanged the usual pleasantries. "A lot of firms give second-round offers. In other words, if a person they want to hire declines a job, they offer it to someone else from a pool of runner-up candidates."

I nodded. This was a common practice.

"But at McKinsey, we don't do this. If someone turns down a summer job with us it's gone; nobody else gets it." I nodded. *What was this guy saying?* The partner continued. "I have no idea how you did in your interviews today. But if you happened to do well, and if we happened to offer you a job, you may be more tempted than most people to turn it down. After all, you've already done consulting, and the idea of trying something new might be appealing." I considered this and realized he was right. Now that I had the green light from Salomon, the odds of my taking a summer consulting job had probably dropped.

The partner continued. "I don't want to interrogate you about the other things you're considering. But I would like to know more about your interest in McKinsey. Alumni of other consulting firms often interview with us in their first year of school. Many do this just to get to know us better. We encourage this, as it helps us to identify candidates for full-time recruiting the following year."

By now, the subtext of what he was saying was clear. Before they got to the point of assigning offers, they wanted to gauge how much people like me *really* wanted to spend the summer with McKinsey. Because if they gave a former consultant an offer he or she had no intention of actually taking, it would hurt both the firm and another student.

I thought about this briefly. If I did manage to get a McKinsey offer, how likely was I to accept it over Salomon? Not very, I realized. Deloitte and Touche was a somewhat different story, as working there would involve a new type of consulting (operational) in a new city. But McKinsey would be similar enough to Bain, and Salomon so different, that it had become unlikely that I would choose McKinsey if it became an alternative.

So I told the partner that I had an offer in investment banking that I was likely to choose over anything in strategic consulting. He nodded, saying he appreciated my candor. With that out of the way we chatted pleasantly for perhaps a half hour. He gave me his views on the firm, its different offices, and the practice areas that interested me. It was nice to discuss these things with the pressure of interviewing and needing to ask all the "right" questions now gone. I think it was a pleasant change of pace for him too. After all, my interview was held in the last scheduled time slot of McKinsey's fourth and final day at HBS, and he'd probably had enough of recruiting.

Moments after I got home, one of the McKinsey partners with whom I had interviewed called. He wanted to thank me for coming in, and also for being frank about my status in my last interview. He wished me luck on Wall Street or wherever I ended up, and said he looked forward to seeing me when full-time recruiting began in the fall. Now that's how recruiting should be handled, I thought as I hung up. McKinsey, like Goldman, was a real class act.

At that point, there were a number of messages backed up on my answering machine. Warburg had called, asking me to return to their interviewing post as soon as possible. One of my Goldman interviewers had also called, but didn't leave much of a message. It was nice to hear from him, but it was likely he had called just to say no thanks.

The last message was from BCG. It said that a certain Australian partner wanted to meet with me on either Wednesday or Thursday. This was odd, as I thought BCG had already contacted its finalist candidates (and ignored the rest of us) on Sunday. So why were they calling me two days later? Maybe somebody had canceled on their Aussie, and they wanted to fill the gap in his schedule with a second-round pick. They can wait, I thought. I had a busy night ahead of me. As I got up to leave, it occurred to me that I still hadn't heard from the administrator at J. P. Morgan. I swallowed my pride, called again, and left yet another message.

The early evening was another collage of interviews. I met briefly with a senior banker from Warburg, then went to my

American Express interview. The AMEX woman was terrific, but the job sounded a little too much like what I did in San Francisco. After my eye-opening interview with McKinsey, I realized that I probably shouldn't pursue it much further. When I got home there was a message from Warburg asking me to come back yet again, so I numbly went in for a third time. I finally started on the night's cases around ten. Around midnight I remembered the call from BCG, so I phoned in a message saying I could only meet with their Australian on Wednesday, as I would be in New York on Thursday.

Not surprisingly, the subject of interviews dominated the next day's lunchtime chatter. I sat down next to Sandra, who was looking happy and relaxed after her weekend of skiing. Somebody mentioned that between a third and a half of the people in our section had received offers by now. This, of course, made some of those who hadn't rather anxious. Carter was feeling particularly abused. He had already been through one last-round interview clear down in New York, but had missed the job by inches. The contrast between his frame of mind and Sandra's could hardly have been starker.

"Here comes the rocket scientist!" Sandra announced gleefully as William Simmons maneuvered his tray to an empty spot across from me. I looked up at him quizzically.

"Quite a comment in BGIE today, Rob," he boomed in a naked attempt to change the subject.

"We didn't have BGIE today, William. Exactly what qualifies you as a rocket scientist?"

"I meant HRM," William stammered, backpedaling furiously. "In which I liked your point. Your comment, that is."

"I didn't even raise my hand in HRM. Talk."

William grudgingly talked. Long enamored of England, he indicated an interest in McKinsey's European offices when he sent in his résumé. Fate smiled upon him, and on Friday he found himself opposite a partner from McKinsey's London office. He didn't quite click with the guy from the outset, and things really unraveled once the case started. The partner requested a tricky cash flow analysis, and William drew a blank. The guy kept pressing him on it, and William flailed away unhappily for perhaps a half hour.

The moment the interview ended, William left the Guest Quarters in a dark mood and sulked all the way back to campus.

When he got home, he loosened his tie, watched some TV, and started feeling better. But all the while he was plagued by the uneasy feeling that he'd forgotten something. Later that evening it dawned on him—he had been scheduled to have three interviews with different representatives of McKinsey Europe. He had skulked off after one. Somewhere deep in the Guest Quarters were two jilted McKinsey partners who would not soon forget his name. Oops.

When I got home from lunch, there was a message from BCG asking me to meet with their Australian partner on Thursday. I called the recruiting coordinator again and left another voicemail reminding her that I'd be in New York on that day.

Next I called Goldman. "Hello, Robert!!" my interviewer chirped merrily. "Do you mind if I put you on hold for just a second?" What could I say? The line went mute.

After a couple of minutes I started reading a BGIE case. After a few more he got on long enough to say "Just a moment, Robert." Again, the line went mute. The minutes resumed their march.

After a while I grew optimistic. Nobody would put you on hold for this long just to ding you, I thought. Particularly not on a long-distance call. He must have good news for me!

"I'm afraid I don't have very good news for you, Robert," my interviewer corrected me moments later. He gave me a nice consolation speech, rounding it out with the inevitable Sports Analogy. "Y'know what it's like, Robert? It's like that girl . . . Bonnie Blair." He paused meaningfully. Who the hell is Bonnie Blair? I pondered. "Do you know how much she beat that Chinese girl by in the Olympics?" I didn't dare guess. "Twenty-five one hundredths of a second! Three gold medals, and the total time she beat her by was *twenty-five one hundredths of a second!*" He paused again, allowing me to marvel at this. "And that's what it was like with Robert Reid. It was like the Olympics. It's not like somebody else got a *nine* . . . and Robert Reid got a *two*! No, it wasn't like that at all! It was more like Bonnie Blair . . . and that Chinese girl." I wondered if he realized that I hadn't even made it to the second round.

He reminded me of the dinner Goldman would host at HBS in April, advised me to spend time with the reading list he'd given me, invited me to call if I ever had any questions, and urged me to reapply next year, when they'd have far more spots to fill. Sure, the call was a trifle odd (especially the Bonnie Blair routine), but I appreciated it nonetheless. Few firms gave such earnest attention to candidates who got KO'd in the first round. Besides, my interviewer's warmth seemed genuine. And so what if he came off as being a touch eccentric? When you got right down to it, so did most of us.

That afternoon I came home to yet another call from BCG. Now the woman wanted me to come in at eleven Thursday morning, before my flight to New York. This represented a hopeless conflict with my classes, so I called back, and left a message saying that we were clearly at an impasse, but thanks anyway.

The next afternoon I flew to New York to visit Salomon. The trip went beautifully. I hung out with Minouli and Jack, by now my old friends, and also saw Stanton, the managing director I first met in September. They arranged for me to visit their Capital Markets group, and also introduced me to some industry-focused people. Among them was Roger, a senior banker who was extremely well-versed in interactive media.

The bank, he said, was particularly interested in the convergence between the media, telecommunications, and computer industries. They were on the verge of publishing an extraordinary research report on this subject, and might soon arrange a major conference for the industries' key players. If I came for the summer, he said, he'd do his best to arrange for us to work together. Salomon's starting to look good, I thought as I walked out of his office. I could learn about emerging technologies from this guru, learn about finance from everybody, spend a couple of months in New York, stay reasonably close to my family, hang out with the hundreds of first-years who would be in the city over the summer, and eat some great hot dogs.

Jack and another associate took me to an elaborate dinner early in the evening. As we glanced through our menus, the thunderheads gathered, the wind howled, and the rain splattered spitefully on the pavement outside. It was a truly black and tempestuous evening by the time the salads arrived. A quick call to the airport confirmed that the Boston shuttles were no longer chancing it. I was stranded. "A night in the Marriott! We better make it as painless as possible," counseled Jack, calling up another bottle of wine. By the time the dessert menus arrived, we were all punchy and animated. I asked the waiter to recommend something with chocolate, and he said the Statue of Liberty Chocolate Variation had plenty.

"Good lord," said Jack, looking at the menu. "At twenty bucks it better!" I glanced at the dessert's description. Twenty bucks, all right. The fine print beneath the price read "Without Statue: $10.00." Here was the clincher—this statue had to be seen. We ordered the complete Variation *avec statue*. The dessert came along with a fancy white box that could have concealed an umbrella. Inside was a tiny chocolate Statue of Liberty which measured perhaps three inches from torch to toe. I gazed in shock at this diminutive icon. Ten bucks! Only in New York.

The statue was my only luggage on the gritty-eyed six-thirty flight back to Boston the next morning. I could have slept in, attributed my absence to an Act of God, and perhaps even gotten away with my grades unscathed. But I didn't want to miss class, as today was our last session of HRM with Karen Trumble.

I knew that I would miss both the course and its professor. While sometimes dated, HRM cases loaned themselves well to generating excited discussion, and Trumble certainly knew how to make the most of them. While her class had gone well, Trumble hadn't always had an easy time with Section I. As our section chair, she had frequently been stuck between us and the administration; at times, an unpleasant position. As happens in all institutions, the higher powers at HBS at times handed down pronouncements that were unpopular with the rank and file. And as the messenger of these unhappy tidings, Trumble was often left dealing with a surly lot. But in the end she gave us a warm and memorable farewell speech. I was very happy to have made it back to Boston in time for it.

When HRM let out, the post–Hell-Weekend weekend was finally upon us. Free at last! Tomorrow would be the first class- and interview-free day in two weeks. I celebrated by placing one last call to J. P. Morgan. This time I finally caught the unreachable assistant at her desk. After some negotiating, she told me that someone could, in fact, meet with me on Tuesday afternoon. I decided to doublecheck on an important detail before hanging up. "Should I just save all my receipts and submit them to you after the trip?" I asked.

There was a long pause. "Sir, you'll have to pay for this yourself. We don't pay for people to fly down for first-round interviews." I looked at my expense report from the Salomon excursion. With plane, cabs, and my storm-induced hotel stay, it came to over $600, a king's ransom for a student. I thanked the woman for her help and declined the interview.

I paused for a moment after hanging up. It's over, I thought. Hell weekend is over! In many ways, this period had conformed closely to my expectations. But in a few important respects, it had diverged dramatically. A few months before, I had worried that employment decisions for many of us would be driven mainly by the allure of prestigious firms or industries. This concern now seemed to be unfounded. Few if any of my friends had approached Hell Weekend the way so many of us had approached job interviews during college. Those who had steered toward risk-averse paths like management consulting generally did so after seriously weighing many alternatives. Few were attracted to these fields solely for their elite aura.

To the extent that there was a de facto ziggurat of prestige associated with employers, it seemed to exist within industries as opposed to across them. Future consultants may have pursued McKinsey more eagerly than Arthur Andersen's consulting arm. But comparing McKinsey's snob appeal to that of a marketing firm like Nestle or a technology firm like Microsoft had become meaningless. Those of us who were prone to let our quest for peer approval influence our decisions were therefore less likely to get funneled into a specific industry, career path, and lifestyle. The Lemming March may have carried some of us along for years. But its worthy old soldiers were finally discovering forks in the road, pondering their choices, and going their separate ways.

It was hard to say exactly why this was happening. The fact that we were more mature and attuned to what was out there than we were as college seniors had something to do with it. The fact that our school had made us better aware of a multitude of companies and industries surely did as well. But perhaps even more important was the mix of people at school. The competitive quest for prestige that summoned so many of us to fields like consulting and investment banking spoke to a relatively homogeneous group back in college. Most of us were single, American, in our early twenties, and attending schools frequented by recruiters from MBA-dominated firms.

But married people, foreigners, and thirty-somethings all

formed substantial minorities at HBS, and hundreds of people had attended undergraduate schools where the likes of McKinsey and Morgan Stanley hadn't recruited. With so heterogeneous a group, it was unsurprising that a widely held consensus about which industries and employers were most attractive never emerged.

That night, a few dozen of us dragged Jerry and his wife Melissa to a microbrewery near the Fenway. He turned 31 that day, and we knew he was in a mood to go out. And a birthday wasn't the only thing he had to celebrate, as a few days before, he had received an offer from McKinsey, by now his first-choice company.

Around ten, we finished dinner and decided to head to a bar on the other side of town. By then the chilly Boston air was muffled in a snow that fell as thick as any I'd ever seen. Sandra, Hans, and I skidded hysterically across town in Hans's car before sliding to a halt near the Boston Common (Carter was not present, having decided, in Sandra's words, to "stay home and sulk" about his lack of a job offer). The far side of the street was but a distant, grainy blur. Hell Weekend and its aftermath slipped away beneath the night's ivory sheen as we forged our way into the shadows that somewhere concealed our friends.

16

DECOMPRESSION AND THE VACATION THAT WAS . . .

I PASSED THE balance of the weekend taking it slow and quietly gathering what remained of my wits. I didn't need the rest for what I had just been through so much as for what lay immediately ahead. With recruiting's fullest fury now spent, HBS was readying to unleash its heaviest academic blow since December. The next week would begin with three consecutive three-case days. These would be followed by a sixteen-day period featuring a midterm, two finals, eighteen cases, and the start of two entirely new courses. This little trial would end on March 22, the deadline by which many companies (Salomon and Deloitte & Touche included) wanted responses from their offerees.

During this hectic time, people with multiple summer offers would have to squeeze in visits to faraway offices before making their final decisions. People without offers would have to continue interviewing. People with offers but still considering other options would have to rush the completion of their job searches before the twenty-second. To reduce the strain of all this, HBS had scheduled precisely one day's respite in the form of a class-free "recruiting day." Other than that, our normal *moral obligation* to attend every class, every day would be in full effect.

Rick and I surveyed the previous and coming weeks' intensity over Sunday dinner. He had already landed one offer in a

Sales & Trading summer program, and now seemed on the
threshold of getting another one. He was pleased about this,
but was a little down about getting dinged by Goldman Sachs,
the firm that had initially interested him the most. We both
agreed that the best thing about Goldman recruiting was how
"personalized" their process was, clear through to the rejection
phase. "I really had a great conversation with my interviewer
when he called with his condolences," Rick said.

"Yeah, me too," I agreed.

"And you know, the guy had an interesting analogy for how
I did in the interviewing process. A bit corny, but interesting."

"What was that?" I asked, suddenly suspicious.

"He said it was like . . . the Olympics. You know, when the
difference between a gold and a silver medal is just a hundredth
of a second?"

Monday kicked off with Finance. For the past several
weeks, this course had lurched along at a steady, if at times
dreary pace. Our study of Financial Forecasting had flowed
into several cases on Financial Policy, which focused on capital
structures (i.e., the proportion of debt and equity used to finance a corporation's assets). This in turn led to a unit on
Financial Institutions and Financial Markets, which surveyed
some of the major players in the industry. Callahan was a very
competent teacher, but didn't spark a snappy section rapport
like Toddson, Patterson, and some of our other professors. She
also entered the classroom with a clear idea of which points she
wanted to cover and in what order. Those who strayed from
her agenda at times saw their comments shunted aside.

Callahan also rarely confined her cold calls to the opening
moments of class. This brought an element of danger and caprice to the classroom that we hadn't seen in the first semester.
On some days she would subpoena several students into the
discussion without provocation. People were often caught un-
awares, which yielded a good deal of embarrassed stammering.

After Finance, Carter and I sat down with William Simmons for lunch. By now, William was pondering a predictably
stellar set of job offers. Goldman Sachs. The Boston Consulting
Group. McKinsey. Ah, yes . . .

"McKinsey?" marveled Carter on hearing this tally. "I
swear, there's no justice!" After William forgot about those two

interviews with the London office, the smart money had been on him getting dinged by McKinsey worldwide.

"I should point out that McKinsey Europe removed me from consideration," William replied consolingly.

"Yeah, but McKinsey New York's part of the same company, and you got an offer from them!" Carter shook his head in grudging admiration. If anybody could pull off a stunt like William's London debacle and still get an offer, it was William himself. "Hell, I'll be lucky to get a lifeguarding job this summer!" Carter's list of dings had grown yet again, and he still had nothing to show for his efforts.

My own job search was not quite over. I still had to visit Deloitte and Touche in Detroit. And IBM's Fireworks group remained an unresolved possibility. At the end of the previous week I left a message with my Fireworks interviewer, indicating that I'd received two offers to which I had to respond soon. He called back and said I was still in the running but that no decisions had been made. With the March 22 response deadline now looming, I was anxious to get the final word.

Otherwise, recruiting was now over for me. I hadn't heard a thing from Warburg, a likely sign that they were no longer considering me. American Express was also no longer an issue, as I had declined a second-round interview with them.

As I was heading out of the cafeteria, I ran into Hans. "Congratulations on Hell Weekend," I greeted him. By now it was widely known that he had received offers from both McKinsey and Bain. "You must be very pleased."

"Yes, I am certainly happy," Hans replied unhappily. "But still, I feel perhaps guilty.

"What do you mean?"

"Well, look at the people in our section. Many of the brightest people, from the Americans I mean, did not manage to get the jobs they wanted. Now I have two attractive offers." I tried to tell him this was nonsense, that his notoriety had nothing to do with his job situation, but he pressed on. "Face it, it's easier to get one of these jobs if you're European. It's a question of supply and demand. Look at the consulting firms, for example. Their business, it booms in central Europe, particularly in Germany. They're crazy for people to staff those offices. And they can't take just anybody; they

need people with the MBA perspective, because that's the
nature of their work.

"Now look at the supply. How many native German speakers come out of HBS every year? Until a few years ago it was
maybe four or five Germans, with sometimes an Austrian or
Swiss. Now it's close to fifteen Germans. But look at McKinsey
and BCG, and how many German speakers they need. Then
you have the investment banks! You cannot deny, these are
truly favorable conditions. So it makes me most uncomfortable
when I look at people, Carter, for instance, who did not get the
jobs they sought, and may have had they merely been European."

I thought Hans was overstating the importance of national-
ity in the job search, as I knew several very capable Europeans
who emerged from Hell Weekend every bit as empty-handed
as Carter. Still, his point was well-taken. The consulting firms,
at least, had international recruiting processes that differed
substantially from their domestic counterparts. Perhaps this,
coupled with the supply-and-demand principle Hans had cited,
made it somewhat easier for Europeans to find work.

As Hans and I were chatting, Sandra came by to say hello.
She now had that hollow-eyed look the rest of us had sported
about a week before. The past few days had been the peak time
for marketing interviews, and Sandra had just been through
her own scaled-down version of recruiting hell. I asked her how
it went.

She shook her head sadly. "I'm getting the feeling that
some of those companies don't even *want* to hire first-years for
the summer."

"What makes you say that?" I asked.

"It's almost like they're going through the motions to maintain a presence for second-year recruiting. One company I
talked to made their hiring decision after *one* round of interviews. A twenty-five minute conversation!" She shook her head
again. "But I have to admit I'm biased. They didn't like me a
bit."

She fared better with Procter and Gamble. "Their interviews were actually pretty engaging," she reported. "They were
a lot like consulting interviews. In the first one, they told me to
imagine I was marketing detergent. R&D had developed a new
ingredient that would make clothes softer, and they wanted me

to say if I'd recommend adding it to a high-end, middle-end, or low-end brand. They weren't looking for a specific answer so much as for how I approached the problem. In my second-round interview they asked me how I'd strategize giving trade allowances for diapers. I choked on that one, and they didn't ask me back."

"Sounds like a tough couple of days," I said. "At least you had your faithful partner by your side to warm your tea and bring you your slippers after the marketing firms had beaten you up." This, of course, was a facetious reference to Carter's unhappiness about Sandra's absence during Hell Weekend.

"Who, Mr. Quid pro quo?" she answered. "I hardly saw him all weekend; he probably thought he was getting me back for abandoning him in his hour of need." The forcefulness of this response surprised me, and I decided not to press for details.

The next morning, several hundred of us crowded into Baker Library for the HRM exam. I arrived early, avoiding a repeat of my last-minute, musical chairs-like scramble for a seat before the Marketing final. The test's case concerned the plight of Dick Freeman, manager of a new factory in the Ball Bearing Division of his company. Dick was finding it tough to meet the ambitious production goals handed down to his infant plant from headquarters. How could he overcome this challenge without compromising the innovative *team concept* around which his workers were organized?

I worked steadily, barely leaving time to spell-check my essay before the exam period ended. As soon as my test was printed, I raced out to the cab stand behind campus. Friday would be the last class-free Recruiting Day of the month, and I was taking the opportunity to visit Deloitte and Touche's Detroit office. I reflected on the morning as the taxi zipped to the airport. It had been a long time since I felt so confident about my performance on a test. If I'd been out there with him, old Dick Freeman and I would have had ball bearings pouring out of that plant like water from an open hydrant! Had I known then of the HRM faculty's peculiar approach to scoring exams, I would have been a lot less confident about my results.

Deloitte and Touche's Detroit office was located in the Renaissance Center (The City Within a City, as my cabbie pointed out enthusiastically). I spent a very pleasant Friday there, meeting with perhaps a dozen consultants, managers, and partners. The overall caliber of personnel impressed me, as did the office's general ambiance. The people seemed very much at ease in their relationships with the company and one another. As my hard-nosed first-round interviewer had pointed out, this was a firm that *expected* people to work their way to the partner level. This may well have precluded much of the up-or-out politicking and one-upmanship that plagued more Darwinian organizations.

Compared to Salomon, Deloitte and Touche had many merits. The firm offered a saner work week, a more affordable metropolitan environment, and it paid a bit better. Still, I ultimately decided that taking their offer would not be the right thing to do. Because while Deloitte and Touche was certainly unlike Bain, Salomon was radically different. Working on Wall Street would expose me to a range of responsibilities, concepts, and personalities that were not found in any consulting operation. I had always felt this summer should be a time for experimentation, so experiment I would. When I got on the plane back to Logan, Salomon was definitely looking like my summer employer. But of course, there was still no word from Fireworks.

It was quiet when I got back to campus on Friday evening, as many people had cleared out for the three-day break. The rest of the weekend was so slow that our study group actually convened for the first time in weeks. Monday would be a big day, as it would see the start of the year's last two courses; Competition & Strategy (C&S), and Information, Organization & Control (IOC). IOC would focus on information management and its effects on businesses. C&S would focus on, well, competition and strategy. The first C&S case concerned Disney, Spencer's employer of three years. This inspired him to give the study group a twenty-minute lecturette which might even have proved enriching to the C&S faculty. The IOC case concerned Mrs. Fields Cookies, and their innovative information technology (IT) system.

IOC got off to a reasonable start. Our teacher, Priscilla MacIntyre, had been teaching the course and its forerunners since 1989. We discussed the central information system at Mrs. Fields, a system which did everything from telling the corporate office how much batter a certain store was using to estimating each day's sales based on weather patterns and other variables. The issues were interesting, but we covered them broadly rather than deeply. IOC looked like it would be a fun class, but one in which chip shots would proliferate.

The situation in C&S could not have contrasted more sharply. Our professor was Perry Cooperman, who, as the "course head" for C&S, had largely designed its curriculum. This guy was a true hard-liner. In his class, chip shots would be taboo, and absences the kiss of death. He made this second policy unmistakably clear on the first day of class. "If you have more than one unexcused absence in this class, you *will not* get a 1," he warned us sternly. "If you miss more than three classes, you *will not* get a 1 or a 2. At that point, the only possibilities will be a 3 or a 4."

As for chip shots, there was no specific numerical threshold separating a 1 from a 2 or a 3. But it was quickly apparent that any vapid observation in Cooperman's class invited disaster. Our other professors had tended to let most comments pass with a nod or a brief editorial aside. Cooperman wasn't like this. He was more likely to interrogate students after they'd made a point, pushing their analysis further, and gauging how deep their understanding of the case went. His style bordered on confrontational, and intimidated a number of people. Not surprisingly, the man was an instant controversy in Section I. Many students walked out of the first C&S class furious about his attitude and his modus operandi.

I walked out exhilarated. "This," I said to anyone who'd put up with my sermonizing, "is how classes here were meant to be taught!" During his first session, Cooperman simply crucified three of the section's most prolific chip shot kings, leaving all of us squirming and cautious. We would now have to think twice before tainting C&S classes with subtle rephrasings of the obvious, and this would ultimately be to everyone's benefit. Cooperman's hostility toward chip shots was fine by me.

I was less enthused about his intolerant absence policy. My main concern was that it amounted to an invitation to lie to him. Because like HBS itself, Cooperman was forced to allow a few exceptions to his radical stance; family emergencies and personal illnesses were officially acceptable reasons for missing his classes. But what would happen when a coveted summer job depended upon traveling to an interview on a day when C&S

was in session? When a student struggling through a personal crisis needed a day off to think? When somebody's best friend was in trouble and needed help? None of these were family emergencies or personal illnesses, but all were circumstances in which reasonable adults might conclude that their priorities lay beyond the walls of Aldrich Hall.

So what should you do if one of these circumstances arose? Invite a low grade in C&S and confess the truth about your plans? Or should you just . . . fib a little bit (Gosh, Professor Cooperman, I've got this really bad cold . . .)? Ideally, everyone's choice on this issue should have been strictly his or her own business. Moral absolutists should have told the truth, moral opportunists should have rationalized their fibbing away, and each choice should have ultimately been influenced only by the decision-maker's conscience.

Unfortunately, this is not how it works when there's a forced curve. By June, a subset of people in our section would inevitably miss two or more classes for "inexcusable" reasons. Those who told Cooperman the truth would become ineligible for top grades. Those who covered their absences with white lies would still be in the running. In short, the policy would favor the relatively dishonest. Could one fault those who would fib to subvert an uncompromising rule that might otherwise damage their academic standing? Of course not. But then should one punish those who retained their honesty, even in the face of such a rule? Of course not. To me, this paradox invalidated Cooperman's policy on absences.

Despite my dismay over this, I would have preferred a business school swarming with Coopermans to one devoid of them. After all, the man could teach, and that's what we were there for. The second C&S class was at least as impressive as the first. In it, we examined the semiconductor industry. Much of our discussion focused on Intel, the microprocessor magnate. Intel's ongoing dominance of its fluid and fast-growing industry was a marvel to many, and was achieved partly through its faithfulness to a superior business strategy. As a member of that company's board of directors, Cooperman was particularly well-suited to teach the case.

Discussion was enlivened further by his continued probing into the analysis of anyone who raised a point in class. Intimidating as this grilling could be, I still thought Cooperman's approach was the best of any of our professors to date. He elicited thoughtful and penetrating discussions, and kept the self-absorbed tedium of chip shots at bay.

After class I passed by my pigeonhole, where I found a memo from The Bahama Mamas. This was the collective appellation of the female contingent of my spring break group. Fourteen of us from eight different sections were scheduled to spend the first week of April on Harbour Island, an idyllic speck of land in the Bahamas. The Mamas' communiqué was a collection of thoughts on our upcoming adventure:

THINGS TO BRING (MEN)

Plenty of chapstick to keep those lips soft for kissing—NOT!!

Sequined thongs for performances on the beach—DOUBLE NOT!

Alarm clocks to wake up and make breakfast for Bahama Mamas.

Also in the memo:

THE BAHAMA MAMAS DEMAND OF OUR DUDES:

Biceps bulging, stomachs that we can do our ironing on, thighs tight, calves bulging. Egos checked at Logan.

This missive was a retaliation to an earlier memo sent by one of the Harbour Island men:

The following workout is recommended for the women:
• Abdominals, every day
• Thighs and buttocks, every day
• Leg adductors and abductors, alternate days.

To appease those of you frothing with feminist indignation, let me assure you that the men will be diligently applying themselves to a demanding pretrip regimen of curls (12–16 oz., no more than 20 reps per day).

Harbour Island still seemed remote, but would certainly be something to look forward to during the upcoming flurry of exams. At least it seemed that everyone aboard had a sense of humor.

The next evening, the campus was hushed as the first-year class prepared for its long-awaited BGIE midterm. Throughout the day, innumerable conversations centered on the question of what country the exam's case would concern. At lunch I was told, on the grounds of strictest confidence, that it would be Indonesia. My informant darkly requested that I not ask how he knew this. Over dinner I learned that the test would actually concern the Ukraine. Several other rival candidates surfaced that evening, including Bolivia (where Harvard economist Jeffrey Sachs had done some work), Egypt (where a great deal of foreign debt was recently forgiven as a result of the Gulf War), and Finland (the Western economy perhaps most damaged by the Soviet collapse). At least one person swore that Australia would be the subject of the exam, while several others argued energetically for Mexico, Nigeria, and Morocco.

Right before I went to bed, two fellow McCulloch residents informed me that the test would surely be on Venezuela. Every few days, they said, some bureaucrat went through Baker Library withdrawing country background packages from circulation. Countries featured in the following week's BGIE curriculum were always banished from Baker in this manner. This, my neighbors said, was done to prevent overly diligent students from getting an *unfair advantage* in class participation by reading these files. A friend of theirs was Venezuelan. That afternoon he had visited Baker to check up on the homeland, and discovered that his country's packet was absent from the stacks. There was no doubt about it, they told me solemnly. It would be Venezuela.

Nobody warned me to expect a test on Singapore, but this was the subject of the next morning's exam (we had a case on Venezuela right after the midterm; had my would-be informants looked a page or two ahead in the syllabus, they would have realized that this was the cause of the Baker information pack's abduction). The case was long; fifteen pages of text and twelve lengthy numerical exhibits. We were asked to assess the effectiveness of the country's national strategy, and to write out some advice for its new leaders. The case was a comprehensive and quite intricate discussion of Singapore's political economy, and it left me feeling truly stymied. The idea of opening a discussion about it in class would have been daunting enough; writing a four-hour essay about it was a dizzying prospect.

As soon as the exam was over, several of us adjourned to the Samuel Adams brewery. The company's founder was an HBS alum, and agreed to take Section I on a tour of his Boston facilities. During the drive over I finally made up my mind; it would be Salomon for the summer after all. When I last spoke to him, my contact at Fireworks said he still needed some "necessary approvals" before he would be able to make a final decision. Intriguing as his group sounded, I was by now aching to resolve my summer plans. It was time to let go of Fireworks.

But more importantly, I was by now quite excited about the experience Salomon was offering. As soon as we got to the brewery, I found a phone and called my buddy Minouli. He was glad to hear the news, and promised to spread it to the appropriate parties. Meanwhile, he advised me to enjoy the tour and the product at Samuel Adams while I could. It would be a busy summer.

I practically skipped through the facility to catch up with the section. I finally had summer plans, and was bursting to tell the first person I saw. This turned out to be Hans.

"Well, congratulations," he said. "I only just now made a similar decision." He had accepted McKinsey's offer in Frankfurt.

I knew that Hans had been holding off on committing for a while. He had long hoped to get a job with a European industrial company, something he only gave up on the day before. "Here it is late March and nobody's even given me a real opportunity to interview," he lamented. "Meanwhile I have this crazy American tuition bill, and McKinsey will pay me well to spend the summer with them. What else can one do?" But he had not exactly resigned himself to his fate unhappily. "I think it will be a lot of fun working for McKinsey," he acknowledged. "I will learn many things, and may even like it enough to go back to after second-year."

By now most (but by no means all) of my classmates had also received and accepted summer job offers. To investigate this subject, *The Harbus* had recently polled a representative sample of 164 students. 75 percent of those surveyed had participated in Hell Weekend recruiting, and 60 percent now had summer jobs, with average weekly salaries in the $1,500–$1,750 range. On the extremes of the salary spectrum were three students who had taken jobs paying under $500 per week and five who would earn over $2,000 per week. Despite isolated grumbling about "quotas" in hiring, a regression analysis of the survey data showed no apparent correlation between gender, race, and success in the job market (although the article's writers presented their findings with the jaded, ME-induced caveat that "you can take our model—like all statistics—with a grain of salt"). The only people who may have been slightly favored in the recruiting process were international students, as a slightly higher percentage of this group already had summer offers.

A few disturbing trends were revealed by the survey. A full 25 percent of respondents had encountered interviewers who had inquired directly about grades, despite HBS's explicit prohibition of this. Some of the worst offenders in this area were reported to be Morgan Stanley, Lehman Brothers, and (not surprisingly, given my own experiences) S. G. Warburg. More distressing, no fewer than 14 percent of students admitted to having lied during the interviewing process. Some of these untruths were perhaps innocuous fibs (one respondent wrote that his lie was saying that he had "loved" his old job). But still, this statistic indicated that scores of people had deliberately misrepresented themselves in the interviewing process.

By now we only had one exam (and one more printing fiasco) to go before the journey to Harbour Island, and it was looking like an easy glide to the end of the week. One evening, HBS's fourteen future Harbour Islanders gathered for a predeparture orientation meeting in Kresge. Spencer and George from my study group were also on hand, as were a number of other people we all knew from various sections.

Eventually we adjourned, having laid some vague plans to gather lots of groceries and rally on Harbour Island no later than Monday. It would have been fun to head over to Cambridge at that point, but we had the small matter of the ME exam to worry about. The final was two days off, and people were eager to get an early start on relearning all those formulas and statistical tools.

I pondered ME's impending final as I walked back to McCulloch. Few in Section I would be sorry to see the last of the course's pedantic, quantitative cases, but most of us would sincerely miss Flanders. No other professor was likely to play us *Simpsons* clips in class to illustrate case points. And not every professor was as approachable and as nice as he. The sad news was that Flanders wouldn't return to Harvard with us in September. He had been offered a position with the well-regarded MBA program at Emory University in Atlanta, and had recently decided to accept it.

At our last meeting, Flanders honored a long-standing request to bring his guitar to class and entertain us. He played "Hesitation Blues" by Jefferson Airplane, as well as a song he wrote in the itinerant musician days of his youth. Not to be outdone, the section serenaded him with a song from its own pen. Sung to the tune of the *Gilligan's Island* theme, it went on for minutes and was entitled simply *Tim's Song*:

> *Just sit right back and you'll hear the tale;*
> *The tale of an ME prof*
> *Who came to teach us numbers*
> *And other boring stuff*
>
> *This Prof was not a normal guy—*
> *He had a prior life*
> *He had this really long hair*
> *And may have had some lice*
> *(and may have had some lice)* . . .

Flanders listened patiently to our grinding, wordy dirge, wished us luck on the test, then quietly took his leave of Section I and Harvard Business School.

The exam, a crazy rush of all the disparate topics we had studied in ME, drove home how much of a grab bag the course had really been. Tyler had warned me of this back at the beginning of the semester. Students, he said, had long complained of ME's disparate and haphazard nature. Rumors were by now circulating that the course would be a victim of the school's ongoing reevaluation of its own curriculum. Some said ME and everything it covered would soon be banished wholesale from

the program. A rival rumor had it that the topics covered in
ME would be broken out and redistributed to TOM, FRMA,
and other related courses.

Once the exam was over, the race was on to leave campus
for break. Most sections had one or two big trips attracting
substantial numbers of their members. A large contingent from
Section I was off to Jamaica. Section C had almost twenty students convening in Park City, Utah, while a big hunk of Section
E would be in Vail. Carter and Sandra were off to an unspecified
island on a smaller couples trip. I hoped the week away would
help them mend some fences after the past few weeks of frayed
tempers between them. Ours was the most sectionally diverse of
the dozen or so large groups heading out of HBS that weekend;
Section H alone would be unrepresented on Harbour Island.

The week passed quickly in a relaxed and amiable spirit.
Airtime, Hell Weekend, First-Year Honors, and Section Dynamics were now remote trivialities. We were all happy that this
was not a section trip. There were no cliques, hidden rivalries,
or other attendant baggage down on Harbour Island. And for
all of us, there were enough new faces along to lend the week
something of the heady air of Orientation. The sun didn't hurt
either.

On Sunday we departed separately or in small groups, as
almost everyone had slightly different itineraries based on the
frequent flier programs or cut-rate airfares they had tapped to
get down there. I left early in the morning. I lacked a confirmed
seat from Miami to Boston, but hoped to wait-list onto a flight
once I got to Florida. I knew the odds of this weren't good;
countless thousands of other students were also heading home
after a week in the sun. It would be easy to get home on Monday,
but this would mean missing a day of classes. I didn't want to
do this. It was Forbidden and Immoral. More significantly, C&S
was meeting on Monday, and missing it would bring me within
three absences of an automatic 3.

I had foreseen this situation weeks before when I made my
reservations, and had indeed tormented over it more than once.
My seat was unconfirmed because I was traveling on a free ticket.
Had I been willing to pay around $500 for a normal ticket, I
would have been guaranteed a spot on the Sunday flight. I came
very close to doing this, but ultimately decided to take a stand.

The fact I was even considering paying $500 that I didn't have for eighty minutes of C&S "face time" demonstrated how badly seven months at HBS had brainwashed me. Feeling like the guy who stood in front of the tanks in Tiananmen Square, I called the airline and told them to give me the unconfirmed ticket.

Several weeks later when the Miami check-in clerk told me I could more easily book a Sunday flight to Jupiter than to Boston, I was feeling a touch less brazen. I tried, I told myself sheepishly as I shambled toward the exit. I did everything I could and I'm stuck here. But as I waited for the shuttle bus to South Miami Beach, I was suddenly overcome by a giddy feeling of . . . delinquency. *This is it!* I thought. *I'm playing hooky!*

In South Miami Beach I found a sun-flushed ghetto of restored deco buildings, long-legged models, Euro-trash playboys, and gawkers like myself. I had wanted to see the place for years, and so felt I couldn't have picked a better place to get stranded. I checked into my hotel around two. I had a confirmed seat to Boston early in the next evening, which would give me more than a day to see the sights, touch up my tan, read a book, and write some letters.

Four o'clock, Sunday afternoon. The weather channel said it was clear and sunny in Boston. Who could possibly be in their office at such an hour, on such a day, at the end of a vacation week? Clearly nobody. It was an ideal time to phone in excuses to my professors.

The first class on Monday would be Finance, so I started with Susan Callahan. The phone rang three times, then: "This is Susan Callahan. Please leave a message and I'll get back to you." I explained my situation, apologized profusely, vowed to never make such poor travel arrangements again, and promised to be at her next class on Thursday. Next I called Patterson and did the same thing. Lastly I called Cooperman.

The ring of the telephone was almost immediately supplanted by a voice. "Hello?" it said. *Cooperman!*

A wiser man might have asked for Hirotaka in a *faux* Japanese accent, apologized for dialing a wrong number, and hung up. This idea regrettably did not occur to me.

"Hi, Professor Cooperman . . . This is Rob Reid from Section I. I'm a little marooned . . ." I briefly explained my situation. Maybe he'll say not to worry about it! I thought frantically.

Maybe he'll say he's blowing off class himself to go golfing because it's such a boring case! Of course this wasn't likely; Cooperman had *written* the damn case.

"I see," he said when I was done. "You realize that C&S doesn't meet until 1:00 tomorrow."

"Uh, yeah." *What was he getting at?*

"I can't imagine there isn't a flight from Miami to Boston that would get you back by then."

"Yeah, uh, great idea, great idea, I'll check. Hope to see you tomorrow!"

I hung up and thought for a moment. Maybe American had no early flight, or maybe they did and there weren't any seats left for people on free tickets. If this was the case, I could have my day in Miami with an easy conscience and a quasi-excuse.

I nervously called the airline. "Yes sir, there *is* an early flight, and there's plenty of room on it for frequent fliers!" the reservations clerk chirped with rattling glee. I told her I'd call her back.

What to do? Leaving in the morning would mean going to bed at 10:00. It would mean not seeing the shopping district when the stores were open. It would mean missing a day on the beach. And for what? An hour and twenty minutes in Aldrich Hall! This was ridiculous. I was twenty-seven years old, and if I wanted to swap eighty minutes of chip shots for a whole day in an interesting place I might not see again, it was my right! And what made C&S so special anyway? What made it more important than all the other classes that were (ever so slightly) more tolerant of absences? And what gave Cooperman the right to demand that I, a *tuition-paying student,* race back like a chastised child for his lousy class? I was going to take the late flight, dammit. If being an obedient HBS student for one extra day wasn't worth the $500 a confirmed ticket would have cost me, it certainly wasn't worth this!

I was lucky my hotel was in a busy neighborhood, as this made it easier to find a cab at 4:30 A.M. The morning flight was a bit behind schedule. If it had been running any later I would have been late to Cooperman's class. I briefly toyed with the idea of pleading with the pilot for an excuse note. But we landed just early enough for me to squeak into the classroom by 1:00, making this unnecessary. The day's class discussion went reasonably well, but I was too groggy to pay much attention to it. Still, I managed to squeeze in at least one quick comment of my own, and at the end of the day I was still four full absences away from an automatic 3.

17

THE GREAT THAW

ABUSED AS I felt by Cooperman's intransigence, I could think of one thing that may have caused it. Perhaps he had adopted his hard line as a result of perennially teaching in the spring. The student body was by now more difficult to cow with threats of cold calls and 3s. Combined with the effects of warmer weather, this surely made teaching more of a challenge than it had been in September. People were just relaxed now, which made aggregate preparation levels slip noticeably. And after our winter grades came back in early April, most first-years relaxed even more.

To advance to the second year, one needed a grade 2 or better in thirty-nine units of class credit (Marketing, TOM, BGIE, ME, and Finance counted for eight credits, the rest for five). Put another way, one could have up to thirty-one credits' worth of 3s and still clear the hurdle. After April 13, all but four classes had concluded and filed grades. There were now only twenty-six credits of class grades outstanding, so anybody who had received fewer than six credits of 3s during the year was virtually guaranteed to advance to the second year.

This was a popular topic of discussion after the ME and HRM grades were released. People who were now safe from accruing that critical mass of 3s were said to have "made tenure," and were generally expected to party more and work less.

Carter, regrettably, was in the untenured group. Uninspired exam performances and a general lack of class participation had earned him 3s in both HRM and ME. He now had 26 credits of category 3 grades. If he got six more from our last four classes, he would "hit the screen." It would then be left to the Academic Performance Committee to determine whether he could return to the program in the fall.

"At this point, I'd feel better if I had more faith in the grading system," Carter said to me one day. "I know I don't speak enough in class. And I plan to change that from now on. But what if I start speaking and the professors just don't notice? You know that happens sometimes."

He was referring to the widely rumored phenomenon of inaccurate grading of class participation. Certain professors, it was said, sometimes left class with an incomplete idea of who had said what. This, of course, was not difficult to imagine. Any given class could include fifty, seventy, even a hundred individual student comments. One would need an extraordinary intellect to be able to mentally reconstruct eighty minute dialogues every day, and errorlessly attribute their components to ninety different participants. Occasional minor misallocations of commentary credit were therefore to be expected.

Unfortunately, several anecdotes swirling through the first-year class indicated that truly dramatic blunders occasionally happened as well. Somebody from another section told me a particularly disturbing story. He had received a warning note from a professor indicating that he was in the bottom 20 percent of his section with respect to class participation. This astonished him, as he had been a frequent and competent contributor throughout the semester. He raised the issue with his professor, and was told that he hadn't uttered a word in the past few weeks. The student was taken aback; he had made numerous comments during this period, and could even recall precisely what he had said and when. Eventually his professor shrugged his shoulders helplessly. "Look, you're a Mike. There must be over a half dozen Mikes or Michaels in your section; I just can't keep you guys straight."

Another memorable story concerned a fellow whose seat had been switched a few days into the second semester. When he received an unexpected warning note about his participation in a certain class, he went in to see his professor. To his utter astonishment, he was told that his "attendance problem" was imperiling his grade. It turned out that the professor had not updated his seating chart after the student had moved. He assumed that the student was now cutting every single class, despite the fact that hardly a day went by when he didn't call on the guy.

Of course, there were also stories of "positive mutations." Several people bragged of getting class participation reports that praised their "exceptional contributions" to case discussions in which they had never uttered a word. But nice as it was to imagine that the good boo-boo's canceled out the bad ones, nobody wanted their own grades influenced even slightly by such caprice. This subject was now a touchy one with Carter. "For a normal person, a screw-up could mean a 2 when they ought to get a 1," he pointed out. "Big deal. But for me it could mean hitting the screen!" This was a big burden for a guy who meanwhile had to deal with the unsurprising consequences of a dangerously narrow job search.

Having struck out completely with the investment banks, Carter was now frantically searching in what he called "the Save the World sector" for summer employment. But even this was no simple task. Big multilateral bodies like the World Bank had Byzantine application processes that took months (and often broad webs of personal contacts) to pursue to fruition. And smaller homegrown organizations like Teach for America were rarely able to make firm job offers until a few weeks before the start of summer. Worse, Carter found that most of these places seemed to be awash with applications and expressions of interest from people much like himself. Unpopular as it might have been at Harvard Business School, the Save the World sector certainly had its adherents throughout the rest of the country.

But Carter's greatest sorrows by far concerned Sandra. Their testy relations had gone from bad to worse over spring break, and they spent their last few days on their remote, idyllic island "just as friends." "And believe me, that's no easy situation when you're sharing a room, sharing a bed, and living on a beach with three other couples," Carter recalled mournfully.

He felt that things had fallen apart for a lot of reasons, but principal among them was the stark difference in how the two of them had fared at HBS. "People who do well here just don't understand what a nightmare this place can be for someone who's having a hard time. It seems like half the people around here go out every night, hardly read their cases, and still sound great in class. And believe me, it's not easy having that rubbed in your face every day. Some people moan about hangovers over lunch, kick around the golf course all afternoon, and still get 1s and 2s without any problem. Then they brag about this as if HBS is a great big joke on the rest of the world, and *they're* suddenly in on it."

"Was Sandra really that tough to take?" I asked. This just didn't sound like her.

Carter shook his head. "No, but a lot of people around here are, and that was the context of our relationship. Because when you're bumping into these hungover golfing Baker Scholars every day, it can be tough to come home to someone who's a complete natural at this stuff, someone who's ready to go out by eight every night, someone who rips through her cases in a half hour, then sounds like a Nobel laureate in class. But of course," he added with a woeful look, "I've found out it's much worse not coming home to someone like this."

At least academically, Hans's picture had recently improved as much as Carter's had deteriorated. He ended up with 2s in both of his winter classes, and things were looking really good for the Spring. In C&S, he had become one of the section's more informed and persuasive speakers, and Finance was clearly his strongest class yet. While it was still theoretically possible for him to hit the screen (this would mean getting 3s in three of the four remaining classes), this seemed to be a very unlikely prospect.

Along with Jerry, Sandra, and Rick, I was now safely among the tenured ones. In fact, a 1 in ME had given me ideas about making First-Year Honors. Meanwhile, my 2 in HRM kept my aspirations firmly clear of Bakerdom. I was frankly surprised by both of my winter grades. I had a good grip on the principles explored in ME, but had never been exceptionally vocal in Flanders's classes. The 1 he gave me was therefore a pleasant surprise. In HRM, by contrast, I often had strong views about the issues imbedded in the cases, and was a frequent participant in case discussions. I also felt good about the final exam I wrote. For this reason, curiosity moved me to visit Trumble's office to find out exactly where my performance had fallen short of 1 caliber.

Unlike most of our professors, Trumble did not make available a statistical summary of the section's class participation and test grades. It was therefore impossible to tell how I had ranked along either of these parameters. I did get a glimpse at the grading criteria for the exam, however, and what I saw astonished me. Stapled to the front page of my test was a three page *checklist* drawn up by the HRM faculty. On it were dozens of issue areas and observations about the exam case. Test takers had apparently received points for those checklist items that their essays mentioned, and none for those that they neglected.

I could understand why someone would use an answer key to grade an exam in ME, as it was, at its roots, a course in math. I could also understand why a professor might use a summary of key points as a rough guide in evaluating a TOM essay, as this field was less subjective than most. But using a checklist to grade an HRM exam struck me as absurd. In doing this, Trumble's department implied that human resources management was (like Physics, say) an objective science, and that HRM cases had right and wrong interpretations. In writing the HRM final, presenting an unusual notion that wasn't on the list wouldn't get you too far. Suggesting, however, that Dick Freeman drop the third shift at his new plant, or move to a five-day work week (both items on the checklist), was worth points.

Just as I finished reading the grading criteria, Trumble herself walked by on the way to her office. She invited me to step in and discuss my grade. The problem with my test, she told me after we had settled down, was that I had "completely missed the TOM issues" in the case. This was perhaps true. At least, I had missed the "TOM issues" as they were perceived by the HRM faculty. The significance of this was quite manifest in the checklist, which said that the "KNOCKOUT grading issue" concerned revising production schedules. The absurdity of making a TOM issue into a "KNOCKOUT grading issue" on an HRM cxam was so acute that I determined I could best retain my frayed temper by not pursuing the subject.

Trumble knew I was upset about the checklist, and did her

best to make me feel better about it. She even offered to give my exam to another faculty member for a "second opinion" on the grade. This was generous of her, and I promised to consider her offer. In the end I chose not to take her up on it. This was largely because I felt submitting my exam to a second review would amount to implicitly accepting the legitimacy of checklist grading. I did not want to do this. I also felt that because I was in generally good shape academically, quibbling over a 2 in HRM would be poor form.

Besides, there were better things to worry about. Our school's extracurricular calendar, diminished by exams and interviews in March, had suddenly picked up a good deal of steam. In the span of a few days there were presentations by the CEOs of GTE and Motorola, as well as one by the legendary LBO wizard Henry Kravis. Of these speakers, Kravis commanded the largest draw by far. He had become an icon in the financial world after a celebrated string of debt-backed acquisitions in the eighties, capped by his victory in the extraordinary struggle for RJR Nabisco. He spoke to us of the transition American business was going through. This transition, he said, was exemplified by the waning of corporate monoliths like IBM and General Motors. The complacency of success, he said, had proven to be an anathema to these once-thriving companies.

"That was amazing," Rick said as Kravis's speech was ending. "It's things like this that really get us our money's worth."

"Yeah, you're right," I agreed. "And that's no mean feat." A few days before we had received grim tidings on this subject in the form of a memo from the director of MBA Program Operations. Tuition in 1993–94, it read, would be $19,750. This $1,200 increase in our term bills would keep Harvard well ahead of inflation, which was hovering only a few notches above zero at that point. Jerry had run some numbers on this. We had paid roughly $45 per class as first-years, he reported. This would sound like a bargain to next year's crop.

"I hope they're charging something like $85 for C&S classes and a couple bucks for IOC," Rick observed when I mentioned this to him. I had to agree. IOC, after showing some early promise, had become a major disappointment for both of us. The technologies that should have fallen in the course's domain were on the brink of affecting some truly profound changes in the business world. But instead of exploring such topics as the rise of interactive media, IOC had instead focused on batch-processing, IBM mainframes, and other tired technologies of the distant past.

Some IOC cases were so shallow that their key issues could be adequately covered in the first several minutes of class. This often left us gasping for pertinent points and observations to fill up the remainder of the period. Professor MacIntyre soldiered on valiantly and good-naturedly, but was hobbled by the watery curriculum she had to teach. The course offered some conceptual frameworks that might have been compelling if taught in conjunction with less dated and more relevant cases. But aside from these, IOC was a singularly uninspiring offering.

The opposite could be said of C&S. This course featured readings by Michael Porter, Kenneth Andrews, and other prominent business academicians. These were well integrated with cases on such diverse industries as semiconductors, water meters, portal cranes, and soft drinks. But perhaps the course's greatest asset was its timeliness. C&S paid more attention to the prominent industries and corporations of the nineties than the rest of our classes combined.

This may have partly reflected the high tech interests of Professor Cooperman, who, as the new C&S course head, had just implemented a sweeping revision of its curriculum. Microsoft, Apple, and Intel were all prominent subjects in his course. So were dynamic industries like cable television, biotechnology, and cellular communications. All of this made C&S a heady survey of emerging commercial technologies.

But Cooperman was no narrowminded technophile. He also brought us studies of exceptional companies in established industries like Walmart, Disney, Swissair, and Cummins Engine. Most of his course's cases were written very recently, and those that were not explored subjects that had retained their relevance to first-year business students. All this was a refreshing contrast to the Neolithic topics explored in IOC.

Another clear winner was BGIE. This was partly because Patterson was so witty, warm, and illuminating a professor. It was also because the cases continued to be fascinating material for reading and discussion. Class had taken on an increasingly qualitative bent after the midterm, with less emphasis on bal-

ance of payments accounting and more on political and historical developments. But this did not make them any less rigorous
than the old TOM sessions on major appliance production. The
complex issues recently explored in BGIE included the role of
oil in the world economy, the advent of the Latin American
debt crisis, and foreign investment in postcommunist Eastern
Europe. In the coming weeks we would examine Germany's
reunification, the North American Free Trade Agreement,
Reagan's economic policies, Clinton's proposed economic policies, global warming, and a host of other timely issues.

Perhaps BGIE's greatest success was that it never lost sight
of its place within the broader HBS curriculum. It could have
easily degenerated into a grab-bag survey of world affairs, a
chip shot festival for frustrated CNN viewers. But the BGIE
faculty kept their course well-attuned to the needs of future
general managers. Its central message came through clearly;
every business, however localized and small, is inextricably
linked to the international political economy. Managers who fail
to appreciate the "BGIE issues" buffeting their enterprises are
asking for trouble.

As BGIE continued its merry tour of the eighties and nineties, Harbour Island tans faded, and the class of '94 settled into
the first-year routine for that brief stretch between spring break
and summer. Having found a summer job and having made
academic "tenure," I now had little to fret about until June.
Most of my friends were by now in similar situations, although
some people were worried about grades, while employment was
still an anxious issue for many others.

But even in April, HBS was not a bad place for a summer
job searcher to be. The weekly updates from the Career Resource Center were still thick with listings of new interviewers
coming to campus. And competition for the remaining jobs was
significantly dampened by the fact that so many people had by
now quit the field. We had always heard that virtually anybody
who wasn't excessively picky would land a good summer job,
and this now indeed seemed to be the case.

Carter found this situation reassuring, and returned to his
job hunt with a verve that he never quite mustered earlier in
the year. "You'd be amazed at the range of job announcements
that crops up around here in the spring," he said. "Movie studios, high-tech startups, small hedge funds; basically anybody

who can't afford to make hiring decisions six months in advance is liable to pass through." While his intensified job search could be a hassle at times, he generally found it to be a good distraction from his other woes, notably his breakup with Sandra and his increasingly perilous academic situation.

This latter worry was becoming particularly pronounced. While Finance was clearly his best subject yet, he found the other three courses to be a bit of a crap shoot. "I now get up every day thinking, just one 3, and I could hit the screen," he said. "This doesn't exactly make for a relaxing morning." Meanwhile, his sorrows about Sandra had yet to diminish. "It's not easy to put somebody out of your mind when she sits a couple rows away from you for three or four hours a day," he said.

Sandra was holding up better, although she was also upset by the demise of their romance. In general, she agreed with Carter's assessment of its causes. "It just isn't easy to have a relationship here when one person's getting by fairly easily and the other one's struggling," she said. "It'd be a different story if we had been going out for a while before we got here. But the strain was too much for the getting-to-know-each-other stage of our relationship. I tried to be understanding and helpful. But after a while, it seemed like all he ever wanted to do was hang around and pout."

At least things were going well for Sandra on the employment front. Her alumni network campaign had by now yielded ample fruit in the form of three offers. Shortly after break, she decided to accept one from a rapidly growing producer of educational software. Her role would be to help position their new line of CD ROM-based interactive learning products. She chose this job over two others with less technical companies, and was relieved that her five-month search for a ten-week position was finally over. It was impressive that her job search resulted in so formidable a set of employment options. The fact that she achieved this entirely through the alumni network and her own initiative was more impressive still. It was also good news for all of us who had thoughts of tapping the HBS network ourselves one day.

At that point, the realities of summer employment were beginning to loom larger for me as well. The second Friday after Spring Break was a class-free "recruiting day." Salomon Brothers, well-attuned to Harvard's schedule and militant intolerance for truancy, chose that day for its pre-summer orientation program. The bank's "Summer Associate Class of '93" was much larger than I had expected. All told there were over thirty of us, and we were just the investment bankers; Sales & Trading had also hired their own crew.

Even more surprising was the number of schools represented in our group. Salomon's New York office had drawn on no fewer than nineteen MBA programs in three countries. Harvard's delegation was the biggest with five hirees, followed by Wharton with four. There were people from all the programs I know Salomon recruited from, like Stanford, MIT, and Chicago, as well as from such diverse schools as the University of Western Ontario and Notre Dame.

The day's agenda included welcoming speeches, presentations about the summer program, and panel discussions on various aspects of the job. A prominent theme was that we should expect to *work*, and work hard. We were also reminded that not all of us would receive full-time offers at the end of the summer. The program would certainly be fun; summer associates were typically assigned to the more glamorous deals, and there were plenty of social events in the calendar. But this would be no vacation.

I got a chance to talk with my new colleagues over dinner and drinks later that evening. I generally liked the people I met. The group was overwhelmingly male (perhaps 80 percent), and most of us seemed to have graduated college between 1987 and 1989. Virtually everyone came from non–investment-banking backgrounds, although several people had worked in commercial banks. Conversation centered on school, speculation about work at Salomon, and the merits of different neighborhoods in New York. It was late before I found my way back to the Marriott. By then I was excited about spending a summer in New York, and knew that I'd landed with a good group of people.

The next Monday was the day of the Boston Marathon, a holiday throughout our city. Many businesses in the area closed to let their employees run or cheer on friends and family members. But Harvard Business School shunned the occasion en-

tirely; Monday was a normal three-case day, despite the fact
that over fifty students (no fewer than nine from Section I)
were participating in the big race. This conflict could have been
avoided easily. Had our recruiting holiday been scheduled for
Monday rather than Friday, the runners could have competed
without missing class, and many of their classmates might have
been there in person rather than spirit.

With so many people now absent for so good a reason,
many expected that even HBS would allow them just one day's
collective grace from its stringent attendance rules. No such
luck. Rather than granting a general amnesty to runners, the
Administration left it to teachers to set their own individual
policies for marathon-related truancy. The race conflicted with
Finance, BGIE, and C&S. Patterson was willing to excuse our
section's runners, but Callahan and Cooperman were unaccomo-
dating. Everyone in Section I who skipped their classes to run
the race they had spent months preparing for would therefore
have their grades penalized.

The race didn't make the school stand still administratively
either. On marathon Monday it was revealed that the saga of
our sections would have a substantially different finale than we
had expected since September. For years, a fixture of the second-year curriculum had been a course called Management
Policy and Practice (MPP). Like the twelve first-year courses,
MPP was a graduation requirement that everybody took with
their sections.

My second-year friends were unanimously positive about
having a fall semester course with their old sectionmates. It
provided a thread of continuity with the first year, and enabled
the sections to regain their cohesion and collective identity after
the summer apart. People were far less enthused about the
content of the course itself. MPP, I had heard, was a vaguely
focused survey of nebulous managerial "soft issues." Punctuated by chip shots, it was widely criticized by veteran students
who had by now lost their tolerance for academic fluffery.

All this would now end. The administration and faculty
had finally heeded the widespread groaning surrounding the
course, and Monday morning brought a memorandum announcing its demise. Two courses were now offered in its stead;
the General Manager's Perspective (GMP) and Global Strategy
and Management (GSM). As second-years we would be required

to take at least one of these classes. They would not be section-based.

It was certainly good to have a widely derided requirement eliminated, and it was nice to be offered a choice. Still, I regretted that our sections would lose the infrastructure for retaining their integrity into second year. Since none of us had suffered through the academic side of MPP, most people focused on this second aspect of the change. "There goes any chance Section I had at regaining some spark next year," Rick observed wryly after reading the memo. "Too bad nobody bothered to ask how *we* would have liked it handled."

Rick was right on this. There had certainly been no student plebiscite on the MPP issue. Far from it; most of us had no inkling that the change was in the works before it was announced. The final decision was made at a faculty meeting a few days before, along with several others of comparable import and secrecy. Monday's *Harbus* put forth the details of what amounted to the broadest change in the first-year curriculum in years. No fewer than five of the twelve first-year courses would be affected.

The rumors about ME's shaky status were at least partially true, as the faculty had voted to eliminate this course along with MPP. But like the amoeba that splits rather than dies, ME had left two heirs to carry on. The first-year curriculum would now feature "Data and Decisions," covering the analytic and quantitative side of ME, and "Decisions and Negotiations," covering decision trees and other topics (the courses were later renamed to Data, Decisions, and Negotiations, Parts I and II). Whereas ME had run for thirty-five sessions, its progeny would together run for forty-five. Like the phoenix arising invigorated from the ashes, Flanders' course would effectively live on, bigger and stronger than ever.

HRM, OB, IOC, and FRMA would meanwhile get diced and sliced in a somewhat more intricate manner. Bits of HRM and IOC would be extracted and combined into a new course called Work and Organization in the Information Economy. Meanwhile, certain fragments of HRM would be spliced with the OB curriculum to create Leadership and Organizational Behavior. Finally, selected chunks of IOC would be woven in with FRMA to create a slightly longer course (eight units of credit instead of five) still operating under the old FRMA mantle. Not yet decided upon was a proposal to switch MC from a graded course offered in sections into an ungraded one offered in seminars. How the implicit demotion in importance brought by the elimination of MC grades might address the inadequacy of communications' training at our school was unclear.

A number of students viewed this seemingly sweeping change as little more than window dressing. "Who do they think they're fooling?" Jerry marveled after reading *The Harbus* article. "Even with all these new courses, they'll still probably end up teaching the exact same cases they taught us this year!"

After an initial stir of surprise, the course changes quickly dropped from the campus's attention. The third-snowiest winter since Boston began keeping records had finally relaxed its icy grip, and people's minds were on things other than the fate of HRM. Tennis courts, golf courses, and other outdoor distractions now beckoned many, while others just opted to splay out on the grass basking in the long-awaited springtime sun. The big lawn in front of Baker Library became known as Baker Beach, where scores of students could be found languidly flipping through cases on sunny afternoons.

Other people threw themselves into on-campus activities like *The Harbus* and the pre-professional clubs with renewed vigor. The end of the week brought the fruits of a particularly demanding student undertaking in the form of the twentieth annual HBS Show. As was traditional, the Show was an original musical-comedy farce, with script, music, and lyrics penned by students. Scores of people had invested countless hours in its careful development since late autumn. Section I didn't have any performers in it, although a few of our number were involved in backstage operations like costume design, lighting, and (surely a grueling post) cast party planning.

Most of the performances sold out, and our section was lucky to get seats for the popular Friday evening show. The first thing that struck me after the curtain rose was how much work had gone into the thing. The elaborate set was designed and built by HBS students. There were dozens of speaking and choral parts, and all the music was played by a live band. It was clear that everybody on stage had worked long hours perfecting lines, delivery, and choreography. And I couldn't even guess how many evenings and weekends had gone into writing the script and music. Perhaps the most scarce commodity any HBS

student has is time, and this show was the product of an awful
lot of that.

The following week brought a distraction of a very different sort, when Goldman Sachs sponsored its consolation dinner for dingees from its Sales & Trading program. This was
held at the Harvard Faculty Club over in Cambridge. The
first person I saw after I arrived was Rick, who had come
much closer to a Goldman offer than I had. He had come to
this event hoping it would be an entré of sorts for next year's
interviewing cycle.

"Looks pretty grim," he observed as soon as I spotted him.
"No name tags." I glanced around the room and saw that he
was right. This was the first invitational recruiting event I had
attended that didn't have a little table of laser-printed name
tags for the company's guests. "No sign-in sheet either," he
added. I scanned the room and again found he was right. "In
other words, they don't give a damn who comes here tonight
and who doesn't," he concluded gloomily.

"Deep breath, Rick," I counseled. "Maybe somebody in
their recruiting department just dropped the ball on those
things."

Rick looked at me incredulously. "Please. This is Goldman
Sachs. Goldman doesn't *just drop the ball*." He continued in his
line of reasoning. "Another piece of evidence. Go talk to a
Goldman person, if you can find one. You'll discover that they
didn't exactly bring out the big guns for us." A few minutes of
halfhearted mingling confirmed this. I talked to two Goldmanites, and both were less than one year out of college. Not only
had the firm left most of its bigwigs behind, but the people
they brought along were several years *behind* us in the career
trajectory. I spent a few minutes advising one of these neophytes on how to pitch his essays when he applied to HBS. This
was the only substantive talk I had with a Goldman person all
night.

Of course, this was most understandable, as Goldman
had been going full tilt with their recruiting program since
the autumn. Simply by lasting this late into the year they had
outdone almost every other firm on campus. If they wanted
to take things a little easier at this point, one could hardly
fault them.

Soon the affable fellow who had interviewed me a few

weeks before called the dinner to order. By now there were perhaps two dozen guests and a handful of Goldmanites on hand. "Okay, everybody have a seat!" my interviewer directed. "Let's try to make sure we get at least one Goldman person at every table!" Evidently, there weren't quite enough of them to go around; the table Rick and I found toward the front of the room was occupied only by fellow dingees. Rick would clearly not get much of a jump on his full-time job search this evening.

It turned out that the dinner wouldn't have helped his networking aspirations even if our table had been teeming with the biggest of bigwigs. Shmoozing and conversation reigned nowhere that night, because no sooner had the salads been served than a lengthy presentation began. Several people stood up to speak about their departments and what a terrific organization Goldman was. Many of them used overhead slides to punctuate their remarks. The wordy presentation, the dinner, and our fleeting moments with Goldman Sachs ended more or less simultaneously. When the last speaker was done, my interviewer stood up and made some closing remarks.

"We invited you tonight," he began, "to let you know that we still love you, that we still like you. . . ." He went on to say that Goldman was "very, I mean *extremely*" interested in keeping up the recruiting dialogue with us in the coming year.

"Yeah, right," Rick whispered sullenly. "They're just doing this to make sure we'll think of them if we ever need private bankers!"

"You know," my interviewer continued, "sometimes you really want something . . . and you don't get it. But y'know, a lot of people . . . important people . . . in world history . . . have been down sometimes. And do you know what it's like?"

"Bonnie Blair!" I whispered to Rick.

"It's like Deng Xiao Peng," my interviewer intoned meaningfully.

"Close!" Rick whispered back.

"Deng . . . He was down before. I mean, *way* down. But do you know where he is now?" He scanned the crowd dramatically. "He's on top. On the *very* top."

"Someone oughta tell him Deng stepped down a while ago," Rick observed wryly.

"Yeah, but they say he's still pulling the strings. Besides, the guy's on a roll. Let him run with it." After all, I couldn't wait to see who Rick and I would be lumped in with next. First Bonnie Blair, now Deng Xiao Peng. Mick Jagger, George Washington, and perhaps even the Buddha himself could not be far behind.

18

THE LAST BELL RINGS

BACK IN MARCH, the start of our last two courses (IOC and C&S) had brought a brief surge in the interest levels most people brought to class. This was augmented somewhat by spring break, which let us clear our heads and come back rested and ready for action. The C&S/IOC/spring break revival lasted for maybe a week, and it had been downhill ever since. By late April, people were vaguely indifferent toward classes. By early May, they were militantly apathetic. Even the still-unemployed were counting the days until our last final exam on June 2.

The whole drill was just getting old. Jerry summed it up nicely one day at lunch. "Whenever I open up a case these days, I pretty much know what it's gonna be like. Even if we've just started a new Finance module, even if we're into a new segment in C&S, I can pretty much predict what the text will say, how the exhibits will be structured, and even what my conclusions will be. In class, I can guess what 95 percent of the people in the section are gonna say before they even start to talk. I know how the professors are gonna respond to them. I know what they'll write on the board and what they won't. I've been sitting in the same damn seat since January, looking at the same faces, hearing the same voices making the same arguments, passing the same notes, and drinking the same Kresge coffee to keep my eyes open. And if I hear Magnus

start one more comment with the words 'In Sweden,' I swear
I'm gonna belt him!"

"Aw come on," I reproached. "Magnus doesn't talk about
Sweden all the time . . ."

"I know. I didn't say I always know what people are gonna
say, I just said I know *95% of the time*. And Magnus does always
talk about Sweden, dammit. And Miguel always prattles on
about Venezuela. Wendy's always blabbering about her earth-
shattering work at McKinsey. And Walter can't shut up about
what he learned on Wall Street. You can always count on Justin
to make some inane point about the case's ethical issues. And
then Garth's sure to chime in with some ridiculous homily about
how people have to look out for themselves. Maxwell starts
every comment by saying, "When I read this, I hadda ask myself . . ." Tina starts every comment by saying, "Yeah, I
mean . . ." Erin starts every comment by saying, "Wellllll, I
think . . ." And Stanley, Mitchell, and Sue Ellen have spoken in
every single class on every single day since mid-March!"

Luckily for Jerry and the other lethally bored members of
the section, an anonymous wit's inventiveness brought us all a
much-needed moment of comic relief later that week. During
a particularly dry Finance class, a guy from the Right Field
Warning Track named Todd raised his hand. Callahan spotted
him. "What do you make of this . . . Odd?" she asked, a puzzled look crossing her face. There was a short pause, then the
room erupted in laughter. Somebody had subtly altered Todd's
nameplate with a tube of correction fluid so that it now read ODD.

As Odd fielded the question, I examined some other nameplates. Seated in front of Odd was a guy name Farzan, who had
now become TARZAN. Two seats to Tarzan's right was a fellow
called Chan, who was now named CHA. I glanced about the
room. At one seat, the respectable family name Roth had been
degraded to ROT. Across the room, a guy named Doug was now
simply UG. A particularly clever alteration was dealt to a Sky
Decker named Christoph. The first two letters of his name
had been obliterated along with the right leg of the letter "R,"
yielding PISTOPH. Other victims included two Bill's renamed to
ILL and at least one EVIL whom we had previously known as
Kevin.

While they may not have been the work of a comedic ge-
nius, the alterations gave us all something to chuckle about.

And somewhere in the room, a clever little vandal had found something to mull over when class got slow. I could almost hear those diabolical plans being hatched. ROB REID . . . *Now what can I do with that one?*

Outside of class there were, as always, plenty of things to save us from boredom. Suddenly prominent among these was a series of administrative chores associated with our transition to the second year. A big issue for many of us was now housing. Very few second-years typically remained in the dorms, and only one dormitory (Morris) was available to us. Morris had a more modern and luxurious feel than McCulloch, but at age twenty-seven I was determined not to spend another year in a single cramped room.

If there was a "cool" thing to do second year, it was to live off campus with a few other people. Hundreds did this every year, and several apartments had become famous perennial off-campus roosts. The largest of these housed upwards of ten students. I was invited to join one of the smaller households, but decided not to. I had grown too fond of life in the shadows of Kresge, Aldrich, and Shad to seriously consider commuting. Driving and parking in Cambridge was a nightmare, and the thought of starting my winter mornings with an Arctic march across a Charles River footbridge held no allure. Living on campus, any campus, is the apogee of convenience short of living at home with doting parents. I would spend the rest of my life in the big unfriendly world, and saw no reason to rush off to it now.

This left me one realistic housing option in the on-campus apartments at Soldiers Field Park. SFP's principal drawback was its extravagantly high cost, which was made all the more onerous by our school's insistence on collecting rent for twelve months out of the year. This placed the burden of a natural nine-month occupancy cycle squarely on the shoulders of its debt-laden students. Lessees who didn't spend the summer in Boston (perhaps 90–95 percent of the class) had to find subletters (not an easy task, and it was certainly a buyer's market) or resign themselves to paying double rent for three months. Despite this drawback, I steeled my nerves and entered the housing lottery for a one-bedroom apartment in Soldiers Field Park. Rent for the dwelling I was eventually assigned exceeded the most I ever paid *while employed* by roughly 30 percent. Still, I sullenly reminded myself, it beat Morris.

That weekend brought another milestone heralding the end of our first year in the form of the annual Newport Ball. This event was held, as the name would suggest, in Newport, Rhode Island. The dance itself took place on Saturday night, but the whole weekend was thick with collateral activities. I headed up on Friday afternoon with Alistair and several of his buddies from Section C.

Alistair's family had a spacious home near Newport, and our group crowded into it for the evening. The next day was one of lazy anticipation. Many of our classmates spent the afternoon on the links, but most people chose to explore Newport. I was in the latter group. A few of us rented bikes and pedaled about, marveling at the summer retreats of long-dead plutocrats. The dance itself was held at Belcourt Castle, one of Newport's larger "summer cottages." It was a dramatic setting for the black-tie affair, and the first-year class dutifully behaved itself far better than at the Holidazzle.

After the brief respite of Newport weekend, it was back to a frantic schedule for me. My calendar had become truly cluttered, a situation which was largely my own doing. A few days before, I had confirmed with Salomon that I would begin work on the morning of June 3. This would be about nineteen hours after the end of my last exam. I would have liked a couple days off, but there were three start dates to choose from and this one best fit my schedule. I now had to carefully tie up every conceivable loose end and administrative chore before exams got started.

Most prominent among these was choosing my second-year courses. There were about sixty alternatives to ponder, ranging from the pragmatic (Measurement and Management of Product Costs) to the esoteric (The Business World: Moral and Social Inquiry Through Fiction). Certain classes were so acclaimed that almost all the first-years knew of them. Among these was Entrepreneurial Finance, a class Tyler had warned me would be almost impossible to get into. "I ranked it as my number one choice last year," he explained, "and still didn't get into it. There aren't a whole lot of classes that'll do that to you."

The ranking system he referred to was at the heart of

second-year registration. Each of us would soon submit a roster of classes for each of our last two semesters arranged in order of preference. If a certain class was listed by more people than could be accommodated (as happened in approximately 25 percent of all cases), those who ranked it as their number one choice would be let in first, followed by those who ranked it second, and so on. Courses ranked first by more students than could be let in would be filled by lotteries among the people who put them at the top of their lists.

In the middle of May, a guide describing the second-year courses was distributed. The course guide was traditionally accompanied by a booklet of student ratings of the various classes and professors. This second document would be a valuable one, particularly to those people who didn't have wide networks of second-year friends to turn to for advice. Unfortunately, the school was quite slow about distributing it. Four days before we were to file our course selections it still hadn't come out, so I stopped by the registrar's office to ask when it would be released. "Oh, your guess is as good as mine," a man behind the counter fretted. "This is the *first* year our office has had to put this thing out, and be*lieve* me it was just *dumped* on us. I don't know *when* we'll get it done."

"Well, do you think it'll be soon?" I asked testily. "It won't do us much good after Tuesday."

"Be*lieve* me," he answered. "*Your* guess is as good as *mine*."

This meant we were all going at it a little blind when we started piecing together our second-year schedules. I began by considering the fall semester. Entrepreneurial Finance was definitely on my list, as the topic was interesting in its own right and the professor's teaching acumen was legendary. I had also long since decided to take The Coming of Managerial Capitalism. This was a survey of American business history, and focused on how managerial structures had evolved in response to technological, legal, and competitive change. It would be a qualitative course, and I wanted at least one of these each semester. I also enjoyed reading history, and it was a rare course at HBS that involved this. Our own Nick Patterson taught this course (in itself a major endorsement for it), as did another professor who was a Pulitzer Prize-winning historian. Much as I enjoyed Patterson's teaching, I decided to sign up with the other professor for variety's sake.

Another legendary second-year course was called Coordination, Control, and Management of Organizations. CCMO was known as much for its professor as for its content. The course was taught by a leading thinker on the subject of "agency costs," a fashionable notion in business literature at the time. He was also said to be a truly gifted teacher. For this reason I signed up for CCMO as well.

This left me with one last elective to choose. Tyler had spoken well of Industrial Marketing. Amos recommended Negotiation Analysis. Other highly regarded classes included Power and Influence and Moral Dilemmas of Management. All of these were said to be well-taught, "*neat* courses." As I mulled over these options, it suddenly struck me how easy it would be to just fill my schedule with random, disjointed, neat courses. This could be fun, but would probably land me at graduation with something less than $80,000 worth of hard knowledge and skills. A moment of pragmatism was clearly in order here.

When I thought about it, it seemed that the two "rigorous" disciplines one could best study at HBS were finance and operations management. Of these, finance was the most salient to me. After all, I was going into investment banking for the summer. And my long-term business aspirations centered more on corporate-level governance than factory floor trouble-shooting. Given this, Corporate Financial Management seemed to be my best choice for a fifth class. Combined with Entrepreneurial Finance and my spring semester classes, this would hopefully constitute something akin to a "major" in Finance at HBS.

We finally got the student ratings of the second-year courses exactly one day before we were originally required to submit our course selections. This deadline was pushed back from Tuesday to Wednesday, giving us a full forty-eight hours to consider how the courses were viewed by our predecessors. There was quite a bit of data to digest. Students had been asked to evaluate every section of every course along twenty-four parameters.

The questions they were asked ranged from the trivial (*How helpful did you find the films?*) to the epistemological (*What was the educational importance of the course?*). The results of these surveys were now summarized in an eye-numbingly formatted 15-page book. Not a shred of statistical input was left unlisted. All told, there were 14,448 cells of data for the analytically inclined to absorb, process, and assess. A cursory survey of the book showed that all the professors and classes I was considering had been highly regarded.

Particularly impressive were the ratings for the Entrepreneurial Finance professor. The students in one of his classes had given him an average over-all rating of 4.9 (on a five-point scale) as a professor. This settled the question of which class I would rank as my number-one choice for the fall semester. Entrepreneurial Finance was a clear winner, and if I didn't list it first, I wouldn't have a prayer of getting into it anyway. I gave The Coming of Managerial Capitalism my second preference, as I knew both the class and the professor had been popular in previous years. CCMO came third. I was pessimistic about getting into it with so low a priority, but figured it was worth a try. I listed Corporate Financial Management last, primarily because I knew there would be enough space available in it to satisfy all comers.

When I finalized my course preferences it was very late at night. But this didn't worry me, because for the first time all year I planned to *sleep through a scheduled class* the next morning. This class was actually a lecture in Burden Auditorium, so I figured my absence wouldn't be documented and penalized. Executives from Frito-Lay, the subject of three wearying IOC cases, were scheduled to speak.

I skipped their lecture almost on principle. First, IOC had disappointed me as a course. Second, I hadn't enjoyed the Frito-Lay case series one bit. But perhaps most important, this was a rare chance to indulge myself in a limited, senseless, nay, *pitiable* act of rebellion. By unyieldingly demanding my presence at all classes, by tugging a leash and yanking me in from distant Miami, by lecturing me about the *morality* of perfect attendance, HBS had all but guaranteed that if I ever thought I could get away with cutting a class, by God I was going to do it. My petty rebellion was by no means unique. Around ten o'clock, I ran into perhaps a dozen of my sectionmates while I was getting coffee at Kresge. None of us had attended the Frito-Lay lecture.

This turned out to be a wise move. MacIntyre began our next "normal" IOC session by apologizing for the caliber of the speech the people from Frito had delivered, which she intimated had been uninspired and content poor. This amounted to a benediction of our truancy, and I resolved to sleep in at every opportunity thereafter.

The next item on MacIntyre's agenda that day was our IOC group projects. A few weeks earlier, we had been randomly assigned to teams and given a hilariously vague assignment. We were asked to create a twenty minute, five-slide presentation on the subject of "business transformation" by late May. This was basically all we had to go on. Over the past few weeks, I heard of nobody from Section I (or indeed the entire first-year class) who had done a moment of work on the assignment.

MacIntyre said a few words about the assignment, then asked if we had any questions concerning it. One guy immediately spoke up. "Yeah," he said, brandishing the handout that described the project. "I must've read this six or seven times, and I still don't have the faintest idea of what we're supposed to do." A few people laughed nervously. He continued. "I mean, this has to be the vaguest assignment I've ever seen. What are you looking for? What do you want us to do with it? What on earth do you mean by business transformation anyway??"

By now much of the section was in stitches. Our sectionmate wasn't trying to be disrespectful, but his words mirrored the frustration we all felt about the assignment's vagary and about IOC in general. This annoyance had been heightened by the project's horrific timing. The presentations were scheduled to take place in the midst of exam period, a time when people should have been allowed to focus on their tests.

"So where does this leave us?" he concluded. "I've read the assignment over and over, and the only thing I can think of is that we're supposed to read it for what we think it is . . . and then sort of . . . go with it." At that, several people burst into applause. Pandemonium quickly ensued as dozens of people jockeyed to make their own sardonic quips about the silliness of the assignment.

"When we do the presentations, will *quality* count?" asked one wit.

"Are our intellectual property rights going to be protected?" asked another. "I'd hate to see a Harvard professor make a ton of money off of *my* work."

"Do the people who aren't planning to speak have to attend the presentation?" asked a third.

Throughout all this, MacIntyre did an admirable job of maintaining her composure. This was no mean feat given her position. If she thought the project was a good idea, she certainly had a tough crowd to sell it to. If she thought it was as silly as many of us did, she could hardly undermine her department by saying so. In the best case, she might have allayed some anxieties by laying forth the project's requirements better than the nebulous assignment memo had. But it was soon evident that she wasn't going to do this. Still, the comedians of our section wouldn't let up. Question followed baiting question for perhaps ten minutes.

WHAT A BUNCH OF FOOLS, Carter observed in a note that drifted my way. CAN'T THEY JUST LET THE WOMAN DO HER JOB?

The next day's *Wall Street Journal* indicated that the conduct of one of our schoolmates may have been more deserving of Carter's reproach. A certain second-year, the paper read, was indicted by a New York state grand jury for "*collusive trading* in developing country debt." This story had been kicking about campus for some time now, so the article came as no surprise. Still, it was an inauspicious way for HBS to return to the *Journal*'s pages after the six-month hiatus following the ECN-19 debacle.

It was perhaps appropriate that the week which saw this ethical tumult would end with the launch of the Sadhu Fund, the heir to our long-ago course on business morality. An energetic group had by now spent several weeks arranging its inaugural party. The result was the Sadhu Fund Auction, Cocktail Party, and Dessert Hour, which was held at the Harvard Club of Boston on the Friday night before finals started. The dual purpose of this event was to get our section together one last time, while raising some money to launch our fund.

The night's principal fundraising vehicle was the auction of dozens of lots donated by the students and faculty of Section I. These ranged from fairly mundane articles with definable market values (like a round-trip shuttle ticket to New York on Delta Airlines) to truly whimsical intangibles (like a game of Trivial Pursuit with Nick Patterson, our animated BGIE professor).

The evening kicked off with a cocktail hour. By the time the bidding started at nine, well over 100 sectionmates, partners, and professors were on hand. The first item on the block was Patterson's Trivial Pursuit hour. The bidding started at the asking price of $50, rapidly crossed the $100 threshold, and eventually closed with an amazing offer of $250. This set the tone for an evening in which some truly extravagant prices were paid. The second lot was a weekend for ten at a student's spacious country "cabin." The winning bid was an opulent $1,150. Other memorable sales included $300 for dinner for four at the home of our TOM professor Joseph Stanley, $275 for an aerobics lesson by our FRMA professor Cindy Toddson, and $200 for a cherry pie made by our Ethics professor.

By the end of the night our Fund had over $11,000 with which to begin its ministry to a world of hungry, ill-clad Sadhus.

The post-Sadhu weekend was a quiet one on campus, darkened by the shadow of our last run of final exams. This began at nine Monday morning with Finance. The exam's case concerned a greeting card company known as Friendly Cards. Friendly was considering an investment in an envelope-making machine, as well as the acquisition of another small firm in its industry. This raised the usual host of issues. What was Friendly's cost of equity? Its cost of capital? Did the acquisition make sense? The investment? Could either or both of these outlays be successfully financed? If so, how? What were the implications of this for Friendly's capital structure? Four hours of this was more than enough Finance to last me until Salomon Brothers training started midway through the next week.

Shortly after the test was over, our IOC team met to discuss the unhappy task of defining Business Transformation and its relationship to Information Technology. A tacit sectionwide resolution to minimize all efforts associated with this chore had by now given way to the unsettling symptoms of last-minute intensity. At least one IOC team was said to have held a marathon ten-hour work session. Several other groups had been seen leaving their appointments with MacIntyre dressed in business suits, an uncomfortable reminder of those long-ago MC presentations.

Our team's sentiments about these nerdy displays were unanimous. "How could you ever spend ten hours meeting over this thing," one woman marveled, "when it's just twenty percent of the IOC grade!"

"Yeah," echoed one of the guys. "If we put more than three hours into this we're doing something wrong."

"Well, we've already been here for fifteen minutes. At this rate we'll end up like Gordon's team!"

This grim reference to the ten-hour workaholics fell on receptive ears, and we had the assignment contracted out in no time. With five slides in the presentation and five people on our team, this was a simple matter. Everyone took responsibility for creating one slide, with the notion that we would reconvene the night before our presentation and somehow mold them all into a semicoherent whole. Our first slide, we decided, would broadly define Business Transformation. The next would present some sort of Over-Arching Conceptual Context for examining it. The third (mine) would provide a Theoretical Framework for thinking about Information Technology and its integral role in affecting Business Transformation. The fourth would discuss the Implementational Issues of the Transformation Process. The last would discuss the Risks Inherent in Implementation. This was certainly long on puffery, but then that was how we viewed the assignment itself.

After the meeting, I realized I was famished. I had subsisted solely on a large coffee and a bagel throughout the Finance exam, and still hadn't managed to feed myself. I headed over to Kresge's upstairs grill, where Jerry was enjoying a late and hurried lunch as he scowled over the latest issue of *The Harbus*.

"Have you seen the scandal sheet?" he greeted me.

"Not yet. Trouble in paradise?"

"I'll say." He pointed at an article on the front page. It was about the second-year who had been indicted. "The school's withholding the guy's degree!"

I glanced at the paper. "Sources," it said, had indicated that the indictee would "not be allowed to receive his HBS diploma and attend graduation."

"Whatever happened to the idea of innocent until proven guilty?" Jerry wondered rhetorically. "So the guy's been indicted. He hasn't been convicted. He hasn't even been brought to trial! And how many people get wrongly accused every year in this country?"

"Yeah," I started. "But—"

Jerry was on a roll. "Didn't he study here for two years? Didn't he pass all his classes? Didn't he pay his $40,000 in tuition? And now the school's booting him because he's been *accused* of something!"

"Well it is a serious charge . . ."

"So what? Think of the people who've gotten through this school despite serious charges! Think of that story from last year, the one about the Finance Club. Remember how the guy rigged the election to make himself president? Remember that? Talk about ethically bankrupt! He deliberately undermined another student, he did it on school time, and as a member of a school organization. And the guy's guilty as hell; he admitted to the whole thing! And where's he gonna be on graduation day? Marching on through to 'Pomp and Circumstance'!"

"But they did punish him," I interjected.

"Yeah? What'd they do?"

"They made him write a case about what happened."

Jerry was flabbergasted. "A *case*???"

I shrugged. "Yeah. Maybe that's Harvard's equivalent of making you write 'I will not throw rocks at school' 100 times on the blackboard."

Jerry laughed at this despite himself. "Aright," he said, after a moment of mirth. "But let's get back to the guy who got indicted. What he's accused of doing had *nothing* to do with the school. Most of it happened before he got here, he says he's innocent, and the case is far from closed!"

"So maybe it's a PR move," I offered.

"I'll tell the world it's a PR move!" Jerry glowered. "The SEC's mad at this guy, so HBS is managing its precious goddamn image by kicking him while he's down!"

The indictment wasn't the only scandal gracing *The Harbus* that day. An equally shocking item covered in the issue that day was a memo to the incoming class of '95 which the paper's editors had intercepted and partially reprinted. It was a warning to the newcomers from the administration concerning the "personal computer selection process." The memo began with an italicized commandment:

Do not talk to any of your friends (both present students and alumni) about what you need to meet your computing needs at HBS. Last year many incoming students ignored this memo and instead chose to take the advice of others who were not

> *familiar with the recent changes in student computing in
> the MBA Program. This resulted in many first-year students
> acquiring configurations that did not fit their needs. Specifi-
> cally, several students who purchased laptop portable battery
> operated computers, to be used mainly for exams, did not
> purchase a battery powered printer, leaving those students
> with limited or no printing capability during exams.*

The administration, it seemed, was determined to keep the
printer crisis raging for at least another year. This was a pity,
as there were several more important things that it might have
focused on. The trumpeted Leadership and Learning initiative
was still ticking along, questioning our school's most fundamental precepts. An extensive change in the first-year curriculum
was about to be implemented. And here we had a top administrator investing her precious time in pre-emptive strikes against
the porto-printer renegades of tomorrow. *Do not talk to any of
your friends.* This was too much.

Like two cantankerous old men in a small-town diner vent-
ing their spleens about the state of the world, Jerry and I had
a merry time grousing about the day's unpleasant news items.
Eventually Carter passed by our table and put a stop to this.
"Look," he reproached. "You guys have to admit that *some* good
comes out of this place."

"Oh yeah, like what?" Jerry said this facetiously; he was the
first to admit that HBS had been the ideal waystation on his
journey back to civilian life.

"Like it's gotten all of us good jobs for the next three
months," Carter replied. Jerry and I looked at each other in
happy disbelief. All of us? We had both assumed it would be
the bread line for Carter this summer. "Yeah, all of us," Carter
confirmed. "And not a minute too soon."

He told us briefly about the happy conclusion of his job
search. After chasing a series of leads provided by the Cole
Room and Professor Lubbock's "developing countries" files, he
had just received a terrific offer from a large European bank.
The bank had made a strategic decision to beef up its operations
throughout Latin America, and wanted a summer associate to
carry out a sweeping survey of the region and its opportunities.
This would involve a great deal of travel, and would likely open
a host of doors for Carter's second-year job search.

Carter, of course, was ecstatic. Latin America had been his greatest academic interest since college. And his new job would certainly require a good deal of financial analysis from him, which would help satisfy his principal business interest. "And I owe all of this to my decision to attend Harvard Business School," he said in a mocking tone that evoked a faith healer's Sunday morning testimonial. "Now if I can just find a girlfriend, everything'll be perfect. Assuming, of course, that I can also avoid hitting the screen." Unfortunately, this latter condition was by no means a given, but we all chose to ignore this fact and focus on the first ray of hope to enter Carter's unhappy world since spring break.

The indications were that a number of lives had brightened similarly of late. A survey in the day's *Harbus* indicated that over 97 percent of our classmates had found summer employment by now. The average reported weekly salary was $1,251, and this did not include bonuses or tuition reimbursement plans. In an anemically recovering economy, this was awfully impressive. Assuming the average person would work for ten weeks and vacation for four, my classmates would pull in over $10 million in salary alone by September. Not bad for a few hundred people, largely in their mid-twenties. Thinking of this put a more cheerful spin on my afternoon. So what if certain elements of our administration could be petty and difficult? On the whole, HBS was a damn good place to be.

Two nights later I welcomed my IOC team to the McCulloch penthouse suite for our first and final big push. It was five-thirty and we were all eager to be done by nine. Our slides constituted the disjointed mishmash one would expect from five people who had worked independently within only vaguely agreed-upon parameters. We wasted a few moments sullenly bad-mouthing the assignment and its wretched timing, but then got on with it.

It wasn't long before a strange and unsummoned chemistry began to work among us. One woman's slide discussed The Benefits of Smallness, a "silly little catch phrase" she had concocted earlier that day. Suddenly we had a theme. And the more we discussed it, the more we realized that it was a theme we all sincerely bought into. Smallness. This didn't refer to a company's size, but rather a way of doing business within it. It meant relationship-driven cooperation instead of hierarchically-dictated relationships. It meant entrepreneurialism and front-line decisions in the place of corporate central planning.

The Benefits of Smallness enjoyed by a five-person venture could be exploited by the most ponderous of corporate behemoths. How? Through an effective harnessing of information technology (okay, maybe it was flowing a bit thicker at this point). People thousands of miles apart could share files and data and enjoy warm personal relationships. The informational resources of a central corporate body could be delivered quickly and cheaply to the most remote customer contact point. Bringing the Benefits of Smallness to an organization through the magic of information technology amounted, of course, to Business Transformation.

Our arguments may have been somewhat pat, but they met the assignment's vague criteria. More importantly, what began as a cynical "let's get this over with quick" session had blossomed into a presentation we all felt good about and believed in. The Benefits of Smallness. It had a nice ring to it. If we ever got the chance to sit down and really develop our ideas, we might just come up with something powerful.

The presentation took place the following afternoon and went fine. We would have done better with a few more hours of preparation, but then none of us felt compelled to try for anything more than a 2. We even bucked the trend by presenting in casual attire. It was nice that none of us cared about the grade for once. What mattered was that we had enjoyed this project despite everything, and had actually learned a thing or two from doing it.

The rest of the week was dominated by farewells and some preliminary steps toward moving out. I was only about midway through dispatching my belongings to Connecticut, Manhattan, and the residences of some generous local friends when exam time hit again. Friday's final was in BGIE. In it we were asked to analyze a hand-wringing, Japanophobic article and react to its arguments. It wasn't easy to get it all read and written in four hours, and everyone was ready for the weekend by the time it was over. Monday was Memorial Day, which meant three days' respite before our last two exams. I decided to drive home and see my parents. Since my pre-Salomon "summer vacation" would last exactly nineteen hours, it made sense to do this now rather than later.

I managed to squeak out of Boston before rush hour. Three days later I returned by train, having left my car to pass a lazy summer in rural Connecticut. New York City was no place to keep it, for reasons of security, traffic, potholes, and parking rates that would make even Harvard blush. It was almost eight before I got to my room, having not yet started to study for the morning's IOC exam. I spent hardly an hour preparing for it. I could think of little to do but memorize a few conceptual frameworks and buzzwords; any further effort would have surely been wasted.

The next morning, we were given a case concerning Connor Formed Metal Products, a family-run enterprise headquartered in San Francisco. Connor's products included "coil springs . . . metal stampings, complex wire forms, and assemblies." The company was suffering from a vaguely familiar litany of complaints. Among them was its inability to fully exploit the potential of its worthy old IBM System 36 computers. In short, it was a rather boring company facing tired technological issues. I tried hard to identify with the case's featured manager, Bob Sloss. Bob *Sloss*! Even the protagonist sounded boring.

For the first and surely last time at Harvard Business School, I checked the clock out of boredom rather than panic during an exam. Three hours to go! I returned to my dispirited writing. When the time ran out, I felt I had done all right, but it was hard to be certain. I probably managed a 2. But it could have been a 1, or just as easily a 3. Not even OB left me feeling so unsure about how my performance would be viewed.

I found the C&S exam the following morning to be a more engaging exercise. For one thing, the case was set in 1993. For another, it concerned telecommunications, a more absorbing subject to me than formed metal. But most significantly, it focused upon a company headquartered in Darien, Connecticut. Darien! I marveled. Imagine, an HBS case set in my hometown! It seemed auspicious.

I worked like a banshee throughout the four-hour period, and didn't even have time to proof my work at the end. I printed my essays, signed my exam, and walked down the steps of Aldrich into a sunny afternoon.

And that was it.

It was over.

Eight hundred of us were halfway to our Harvard MBAs,

and at least 97 percent of us were heading to a summer job. Section I had a few bottles of champagne waiting on the big lawn in front of Baker Library, and I stopped there for a while. The first person I chatted with was Rick, who was by now anxious to start his apprenticeship as a Wall Street trader. He said he had nothing but positive feelings about the year. Combined with his less traditional pre-business school experience, he felt the HBS education would give him the "best of both worlds" upon graduation.

"Sure, having an engineering background made me feel out of place from time to time," Rick said. "And I definitely started a little behind in some of our classes. But at this point, my command of the first-year material is as good as anybody's. And meanwhile, I'm still an engineer. I can fit right into that old hierarchy that applied back in college and at United Technologies, and I've also got a new set of credentials that'll let me do a lot of other things too."

For now, this was trading, although Rick had retained an open mind about where he might go after graduation. "The biggest shift in my outlook is that I'm not mentally tied to returning to my old company. And this is the most important thing school did for me. Even if I could have somehow picked up everything we covered in class from books or from people at work, nothing could have broadened my professional perspective like coming here did."

Hans came by just as Rick was heading off to bid some of our sectionmates farewell. "Rick sounds very pleased with the way things went this year," Hans observed, adding that he felt the same way. But unlike Rick, he was more impressed with the education he received than by what HBS had done for his employment prospects.

This is not to say he was indifferent toward his summer job. On the contrary, he had long since overcome his disappointment about not finding work with a large European industrial concern. He was excited for the broad, high-level assignments McKinsey would bring him, and was certainly pleased with his generous summer salary. But this was not altogether new to him, as he held a comparable job before coming to HBS. What he valued more about our school was the method of learning it exposed him to, and the breadth of the subject matter.

"I was considered to have a wide business background back at home," he said, "and in many ways I did. But all my knowledge was of finance, accounting, and certain aspects of law. Classes like TOM, BGIE, and C&S; these are all new territories to me. And they are important subjects to one who wishes to run a successful business. I do not think I would have developed a background in them had I not come to HBS."

There was a plan for a big night in Cambridge later on, but I couldn't make it as I hoped to be in New York by sundown. After taking my leave of Hans and the rest of the section, I headed back to McCulloch, put the last frantic touches on my packing, and zipped out to the airport with a friend of mine who would start at Salomon the next morning as well. Moments after we boarded the plane, we were both locked deep in the throes of a post-C&S slumber.

19

THE SCREEN

WHAT A DAY! It had started at 8:00 A.M., perhaps twelve hours before, and still showed no sign of abating. I was frantically shifting my attention between a massive spread sheet, a stack of financial reports, and a presentation that had been wending its tortuous way through Word Processing since late in the morning. It was hard to believe the C&S exam was only two weeks ago. *Two weeks!* It seemed like—the phone bleeped plaintively.

"Hello?"

"Figured I'd find you at work. You I-bankers. Busy busy."

"Carter!"

"Bad news, dude. Critical mass."

"You don't mean . . ."

"Afraid so. I got the word a few hours ago. I hit the screen."

"Hoo boy."

"Hoo boy" was right. Carter had just learned that he'd gotten two more 3s, thereby missing the screen-clearing hurdle by a wide margin. A familiar piece of HBS folk wisdom had it that *Some hit the screen and go bounce, while others hit the screen and go splat.* This little truism was now alarmingly relevant to Carter. He had two weeks to avoid going splat (i.e., not being allowed to return to campus in the fall). To do this he would have to write an essay discussing his academic situation, and submit it to the Academic Performance Committee (APC). If he could argue compellingly that his performance would improve in the coming year, they might (theoretically) be lenient.

"So what happens if they shoot you down," I asked. "Are you just out in the street with a year's worth of HBS debt and no credentials?" This would be a cruel fate.

"I'm still gathering facts," Carter replied. "I'll call you in a couple days." Considerably rattled, I returned to my spread sheet, stack of financials, and presentation.

The next day I called Sandra in California to see if she'd heard the news. "Yeah, I talked to him yesterday," she said in a worried tone.

"What's gonna happen?"

"Well, I've done some checking. It seems that a lot of people who hit the screen are allowed to come back. So cross your fingers."

Two days later Carter called and confirmed this. "Something like eight or nine people go splat every year. That's out of maybe twenty who hit the screen. So the numbers aren't awful; my petition could just squeak through." Carter had by now gained a better understanding of his academic position from some materials the school had sent him. "They had each of our professors fill out an evaluation form on me," he said. The forms asked for assessments of his performance in terms of class participation, written work, and other areas. Each professor was also asked to give him a precise rank within the section for their class (e.g., 52 out of 91 students).

"It doesn't look all that bad," was Carter's optimistic assessment after he had reviewed his evaluations. The professors who gave him 2s all had very good things to say about him. Indeed, three of them had ranked Carter in the top third of the section. And even the professors who gave him 3s made some positive comments. All of them said that Carter's attitude was positive, that he had exerted real efforts to rectify his problems (by coming to their offices to talk, for example), and that he had shown an improving trend in terms of class participation. This last theme was particularly important, as inadequate class participation was clearly Carter's Achilles heel. "Every professor ranked my class participation frequency as 'very infrequent' or 'occasional,'" Carter noted.

"This is what I have to focus on in my petition. If I can convince them that I'll speak up more often, they won't have a good reason to boot me."

Even if the committee decided against him, the odds were good that Carter would be able to return to HBS within a year or two if he so chose. "A lot of people eventually petition the committee to come back," he reported, "and from what I hear, most of them make it. At that point, they mainly look to see if you've taken any concrete steps toward addressing the weaknesses you had as a first year." Carter, for example, might take a course in public speaking. Someone whose downfall had been numbers might take a quantitative class at night school.

"So I guess I'll find out in a couple weeks," Carter said grimly at the end of our conversation. "Thank God I'll be too busy to worry about it until then." He had a major business trip planned which would take him to Venezuela and Argentina. He would have to work like a madman until then to complete his essay for the APC on time, and would not return until the day before the committee's decision.

Friday, early evening. I was frantically shifting my attention between a massive spread sheet, a stack of financial reports, and a presentation that had been wending its tortuous way through Word Processing all day. I had expected to hear from Carter by now. Might this silence be bad news?

Saturday. I was frantically shifting my attention between a massive spread sheet, a stack of financial reports, and a presentation that had been wending its tortuous way through Word Processing since lunch time. When was the guy going to call?

Sunday, 11:00 A.M. My curiosity got the better of me. I picked up the phone, dialed 1, dialed Carter's area code, and paused. I shouldn't be so nosy, I decided righteously. A guy who hits the screen deserves a little peace and quiet. I put the receiver back in its cradle.

11:30. I made it through the area code and halfway through his phone number before my conscience regrouped and got the better of me.

11:35. I finally caved in. The phone rang once. Twice. Three times.

"Hello?" A sleepy female voice. That Carter!

"Hi, is Carter there?"

"Rob?"

"Sandra???"

"You sound surprised," she teased. "How many other women pick up the phone around here? Wait a sec, I'll get him . . ."

". . . Hey Rob, glad you called, I had to ask you something." I tensed up. This is it, I thought. "What do you know about Corporate Financial Management? I'm trying to choose between taking that and Service Management. They're both supposed to be good classes . . ."

"So you're back?"

"Huh?"

"The Committee's letting you come back?"

"Oh, sorry, I thought I'd told you. Yeah. Anyway, I think I'd learn more in CFM, but the guy teaching Service Management is supposed to be really good too. What's that? . . . Oh, Sandra wants to know if you're interested in spending Labor Day weekend at the Cape. We're getting a house. Couples only though, you'll need to find a date. Like that's really gonna happen, right? Heh, heh. Anyway, CFM sounds good, but . . ."

I smiled as Carter prattled on. It looked like second year would be a fun time after all.

Robert Reid grew up in Connecticut and matriculated at Stanford University in 1984, where he received both a bachelor's and a master's degree in International Relations. After graduating, he spent a year in Cairo, Egypt, as a Fulbright scholar studying both the Egyptian political landscape and modern Arabic. He later worked as a general management consultant in San Francisco, and then as a consultant specializing in privatization in Warsaw, Poland. In 1992 he entered Harvard Business School, where he received an MBA with Distinction in 1994. Mr. Reid currently lives in Northern California and works in the digital media industry.